BETWEEN
THE REVOLUTION
AND THE WEST

Official portrait of Maxim M. Litvinov taken for his sixtieth birthday, 1936. (Photo courtesy of the Hoover Institution Archives, Joseph Freeman Collection)

BETWEEN THE REVOLUTION AND THE WEST

A Political Biography of Maxim M. Litvinov

Hugh D. Phillips

Westview Press

BOULDER • SAN FRANCISCO • OXFORD

Copyright © 1992 by Westview Press, Inc.

Published in 1992 in the United States of America by Westview Press, Inc., 5500 Central Avenue, Boulder, Colorado 80301-2847, and in the United Kingdom by Westview Press, 36 Lonsdale Road, Summertown, Oxford OX2 7EW

Library of Congress Cataloging-in-Publication Data
Phillips, Hugh D.
  Between the revolution and the West : a political biography of
Maxim M. Litvinov / Hugh D. Phillips.
      p.   cm.
  Includes bibliographical references and index.
  ISBN 0-8133-1038-5 (cloth)
  1. Litvinov, M. M. (Maksim Maksimovich), 1876–1951.
2. Revolutionaries—Soviet Union—Biography.   I. Title.
DK268.L5P48   1992
947.084′092—dc20   91-41681
[B]   CIP

Printed and bound in the United States of America

The paper used in this publication meets the requirements
of the American National Standard for Permanence of Paper
for Printed Library Materials Z39.48-1984.

10   9   8   7   6   5   4   3   2   1

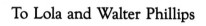

To Lola and Walter Phillips

CONTENTS

Conclusion   177

PREFACE

MAXIM MAXIMOVICH LITVINOV'S LIFE was surely one of the most interesting of modern times. The issue of a couple with a total of six previous marriages, he grew to adolescence within the Jewish "Pale of Settlement" in an atmosphere of uncertainty and insecurity. After serving in the military, he plunged into the Russian revolutionary movement and eventually became one of Lenin's chief underground operatives. After risking his life and liberty in this fashion for almost eight years, he arrived in England in 1908.

There he experienced the relative political freedom of the island that had impressed other revolutionaries, for example, Edward Bernstein, and met his English wife, Ivy. After the October Revolution of 1917, however, he returned to serve the new state and eventually headed the Commissariat for Foreign Affairs during the tumultuous and tragic 1930s. After a brief fall from grace, he was ambassador to the United States during World War II, and during his last years he was, as William Taubman aptly put it, the "first major postwar dissident."[1] Despite a lifetime of dissent, he died a natural death, with his family at his side, in the twilight of Stalin's Russia.

This book attempts to describe and analyze Litvinov's extraordinary life on the basis of the available archival and published materials, and I hope the story will also illuminate aspects of the revolutionary movement and the first decades of Soviet diplomacy. The reader, however, should be warned that these pages do not contain a comprehensive account of either of the last two historical phenomena; Litvinov's activities were a thread running through a larger fabric that is beyond the bounds of this book.

Also, the reader will find lengthy passages from only a few of Litvinov's innumerable public speeches. Anyone even remotely interested in the man is probably already familiar with his famous slogan of the 1930s that "peace is indivisible" and with his fiercely eloquent denunciations of Nazism and the West's appeasement of Hitler. These points have long been a matter of public record, and what I have tried to do is to go beyond the speeches to understand the man who made them.

A couple of points about some material need to be made. First, I was twice denied access to the USSR's Foreign Ministry Archive, including an effort in the summer of 1990, in the era of "glasnost," when I got only as far as the foyer. Perhaps in the future I can progress beyond those forbidding walls on Ploshchad' Smolenskaia, where Litvinov's personal papers are deposited. Second, I was able to peruse the papers of Ivy Litvinov, the commissar's companion and wife of almost forty years, and I also interviewed their son and daughter, among others. These sources added significantly to my understanding of Litvinov the man and his politics; on both counts, he was quite remarkable.

Hugh D. Phillips
Bowling Green, Kentucky

Notes

1. William Taubman, *Stalin's American Policy: From Entente or Détente to Cold War* (New York: W. W. Norton, 1982), 133.

ACKNOWLEDGMENTS

THE RESEARCH, ORGANIZATION, and writing of this biography were some of my primary preoccupations for almost a decade. I ran up quite a debt during those years, and it is a distinct pleasure to publicly acknowledge that fact.

First and foremost, I want to thank my parents, Lola and Walter Phillips, who stood by me morally and financially through it all. To them I affectionately dedicate this book.

I also received substantial institutional support. The International Research and Exchanges Board (IREX) enabled me to spend the 1982–1983 academic year at Moscow State University on the Graduate Student and Young Faculty Exchange, and a large part of this book rests on the foundation IREX so generously provided. The Graduate School of Vanderbilt University and the University of Alabama in Huntsville also provided travel funds, and the Kennan Institute for Advanced Russian Studies made possible a month of research in Washington, D.C. My friends Steve and Roxanne Burant and Mike Adcock did their bit to make my stay in Washington a most pleasant one.

The Faculty Research Committee of Western Kentucky University was exceptional in its generosity. Three separate grants enabled me to travel to the Public Record Office and the Hoover Institution and to make a final wrap-up trip to Moscow. The last excursion was also facilitated by grants from IREX and the American Council of Teachers of Russian.

Many individuals have assisted me in my study of Litvinov and Russian history. Hugh Ragsdale first sparked my interest in the field, and I hope that after he has read this book he will not rue having done so. At Vanderbilt University, the late Forrestt Miller supervised the beginnings of this work, an arduous task completed by Francis Wcislo. While at Vanderbilt, I also received great intellectual stimulation from Charles Delzell, Melvyn Leffler, and Holger Herwig.

More recently, I have had the good fortune to be associated with the History Department at Western Kentucky University. Under the leadership of Richard Troutman, a truly congenial atmosphere prevails, which adds enormously to the enjoyment of intellectual inquiry. Although all my colleagues have my appreciation, I want to thank specifically Lowell Harrison, who took time away from his study of Kentucky legal history to read and critique the entire manuscript. Also Drew Harrington, Richard Salisbury, and Richard Weigel gladly offered their help as I wrestled with the French language.

I want to thank Peter Kracht, Megan Schoeck, and Michelle Starika of Westview Press for their kindness and patience in dealing with a novice, and finally, I want to thank Laura, Daniel, and Jonathan. Without their constant attention this manuscript could have been finished in half the time. But so what? For the last few years, they have done half the laughing.

Despite all the assistance, any errors are mine alone.

H.D.P.

One

FROM BIALYSTOK TO BRITAIN

MAXIM MAXIMOVICH LITVINOV, a Bolshevik and Soviet Russia's third commissar for foreign affairs, was born Meer Genokh Moisevich Vallakh on 17 July 1876, the son of a Jewish bank official in Bialystok, a small city near the border between the Russian and German empires in what is now Poland.[1] He later vividly remembered a night in 1881 when two "stranger-men" lifted the five-year-old from his cot and searched through his pajamas and mattress.[2] The police suspected his father of subversive activities, and, although the suspicion was groundless, he was arrested and imprisoned for six weeks on the charge of having ties with "foreign hostile elements." The police raid of the Vallakh home and a subsequent visit to the Bialystok jail to see his father both made deep impressions on Meer.[3] The episode gave the young boy his first experience with the imperial police, and many years later, Litvinov's daughter, Tatiana, would recall that by the time her father had reached adolescence, he had already formed the vague hope that someday he would see a Russia "without prisons."[4]

Young Meer faced other, more prolonged difficulties. His parents had both been previously married three times—he was the eldest son of their fourth union—and apparently their last attempt at wedded bliss was none too successful. Litvinov recalled to his wife, Ivy, that his parents "quarrelled fiercely and frequently, always ending with threats of separation," particularly terrifying remarks in view of their past proclivities. Ivy added that Litvinov recounted these quarrels with a "look of horror on his round face," remembering his childhood fear that "the world is breaking into bits and falling on me." Despite this strain, or perhaps because of it, Litvinov was apparently very devoted to his father. Once, he "yielded to an uncontrollable impulse to kiss his father's hand as it rested on the table beside him." The young

1

Vallakh "picked it up and turned it over in order to kiss it right in the palm" as he later told Ivy in one of his "rare expansive moments."[5] The denouement of this tender and dramatic moment is not recorded in Ivy's papers. It is evident that Litvinov's childhood involved some periods of intense insecurity and turbulence, and perhaps his early domestic situation may account in part for the adult Litvinov's somewhat taciturn personality and his fondness for neatness and order.

Meer did well in the local secondary school, which accepted a limited number of Jewish boys, but his hopes for higher education collapsed one day when his history teacher told him, "You're a very clever fellow, but you'll no more see the inside of a university than I could bite my elbow." Consequently, Vallakh decided to join the army and then enter a German university.[6] The dreams of a German education would go unfulfilled, like so many of Litvinov's hopes, but Ivy felt that he was also drawn to the army in an effort to escape the "claustrophobic atmosphere of Jewish family life."[7] Whatever the motivation, the seventeen-year-old Vallakh left Bialystok for the Imperial Russian Army, a decision that led to one of the great turning points of his life.

Litvinov's military experience was something of a paradox, like much of his professional life. Ivy believed that her husband's "disciplined and innately modest temperament" enabled him to fit in well with army life—Litvinov even enjoyed marching and remained an inveterate hiker. In later years, when people wondered at his endurance, he would reply, "Old artillery man."[8] He also developed a lifelong appreciation for a well-regulated and orderly life, and he got on well with his immediate superior, one Captain Slugov. During his army years, Litvinov also mastered Russian, in which he had heretofore lacked confidence, and began to work on French and German.[9] Nonetheless, there was another side to Litvinov the artilleryman. While Litvinov was serving in Baku, a fellow soldier introduced him to the writings of Karl Marx and of the Russian radical publicists, Dmitrii Pisarev and Nikolai Dobroliubov, material Litvinov devoured passionately.[10]

Litvinov's military career was cut short, in 1898 when he refused to fire on strikers at one of Baku's factories. Captain Slugov managed to cover up Litvinov's first act of defiance, but he was soon dismissed for a "petty violation of regulations." His indiscretions were later forgotten, however, as during World War II, Litvinov's old Seventeenth Baku Regiment was known as the Maxim Litvinov Regiment.[11]

Litvinov's military experience was of great importance. It instilled in him a personal and even professional orderliness and neatness that was later widely remarked upon by relatives and colleagues. According to one source, a Soviet watchmaker working near Litvinov's office in the 1920s could obtain the exact time "according to Litvinov," that is, the regularity of his schedule.[12] Yet Litvinov's military experience also set him firmly upon the road to revolution. Soon he would discover the writings of Lenin and devote his life to the socialist cause, but the first steps were taken in Baku in the 1890s.

Out of the army and unemployed, Litvinov learned of a job opening in Klintsy for an accountant with a knowledge of German. By then Litvinov was fairly fluent in German, but he knew nothing about bookkeeping. He wanted the job, according to his first biographer, N. Kornev, because it would enable him to "establish ties with the working class," so, with characteristic aplomb, Litvinov mailed an application to the factory, noting that he would arrive soon for an interview. Then he bought a book of self-instruction to learn accounting and spent day and night studying. He presented himself to the factory director, breezed through an exam and an interview, and became the new accountant.[13] Determination, confidence, and intelligence characterized Litvinov well before his dramatic years on the stage of European diplomacy in Geneva.

Litvinov soon moved to Kiev, where he obtained a managerial position in a sugar factory. He was now a member of the middle class, with a steady income, but he was chronically without funds because of a side of his life that was wholly unknown to his managerial colleagues in the factory. Most of his money was going to the underground Social Democratic Labor Party, which Litvinov joined in 1898 almost immediately upon his arrival in Kiev. Litvinov's party cell had eight members and joining it was, for Litvinov, the real beginning of his life.[14] His first contributions to the party were his time and money. He bought, set up, and ran a printing press, turning out revolutionary pamphlets and leaflets by night,[15] until in 1901, Litvinov was arrested and received a two-year sentence for operating his illegal press.[16]

Many times the imperial system of imprisonment and exile produced results diametrically opposed to those desired by the officials in St. Petersburg. By later Soviet standards, prison discipline and supervision were often shockingly lax, and opportunities for reading and conversation were usually plentiful. The result was an informal, but effective, school of higher learning for revolutionaries. Litvinov took full advantage of the system to read further on socialism and the history of revolutions, and of great immediate significance was his exposure to the émigré journal from Geneva, *Iskra,* and to the writings of one of its founders, Vladimir I. Ulianov, soon to be known as Lenin.[17] Litvinov read the *Iskra* articles with joyous excitement because Lenin called for a deemphasis of ordinary trade union organizing by the Social Democratic party and demanded a mass proletarian revolution. For Litvinov, Lenin's writings opened "new horizons" and called forth a "thirst for work." Talk, political and linguistic studies, and the humming of Verdi's arias no longer sufficed, and Litvinov resolved to escape and establish contact with Lenin.[18] In deciding to follow Lenin, the young Litvinov made a commitment to violent revolution.

Nine other political prisoners, including the future Soviet leaders and victims of Stalin's terror Grigorii Zinoviev and Lev Kamenev, joined with Litvinov in an attempt to break out, and Litvinov was entrusted with planning the escape. Apparently the group established contact with Lenin because after their escape, imperial police agents told the chief of the Kiev district that it had been learned that the Foreign League of Russian Social Democrats (which included Lenin and the *Iskra* group) had approved the attempt and had prepared false passports for the escapees.[19]

On an August night in 1902, a small group of political prisoners in Kiev's Luk'ianova Prison strolled into the prison courtyard for their daily exercise. Only a twenty-five-foot wall separated them from the world outside, and because political prisoners could receive visitors, Litvinov had been able to arrange for a contact to be waiting on the street. He casually leaned against the wall and watched as the others tried to make as much commotion as possible, running to and fro and shouting over a game of *gorodki* (similar to bowling). When Litvinov heard a signal beyond the wall, he leaped upon the lone guard with a concealed blanket, covered the man's head and wrestled him to the ground. The other escapees flung a flimsy rope made of sheets with a large metal hook at one end over the wall several times before the hook finally caught at the top. While Litvinov held the guard, the others clambered up the rope of sheets and dropped to the street below. Litvinov followed. He recalled years later that the guard had been more or less sympathetic and had resisted only halfheartedly.[20]

Having crossed the prison wall was, of course, not enough. Litvinov and the others were still in danger because the warden immediately telegraphed news of the escape to St. Petersburg and from there the information was relayed to all border points and 295 towns of the empire.[21] The cumbersome and inefficient imperial police system rumbled into operation.

Litvinov had planned that the escapees would make a dash for the Dnieper River where a boat would be waiting, but immediately he ran into trouble. Scrambling down a ravine, he struck a human body. It was Bliumenfeld, one of his comrades, who had collapsed because of a weak heart and the excitement of the breakout. Litvinov was five feet six inches tall, stocky, and muscular, but he was bleeding and frightened and not physically up to the task of carrying Bliumenfeld. All around shots rang out, and the rainy night was filled with men's curses and the beat of horses' hooves as the police swarmed over Kiev. Litvinov decided to remain quiet and wait; he refused to leave his friend in such a helpless situation. After two hours had passed, Litvinov heard some of the searchers returning, and from their violent oaths he knew that none of the others had been caught.[22]

Soon Bliumenfeld felt well enough to move, but Litvinov had no idea where to go—they had certainly missed the rendezvous at the river. Desperate, they crawled on all fours out of the muddy ravine and crossed a vacant lot to the nearest street. Filthy from head to toe and in torn clothes, the two looked like the dregs of Kievan society, so they decided to act out the part openly. Pretending to be drunk, they reeled down the street singing ribald songs. When they spotted a *droshkii* (a two-horse taxi carriage), they hailed it and demanded to be taken to the nearest tavern. Still feigning inebriation, but terribly frightened and nearly exhausted, they staggered into a dark corner of the sleazy inn that their driver had selected and finally fell asleep.[23]

After awaking, Litvinov began to worry. Bliumenfeld knew nothing of Kiev, having been in the city only since his arrest, but Litvinov had the address of a woman, the daughter of a veteran of the Polish uprising of 1863, who might help them. She lived on the other side of Kiev, however, and day was dawning. Unable to travel openly in daylight, the two fugitives, at Litvinov's suggestion, tottered from bathhouse to bathhouse, hiding in the steam-filled rooms as long as possible. That night they reached the woman's residence, and she sent them to a friend of hers who promised to help them escape the city.[24]

The fugitives hid for a few days in the home of their new accomplice and then made their way to the Zhitomirskii highway and followed it to the nearest railroad station. There Litvinov and Bliumenfeld, posing as a land surveyor and his assistant, used their forged passports to obtain tickets for Vilnius, near the Prussian border. Before the train reached that city, however, they disembarked at a small station, where, according to a new plan worked out in Kiev, they met professional smugglers whose job was to get the revolutionaries out of the country. For twenty-four agonizing hours, the two escapees hid in a haystack to avoid the mounted border patrols, who seemed to be ubiquitous. Suddenly the smuggler gave the signal, and they leaped to their feet and began running. Soon a joyous shout told Litvinov that after many grueling days, he was finally no longer inside the Russian Empire.[25]

Litvinov then made his way to Berlin, where he wrote his mother three letters (intercepted by the imperial police) in which he summarized his ordeal. He assured her that he was fine, though physically and mentally exhausted. After resting for a few weeks, he boarded a cramped third-class railroad car bound for Zurich, the headquarters of *Iskra*.[26] He and the other escapees soon met at an outdoor restaurant on the banks of the Rhine where they held a well-lubricated reunion and sent a "congratulatory" telegram to the chief of the Kiev police, General Novitskii. It was signed "Chief of the Escape, Maxim Litvinov."[27]

In Zurich, Litvinov joined the office of the Foreign League of Russian Social Democrats, which had been created in 1901 to aid socialist émigrés and to coordinate the transport of *Iskra* into the empire. Soon Lenin selected Litvinov to supervise the latter activity,[28] and in his new job, Litvinov demonstrated his characteristic resourcefulness. He began by sending packages of the paper to assorted sympathizers and radicals in Russia; since they could always claim that the packages arrived without their ordering them, he felt they were in no danger. As an irritant, Litvinov also sent copies of *Iskra* to high-level government officials. To confound the imperial agents operating in Switzerland, Litvinov bicycled across the Swiss countryside and dispatched the paper from different towns and villages. He later explained that this plan made it impossible for imperial agents to determine exactly where *Iskra* was being published; it also gave him a chance to indulge in one of his favorite pastimes—traveling in and appreciating beautiful landscapes.[29]

According to Litvinov, these methods of distributing *Iskra* were generally efficient, and only a small number of issues fell into police hands. Such a system, however, could accommodate only about 500 copies of each edition, so Litvinov sought other avenues. He used false-bottomed suitcases carried by people traveling into Russia, and he enlisted the help of sailors in the French merchant marine, who would regularly deliver large quantities of *Iskra* from Marseilles to various ports on the Black Sea. Most of the papers that reached Russia, however, were delivered overland by professional smugglers. These smugglers ordinarily extracted high fees for their services, but if they were socialists or simply bitterly hostile toward the imperial regime, they worked for little pay.[30]

This relatively happy period came to an end late in 1903 when the Russian Social Democrats split into two factions—the majority Mensheviks and the Bolsheviks. A choice had to be made, and Litvinov promptly sided with Lenin and the Bolsheviks. Litvinov then accepted Lenin's assignment to return to Russia illegally as an "agent of the Central Committee for the Northwestern Region,"[31] and by early March 1904, Litvinov was once more inside the empire.[32]

Now began Litvinov's most ardently revolutionary period. He established himself in Riga as the Bolshevik chief and worked there as a smuggler and as Lenin's advocate against numerous opponents. Just before the revolutionary storm of 1905 broke over Russia, he wrote to Lenin concerning the situation in Russia following a Bolshevik meeting in St. Petersburg in December in 1904. He said that R. S. Zemliachka, with whom Litvinov was supposed to be working, "does not in the least realize what a sorry and critical situation we are in," compared to the Mensheviks, and she "refuses to come to any agreement with me" but wastes time on "long and boring speeches."[33] Litvinov demanded action. He wanted the immediate preparation of a party congress, to be carried out without coordination with the Menshevik-controlled Central Committee, and he intended that the congress would establish a new Central Committee—"our Central Committee," as he put it. But the Bolsheviks must go even further: "In my opinion, we can and should come out openly . . . to declare that in the present abnormal conditions . . . strict loyalty [to the Central Committee] is impossible. We are being pushed onto the path of revolution."[34]

Litvinov ended his report pessimistically, noting that the Bolsheviks had little support among the masses of workers in St. Petersburg and that swarms of Mensheviks had arrived in the city. Moreover,

> the periphery, if not everywhere against us, then almost nowhere is for us. The broad mass of party workers still considers us a small group of disorganizers, without any forces of our own. . . . I repeat: Our situation is extremely precarious and unsteady. Our only way out is immediately to call a congress (no later than February) and get out a newspaper.[35]

Lenin replied that he agreed with Litvinov "a thousand times" on the need for immediate action,[36] and in April 1905, the Bolsheviks did hold a congress in London. By then, however, the revolutionary situation in Russia was well advanced, with virtually no Social Democratic guidance.[37]

When Litvinov wrote his letter, imperial Russia was indeed a powder keg—Bloody Sunday was only weeks away—but if Litvinov's call for a Bolshevik revolution had been accepted in late 1904, it would almost certainly have failed. Besides the evidence he presented of the lack of popularity and even contempt for the Bolsheviks among the working class, the plain fact was that Russia's workers, though discontented, were not yet ready for violent insurrection. The peaceful demonstration led by Father Georgii Gapon in St. Petersburg, on that January Sunday in 1905, revealed a powerful belief in moderate reforms through appeals to the emperor. Only after Nicholas II's officials responded with bullets and sabers did Russia begin moving toward the strikes and barricades that would mark the summer and autumn of 1905.[38]

Meanwhile, Litvinov, using the name "Felix," continued his propaganda work but apparently to little avail. In October 1905, following numerous strikes, demonstrations, and the spectacular assassination of Grand Duke Sergei, Russia (and the world) witnessed the first successful general strike. Not only was the strike successful, it was carried out despite the lack of overall planning. Paralyzed, the imperial government issued the October Manifesto, whereby Russians received, for the first time, a guarantee of basic civil liberties.[39]

Lenin immediately responded with the publication of a newspaper, *Novaia zhizn'*, printed in St. Petersburg, and Litvinov left Riga for the capital in order to assist in the daily administration and publication of the paper. When he arrived, he found that he was expected to have a paper on the streets within twenty-four hours, despite the fact that he had virtually nothing with which to work— only a contract with a local printing shop. His "office" had neither furniture nor employees. A few volunteers were hastily assembled, but there were no vendors to peddle the new paper. People who wanted it had to come to Litvinov's office on Nevskii Prospect, but Litvinov claimed that the first 15,000 copies "were practically torn from the hands" of his aides, eloquent testimony to the radicalization that Russia had experienced. Within a few days, Litvinov, working around the clock, had contracted for a second printer, organized a circulation department, and even persuaded "a few real experts" to work for him.[40] As one official Soviet publication concedes, "all the practical work of publishing and distributing *Novaia zhizn'* was carried out by the tireless and elusive M. M. Litvinov—agent of the Leninist *Iskra*."[41] The contents of the paper were, of course, Lenin's responsibility, and he contributed material almost daily.[42]

Litvinov was so successful in handling the newspaper that when the editors and administrators of all of St. Petersburg's dailies formed a committee to coordinate their activities to combat the obstacles placed before them by the police and postal authorities, they elected Litvinov as their chairman. All this time, Litvinov, posing as Ludwig V. Nietz, was a wanted political criminal.[43] Soon, however, the government closed the more radical papers, including *Novaia zhizn'*, and the situation became dangerous. On orders from Lenin, Litvinov left St. Petersburg for new and equally dangerous work abroad—the purchase and transport of weapons and ammunition into the empire.

Litvinov was in Paris in early 1906 with instructions to purchase "rifles, machine guns, small arms, and the necessary cartridges." His first order was placed with a Danish arms company, but when told that an officer of the Danish Army must come to Paris to supervise the sale, Litvinov was stymied. To tell the truth—that the arms were intended for revolutionaries in the Caucasus region—was hardly practical; so Litvinov assumed the role of a French-speaking army officer from Ecuador. What he used for credentials is not known, but the deception was a success, and the arms were procured.[44] During the

summer of 1906, Litvinov roamed the Continent and placed orders in
Brussels, Vienna, Karlsruhe, and Berlin. He became an accomplished
imposter (a skill that may have helped him later as a diplomat!); and
equal in importance to his boldness and ingenuity were Litvinov's
charming manners and dress and his, by now, impeccable French. All
of these qualities were to be sorely tested during one week in Karlsruhe.

In that city, Litvinov met with the director of a factory that
produced the type of cartridges the revolutionaries needed. With his
usual confidence, Litvinov told the director of his desire to buy some
of the ammunition and was informed that there were some officers
from the Russian Army in Karlsruhe for the same purpose and that
they were at that moment on the firing range to test the ammunition.
The director concluded with a courteous offer to lend Litvinov his
carriage to take him immediately to join the Russians. Realizing that
there was no alternative, Litvinov graciously accepted the director's
offer and departed. Surprisingly, the day passed without incident as
the fugitive from the imperial regime and officers of the emperor's
army fired round after round and then repaired to a local inn to imbibe
round after round. Litvinov admitted that he even came to like the
officers and politely "accepted" their invitation to visit Russia sometime. Upon parting, Litvinov gave them one of the numerous fake
business cards he carried. Most important, as Litvinov recalled, the
imperial officers had given him valuable information concerning the
latest European firearms and ammunition.[45]

Amazingly, one of the Russian government's leading agents in
Europe, a certain Garting, had informed St. Petersburg that, "Vallakh
. . . has been in Berlin . . . to make arms purchases in large quantities
and to arrange their delivery to Russia."[46] Moreover, Russian authorities had notified imperial agents abroad in June 1906 that Litvinov
was in Marseilles to arrange the transport of arms via the Black Sea.
Despite this information, Litvinov continued to elude capture.

Litvinov's attention turned next to the problem of transportation.
He toured almost all the major European ports, receiving accommodation and advice along the way from friends in other socialist parties,
and eventually decided on Varna, Bulgaria, as the best spot from which
to dispatch arms and ammunition into the empire. Litvinov went
directly to Bulgarian government officials to enlist their help in getting
cargo to "Armenians, who are fighting the Turkish oppressor." Initially

enthusiastic, the Bulgarians later wavered, and Litvinov, with breath-taking recklessness, decided to present his case at once to the Bulgarian war minister, General Savov. The precise details of their conversation are not known, but Litvinov claimed that Savov promised the Bulgarian authorities would not interfere with a project aimed at the Turks.[47]

Litvinov bought a yacht in Fiume and had it refitted for the task, but political squabbling hampered his plans. In April 1906, the Fourth Congress of the Russian Social Democrats had met in Stockholm in an attempt to reunify the party. Lenin had called for a new revolutionary onslaught against absolutism, which the Menshevik majority had promptly rejected; when Litvinov had learned of this, he had resigned from his assignment as a gun runner, but the party's Central Committee had rejected that also. Litvinov recalled that this action had amazed him. He could only surmise that the more radical party elements from the Caucasus, for whom the weapons were intended, had pressured the Central Committee to continue the operation. The money needed to complete the mission, however, was never sent, and in September 1906 Litvinov decided that he must go to St. Petersburg to make a personal plea.

An imperial agent in Paris informed the Russian authorities that Litvinov was returning under the alias "Gustav." The police decided to let their quarry make his way to St. Petersburg where, it was hoped, he would reveal his accomplices. That plan had to be changed, however, because in Vilnius the police assigned to watch Litvinov lost track of him.[48] In panic, they issued orders that Litvinov be arrested "at all costs." He was soon picked up in Vilnius and taken under police guard to St. Petersburg. Upon arriving in the capital, Litvinov escaped. The details of his escape are not known, but we do know that he spent a few days in the city (while on the assumption that he had fled, the police ordered searches in all the other western cities of the empire) and obtained funds from some unnamed Mensheviks. Then he made his way back to Bulgaria.[49]

Finally, in late 1906, after ten months of preparation, Litvinov stood on the beach near Varna and watched as the yacht sailed away, bound for Batum, a Georgian port on the Black Sea. His high hopes were dashed when he learned three days later that the boat had run aground, the crew had scattered, and Romanian fishermen had helped themselves to the cargo.[50]

Litvinov continued to be active within the party, and in August 1907, he became the secretary of the Russian Social Democrats' delegation to the Twelfth Congress of the Second International—a fact that indicates he still maintained good relations with the Menshevik majority despite his personal devotion to Lenin. In November 1907, the head of the Russian police offered "any price" for Litvinov's capture, and the French police arrested him in Paris in January 1908 when he tried to exchange some bank notes that had been stolen by a Bolshevik "expropriation" squad in Tbilisi in June 1907. Litvinov was able to prove that he had been in Paris at the time of the robbery, so the French minister of justice refused the extradition request of the Russian authorities, although he did have Litvinov escorted out of the country as an undesirable alien. Later, Litvinov and the French minister, Aristide Briand, were to meet under decidedly different circumstances.[51]

Disheartened and weary from almost ten years of continuous and seemingly useless revolutionary struggle, the thirty-two-year-old Litvinov arrived in London in January 1908 for a ten-year stay. He carried a letter of introduction from the well-known writer and Bolshevik sympathizer, Maxim Gorky, and using this, he met the director of the London Library, Charles Wright. Wright got Litvinov a job with the publishing house of Williams and Norgate, where, characteristically, Litvinov quickly rose to a position of some responsibility—it seems that he was even called into conferences to give his opinion of the firm's general policy.[52]

In London, Litvinov led a comparatively conventional, if probably lonely, life. But "some time in the end of 1915," his prospects for the future began to change once again, for the émigré had caught the eye of the free-spirited Ivy Low. Years later she recalled that

> I would be disappointed if I did not see him at least once every day, a Pickwickian gentleman, walking stick clasped firmly at his back, who only halted his brisk steps to peer (wistfully I thought) at the caraway rolls and cherry tarts in [the baker's] window. I would have been surprised to know that he kept a lookout for a blackbrowed girl of shaggy aspect, who strode past in deplorably thick-soled brogues with an air of fine detachment.[53]

Soon Ivy learned his name, and its correct pronunciation, when she queued behind him one day at the post office. As Ivy has recorded it, the postal worker said he had a letter "for LITvinov. 'That's me—Lit VEE nov,' said the stranger and held up a large visiting card in confirmation."[54]

As it turned out, the two had a mutual friend, Phyllis Klishko, a former schoolmate of Ivy's who had "married a Russian," and it was she who introduced them. By December 1915, they were sufficiently close that Litvinov told her of "secret presses, of social-democrats and social revolutionaries, of Bolsheviks and Mensheviks," terms that Ivy found confusing at first. She, in turn, confounded Maxim with stories of her youth and the information that she "had never had an hour's [educational] instruction" since she was fifteen.[55]

As their relationship developed, Litvinov strove to eliminate any uncertainties or ambiguities. He told Ivy that "the lives of many men and great sums of money had been entrusted to his keeping, and they had been safe. And [Ivy] would be safe too." But "at the first beat of the drum of revolution," Litvinov told her he would go, even if it meant their separation. Ivy said that was all right because "I would go too, so nobody would be leaving anybody."

Soon came the inevitable meeting with Ivy's family and friends. Her aristocratic mother liked Maxim's "warmth," but "she was chilled by the austere moral core" within him. Like many people, she found him "inaccessible," although Ivy felt this perception in part stemmed from Maxim's uneasiness in "unfamiliar surroundings" and from his "hesitant English." His age and appearance did not help matters. He was thirty-nine to Ivy's twenty-five, but his "stoutness and gravity made him appear considerably older." His clothes were "all wrong, . . . creased and shapeless from neglect and from the newspapers and maps with which the pockets were always stuffed." Nonetheless, Maxim and Ivy's family managed to get along, and "in the end he grew to like my mother, if only for the unflattering reason that she hardly ever came to visit us."[56]

Ivy also introduced Maxim to her Aunt Edith and her husband, a Dr. Eder. Ivy thought Maxim and Eder, sharing many personal traits, were well suited to each other; for example, both were "reticent almost to taciturnity, both had expressions ranging from the grave to jovial." Eder, however, was "engrossed in Zionism and psychoanalysis, causes in which Maxim firmly refused to take the slightest interest." Thus, their meetings "were apt to become irritating."[57]

Litvinov continued to wrestle with his principles and his emotions. As Ivy observed:

> He considered that revolutionaries ought not to marry, and it was against his principles to tie himself down by the laws of a capitalist country to a relationship which should be ruled by feeling alone. . . . And yet, though all these doubts and conflicts could have been resolved by simply staying where we were, we could think of nothing but living together in marriage, proper legal marriage.[58]

And so the conflict was resolved, and Lenin's agent and former gunrunner appeared one day in 1916 at the Registry Office in Haverstock Hill for his wedding, which was "reached in good time to make our first baby legitimate."[59]

The marriage had its difficult moments, owing mainly, it seems, to the very different temperaments of the newlyweds. Litvinov's "inflexible puritanism" clashed with Ivy's "devotion to impulse." Maxim was also "neat as a monk in a cell," and Ivy's untidy ways exasperated him no end. Still, there is no evidence in Ivy's papers of serious marital problems. Indeed, Litvinov once "nodded gravely" and agreed with Dr. Samuel Johnson's observation that "marriage has many pains but celibacy no pleasures."[60] And Ivy seems to have enjoyed one of her husband's greatest pleasures, observing that:

> Maxim's leading passion was the study of guide-books and he could conduct me for day-long walks through parkland and woodland, over field and down, hardly crossing a highroad, only descending to populated districts for a splendid lunch at a country inn known to him by repute or experience. All through our lives together, in whatever country we found ourselves, his happiest hours were spent in drawing up itineraries for ourselves or others. For him a view was something you went a long way to look at.[61]

But where Maxim and Ivy "really came together" was over books. Litvinov "had long given up reading novels" by the time they met, but

Ivy rekindled his interest in such reading material. He discovered the works of Jane Austen and Robert Louis Stevenson, but Anthony Trollope "was the man for him,"[62] as Litvinov believed that a foreigner could learn all that was needed about England's parliamentary system from Trollope's *The Prime Minister*. He "really gloated" over the character Phineas Finn,[63] calling him a "pleasant mediocrity . . . bound to succeed in [English] public life."[64]

During these years, Litvinov's contacts with Lenin became increasingly infrequent and distant. The two men remained in touch, but Litvinov was tiring of Lenin's doctrinaire and futile ways. On 3 December 1913, Litvinov bluntly wrote to Lenin that the latter's recent criticism of Rosa Luxemburg had been "excessively sharp in tone" and had given ammunition to the "Europeans against us,"[65] and in the same month, Litvinov reported that his visit to a meeting of the International Socialist Bureau had convinced him that most of Europe's socialists regarded the Bolshevik-Menshevik schism with "complete indifference."[66] Litvinov himself was losing interest in what must have seemed to him a pointless squabble, and thus he denied Lenin's 1914 request that he represent the Bolsheviks at a congress of the Second International. He wrote respectfully but firmly that he could not be away from his job for the necessary three weeks and that he lacked adequate funds. He added diplomatically that in any case, "only" Lenin could exercise influence at such a meeting.[67] A few years earlier, it would have been inconceivable that Litvinov would have turned down such a request from Lenin, but Litvinov had changed a great deal since 1908. He was now very much settled in London, and, according to his daughter, he had even come to admire the British parliamentary system.[68] In a symbolic act that cut his ties with the past, the former Meer Vallakh became "an English subject . . . naturalized as Litvinoff."[69]

If Litvinov thought he was indeed starting a new phase of his life, he was certainly correct, but it would not be a reasonably comfortable existence with his new family in London. Shortly after his first son was born, the tocsin of revolution reverberated out of Russia and across Europe, and Litvinov's life, and world history, embarked upon new, unknown paths.

Two

DIPLOMATIC BAPTISM

The First Soviet Representative to Britain

THE MARCH REVOLUTION and the collapse of the Romanov dynasty struck Litvinov like a bolt from the blue, and soon he would be named Soviet Russia's first representative to Britain, a task for which he was wholly unprepared. Moreover, he would never receive any formal diplomatic instructions from Moscow; he would simply have to improvise and hope for the best.

It is true that in the days before the outbreak of World War I, Litvinov had suspected that a great war might bring about a profound social upheaval. According to his friend and fellow diplomat, Ivan Maisky, however, Litvinov had said that even if a revolution were to occur in Russia, it would by no means ensure the triumph of the Bolsheviks. "Who knows what prospects will unfold for Russia and the Russian proletariat?" he mused one evening at the home of a fellow émigré, Platon Kerzhentsev.[1]

When war broke out in August 1914, Litvinov made no effort to get to the Continent but remained in London, a relative backwater for Russian political émigrés. He continued as before to work and support his wife,[2] and on Sundays, he made his usual bicycle tours of London and its numerous suburbs. However, Litvinov also played an active, perhaps pivotal, role in the largely apolitical Herzen Circle, an émigré group that he had helped organize. Open to all Russians in London, the group's activities included the organization of chess matches and other cultural diversions, but Litvinov had also initiated a monetary fund to aid any émigré in need.[3]

Litvinov remained very much a political man even though he had grave doubts about Lenin's chances for success in Russia. Litvinov's

17

keen mind and the turbulence around him made it virtually impossible for him to avoid politics, but still, when the news came of Emperor Nicholas II's abdication and the formation of the Provisional Government in March 1917, his reactions were those of a man caught completely off guard.

His wife was in a maternity hospital recovering from the birth of their son, Mikhail, when she received a phone call from her husband. It was March 16, and he wanted to know if she had seen the London *Times*. Replying that she had not, Ivy asked what had happened. Seemingly in a daze, Litvinov simply told her to look at the paper and that he would come for her and Misha that afternoon. Ivy was at a loss to understand her husband's unusual behavior until she saw a copy of the *Times* and the headline that the tsar had abdicated.

In her account of those momentous days, Ivy recalled that the next day they learned that Grand Duke Mikhail had declined to assume the throne. Everything was in a state of flux, including Litvinov's mind, and he rushed to dictate his reactions to his wife while pacing the floor of their small apartment. According to Ivy's account: "17 March 1917, London: I went to bed last night in great excitement. It seemed that the news had opened all the floodgates of my mind."[4] Not surprisingly, sleep was impossible, and at 6:00 A.M. Litvinov rose, trembling with excitement, to see the morning papers.

> Can this really be the People's Revolution? The type jumped up and down . . . as I ran through the paper. I can't remember how I spent the morning; I went about the daily routine almost unconsciously. I tried to shave with the toothpaste and got into the bath without having turned on the tap. What joy! I rushed to the Russian Consulate to ask for a passport and asked them why they hadn't taken down the portraits of the Tsar. The despondent officials said they had received no instruction, that I must apply to the British Home Office and etc., and etc.

Litvinov considered telephoning someone in the new Provisional Government but decided that those officials faced more important matters. He continued: "I remembered how in 1905 I pitied my comrades in exile when they couldn't be with me to observe the joyful spectacle of the revolutionary events. And now I am in the same situation. What a tragedy—to have spent half my life in. . . "—here the paper is torn upon which Ivy took down her husband's reactions, but she remembered that he also spoke of visiting J. Ramsay Mac-Donald, the British Labour Party leader, that day and asking him "how he intended to react to the Russian Revolution." But MacDonald, like the officials of the Russian Consulate, said he had received no instructions.

Despite his preoccupation with the news from Russia, Litvinov's mind also turned to thoughts of his family obligations. At home, he showed Ivy a passage from the Old Testament that he had jotted down during his busy day. It read: "When a man hath taken a new wife, he shall not go out to war, neither shall he be charged with business but he shall be free at home one year, and shall cheer up his wife which he hath taken" (Deuteronomy 25). Ivy teasingly suggested this passage was "unexpectedly humane for the Old Testament." Maxim replied: "No, population measure. The tribe must not be allowed to die out. I wouldn't have been exempted, I already have a son to take my place."[5] Once again he reminded his wife, gently, that if the revolution called, he would go.

Ivy claimed that after the fall of the Romanovs, London reporters continuously pestered her husband, "Everywhere we went—on the street, in the metro, and even at the gate of our home—we ran into them. 'Litvinov, tell us something . . . what do you know . . . if only just a name!' He replied that soon they would hear the name Lenin. The reporters were puzzled: 'Yes, but who is this Lenin?' they asked." Soon, as Ivy observed, the whole world would know the name Lenin. Her husband later remarked to her that "the reporters probably think that even then I knew everything." "And what in fact did you know?" she inquired. "I knew Lenin well," he answered.[6]

Litvinov learned of the monumental events of 7 November, when Lenin and the Bolsheviks seized power in the name of the Petrograd Soviet and in a relatively bloodless coup swept aside Aleksandr Ker-enskii's government, from the London papers.[7] Scanning the *Times* from 8 to 20 November, Litvinov read such headlines as the following: "Maximalist Sedition in Petrograd" (8 November) and "Leninists Claim Victory" (14 November). The latter article must have been especially thrilling to Litvinov—on 12 November the *Times* had proclaimed "Lenin Losing Control," but the most recent of the dispatches from Russia admitted that in Petrograd at least, "what power is exercised is in the hands of the Extremists," that is, the

Bolsheviks and the Left Socialist Revolutionaries. On 20 November, the *Times* wrote of "Russia Under the Bolsheviks" and asserted that the "Leninists" had come to power so easily because Kerenskii and the Provisional Government had fled at the first sign of danger and the majority of the population was passive and indifferent to the whole affair.[8]

Not only did Litvinov learn of the October Revolution from the British press, he also learned a few weeks later of his own appointment as the Bolshevik representative in London from the *Times*.[9] He did not even receive his first diplomatic pouch until March 1918 because the new authorities in Petrograd were preoccupied with other matters.[10] Even for the Soviet representative in London, direct contact with the new government was sporadic.

Meanwhile, Lenin had discovered that the decree on peace, which had been issued on 8 November 1917 and called for a "just and democratic peace," had received a decidedly negative response from the Russian diplomatic corps.[11] Accordingly, on 5 December, the Soviet government sent a communiqué to all embassies and missions asking for a declaration of loyalty to the new regime;[12] a message that was met "with silence."[13] On 9 December, therefore, twenty-eight ambassadors were dismissed, and the process of naming new representatives, which had begun tentatively in mid-November, accelerated. V. V. Vorovskii was the first Soviet appointment, accredited to all of Scandinavia with instructions to "tell the world about events in Russia."[14] His title was "plenipotentiary," more commonly referred to as *polpred*—the Bolsheviks disdained such "bourgeois" terms as "ambassador" or "minister" for the present.

Litvinov was not so lucky. As he told Maisky: "There I was a *polpred* and I had nothing, absolutely nothing—no instructions from Moscow, no money, no staff. I simply had to start from scratch."[15] Indeed, apart from frantic talks then under way with the Germans, the Soviet regime had no foreign policy in the usual sense of the term.

Litvinov initially could only attempt to establish contact with the new government. He did so by means of an unnamed émigré who was returning to Petrograd, giving him a letter asking for instructions and money and even sent to the new People's Commissariat for Foreign Affairs (*Narkomindel*) a code for messages. The cipher, which Litvinov had obtained from a sympathetic member of the Imperial Purchasing

Commission in London, was accepted by *Narkomindel* and sent, with some alterations, to all plenipotentiaries abroad.[16]

Litvinov, despite his lack of instructions, was not a man to sit idly and wait. He wrote to the British Foreign Office of his appointment, only to have his letter returned unopened. Next he demanded that the Russian Embassy be turned over to him; as he expected, this request was denied. Litvinov therefore opened his own "People's Embassy" at 82 Victoria Square. Years later, he came across an anonymous report in the *Narkomindel* archives that accurately described this new diplomatic residence. Traveling through the bleak northern suburbs of London on a rainy night, the unknown correspondent relates, "in the pale light of blacked out lanterns, I found the house and knocked. A young, simply dressed woman with bobbed hair [Ivy] opened the door. The representative of the Soviet Republic, dressed in a shabby brown coat, was drinking tea and serving himself." The room was sparse, its only "decoration" being a bookshelf containing the "*Encyclopedia Britannica, A History of the Paris Commune* and a few other books." The whole place was "in no way different from the home of an English worker's family."[17]

Appearances aside, the new "embassy" was then something unique in modern diplomatic history. Its purpose, as defined by Litvinov, was to serve as a propaganda center that went over the head of the British government to appeal directly to the working class, a tactic often used later by the Soviet government with widely varying results. Litvinov began by issuing a stream of pamphlets urging British workers to join with their Russian counterparts to force peace upon the belligerent governments. The most detailed and important of these tracts was *The Bolshevik Revolution: Its Rise and Meaning*, written in early 1918 and published by the British Socialist Party in that same year.

This propagandistic version of Russian political history from 1905 to 1918 offered a typical mixture of truth, half-truth, and outright falsehood, but one passage was significant. Litvinov reviewed the events surrounding the recently signed Brest-Litovsk Treaty, which nominally ended the war between Russia and the Central Powers. In an important section he revealed feelings about the Germans that were to color his approach to foreign policy through much of his career. Writing with obvious emotion, he described the situation as follows:

> The Germans . . . with a perfidy not easily matched in military
> history, immediately broke the armistice and marched against
> the defenseless and partially demobilized Russians. The
> Bolsheviks gave in and signed the aggravated German conditions
> of peace. . . . Yet what else could the Bolsheviks have done, with
> such a terrible legacy . . . in the shape of hunger, lack of every
> necessity for war, disorganization of the machinery, dislocation
> of the entire transport system, and with all the bourgeois
> elements against them?

Litvinov concluded by blasting the German working class itself, saying
that from this quarter the imperial German government had nothing
to fear if it should choose in the future to march against Soviet
Russia.[18]

The concluding sections of Litvinov's tract are significant for two
reasons. First, he strongly condemned the German workers, the group
that Lenin still looked upon as the potential saviors of the revolution.
But Litvinov, it seems, never cared much for Germany, even after the
1922 Treaty of Rapallo between Germany and the Soviet Union, and
his dislike and distrust of Germany were born, not in January 1933
with the rise of Adolf Hitler, but in the spring of 1918. He believed
that any German government had the potential for expansionism
toward the east and that the German people, including its working
class, would support such policies. Second, Litvinov regarded the 1918
Brest-Litovsk Treaty as a distasteful but absolute necessity, a view that
was fully in accord with Lenin's position. In both instances, there can
be discerned glimpses of the impassioned but nonetheless businesslike
and frank diplomat who later argued before the League of Nations
that Nazi Germany must be met by collective action in Europe for the
eminently reasonable purpose of averting another world war.

The British government, enraged over the loss of its ally on the
eastern front, hardly could have welcomed such antiwar works as *The
Bolshevik Revolution*, but according to Litvinov himself, the official
and unofficial attitude "towards me was comparatively favorable, allow-
ing for the time and circumstances."[19] The British even went so far as
to permit unofficial contacts between Litvinov and Reginald Leeper of
the Political Intelligence Department of the Foreign Office, a man who
had previously taken Russian language lessons from Litvinov.[20] The
government consented to these contacts because of the desire to learn

more about what was happening in Russia, especially in view of some recent remarks by the fiery Lev Trotskii, Soviet Russia's first commissar for foreign affairs.[21]

In late November 1917, Trotskii had demanded the release of the émigré Georgii Chicherin from a British jail where he was being held on charges of sedition. When the British balked, Trotskii made an ominous threat against the lives of the numerous British subjects residing in Russia.[22] Chicherin was released,[23] but by doing so, the British government may have given the Bolsheviks the impression that Britain could easily be blackmailed. In any case, Moscow was soon to try such a tactic again.

But in London, Litvinov continued to meet with Leeper, and on 11 January 1918, the two men were joined by Robert H. Bruce Lockhart at "Lyons' corner shop in the Strand." There Litvinov wrote a "very kind" letter for Lockhart to give to Trotskii when the former arrived in Russia to serve as Litvinov's British counterpart. The letter was written for some reason on a piece of tablecloth, and in it, Litvinov described Lockhart as "a thoroughly honest man who . . . sympathizes with us." Litvinov added that he still had no information from Russia except what could be gleaned from the newspapers. Most important, the two sides, through Leeper and Litvinov, agreed to grant each other certain diplomatic privileges, including the use of ciphers and couriers.[24]

This first diplomatic "conference" between Soviet Russia and Great Britain concluded on a comical note. Litvinov noticed that among the desserts listed on the menu was *pouding diplomate*, and he decided that he should try it, being now a "diplomat" himself. The waiter took his order but returned to say that they had run out of the pudding. Lockhart recalled that "Litvinov shrugged his shoulders and smiled blandly. 'Not recognized even by the Lyons,' he said."[25]

Lockhart's impression of Litvinov was "not unfavorable," though Lockhart found Litvinov "slower witted" than Leeper's other Russian friend, Fedor Rothstein (later Soviet *polpred* to Iran). More significant, Lockhart felt that "in so far as a Bolshevik can be said to differentiate in his degrees of hate for bourgeois institutions, he certainly regarded German militarism as a greater danger than English capitalism." In his diary, Lockhart also bluntly wrote that Litvinov "does not like [the] German government [that] banished him from Germany."[26] For the most part, Litvinov would hold his opinion during his active life.

In retrospect, this January meeting can be considered the high point of Litvinov's strange "mission" to Britain. He continued to meet regularly with Leeper, but Litvinov's standing with the British government began to decline steadily. This deterioration could arguably have been avoided had Litvinov exercised greater prudence and behaved in a manner that the British considered appropriate for the representative of a foreign state rather than as a spokesman for the international workers' movement. On the other hand, had the British recognized Litvinov as an accredited diplomat, perhaps the remainder of his stay in London would have been less unfortunate. On Litvinov's behalf, it must be repeated that, as he readily admitted, he was utterly without experience as a diplomat and therefore had to improvise. Nor did his situation really improve with the arrival of his first diplomatic pouch. When he opened it, he was surprised to find only a pile of the latest Moscow papers, a letter from Georgii Chicherin, now Trotskii's deputy commissar, and a check for 200,000 imperial rubles. The letter, however, was "in the most general terms and gave me no definite instructions whatever."[27] It is true that the Bolshevik leadership was in an extremely precarious position in March 1918, particularly with regard to the question of acceptance of the Brest-Litovsk Treaty with Germany, but still, it seems that if Moscow had really wanted to improve relations with London, Litvinov would have received more specific orders. The absence of any such directive clearly demonstrates that the Bolsheviks' hopes for the future were still pinned to an imminent socialist revolution in Europe. Diplomacy would have to wait.

An important part of the strategy Litvinov worked out for himself was to establish and cultivate contacts with the leadership of the British Labour Party, and an indication of his success in this endeavor was an invitation for him to address a Labour Party conference on 22 January 1918. In his speech, which received wide publicity, Litvinov spoke of the storm clouds of revolution gathering in Austria and Hungary and predicted with certainty that they would spread "over all of Germany." On the other hand, Triple Entente (Britain, Russia, and France) statesmen had been "forced into the open"—doubtless a reference to the Bolsheviks' publication of the secret treaties among the Entente powers—which Litvinov said rather cryptically, will have "an effect on the minds of the workers of the world." He concluded with a call for the British working class "to speed up your pace" toward peace.[28]

The foremost authority on Soviet-British relations during this period, Richard Ullman, argues that this address was hardly a Trotskyist demand for revolution, and he also points out that other foreign socialists shared the podium with Litvinov.[29] Litvinov, however, was also supposed to be the representative of a foreign government, even if that government was not yet recognized by London, and he was bypassing the constituted government in an effort to influence British policy. It is difficult to imagine any regime that would accept such an approach with equanimity; certainly, the Bolsheviks did not tolerate similar tactics on their territory, as Lockhart soon discovered.[30] But the Bolsheviks had the annoying habit of claiming for themselves both the rights of a sovereign nation and the rights that they felt should accrue to the leadership of the workers of the world.

In any event, the initial British reaction to Litvinov's speech was virulent. The home secretary, Sir George Cave, denounced before the House of Commons the continued tolerance of Litvinov's mere presence, putting Cave at odds with his own government's policy,[31] and the owner of 82 Victoria Square suddenly decided it would be a good idea to cancel the three-month lease just granted to Litvinov. The latter took the dispute to court, where the judge ruled that Litvinov had invalidated the lease himself by breaking his pledge not to use the place for propaganda purposes. Fifteen years later, Litvinov insisted to Leeper that he had lost the case because "political prejudices decided the issue in a British court of justice,"[32] truly a bizarre complaint from a representative of Stalinist Russia where "political prejudices" were all that mattered in judicial procedures. Perhaps Litvinov thought the British were above such methods.

The British Foreign Office did attempt to prevent anything so drastic as Litvinov's arrest, despite the readiness of the Home Office to do just that. There were too many potential hostages in Russia, and the Foreign Office was well aware that some of those Britons were engaged in "unsavory activities."[33]

Because of the heated atmosphere in Britain, and cognizant of the growing importance of the United States in European affairs, Litvinov asked Lenin for a transfer to Washington, D.C. Lenin agreed, and Litvinov went to the U.S. Embassy in London with his documents and requested a visa. The request was denied, probably as a result of British opposition, and Litvinov had to wait fifteen years to travel to the United States.[34] Ironically, he was finally accepted as the Soviet ambassador to Washington during World War II, a time when his influence within the Soviet government was nil.

In August 1918, the tense state of relations between London and Moscow reached a genuine crisis. On 4 August, the Soviet government learned of British landings at Archangel, and the next day the Cheka, a forerunner of the KGB, picked up about 200 British and French residents in Moscow, and the French consulate was raided. The internment of the consular staffs lasted only a few days, but upon their release, the consulates were officially closed. The British handed over representation of their national interests to the Netherlands, but Chicherin then announced that no British citizens would be allowed to leave Russia until Litvinov and his staff had left London. Lockhart met with Chicherin and pointed out that no one was detaining Litvinov, and the Dutch in Moscow reported on 23 August that London had confirmed that Litvinov was free to leave.[35]

The next day, according to Soviet sources, Chicherin told the Dutch minister, W. J. Oudenjik, that all British and French personnel could leave Russia only after the Norwegian government had notified Moscow that Litvinov and his staff had reached Bergen.[36] According to a U.S. source, however, the Dutch minister claimed that Chicherin had also insisted that the liberation of the interned French and British citizens "must coincide with the cessation of repressive measures against the adherents of the Soviet authorities in the Allied countries and on the territories occupied by . . . the English and Allied troops."[37] In other words, the internees were hostages, pure and simple. If the Soviet government thought that London could be blackmailed in such a crude way, however, it was quickly enlightened; by this time, the British were thoroughly disgusted with Soviet behavior, and the talks came to a halt.[38]

At this juncture, events occurred that were beyond the diplomats' control. On the morning of 30 August, M. S. Uritskii, head of the Petrograd Cheka, was murdered on the street by a military cadet, and that evening in Moscow, Lenin was seriously wounded by a young Left Socialist Revolutionary. The so-called Red Terror ensued. In Petrograd alone over 500 political prisoners were executed on 31 August and 1 September, and, more significant for our study of Litvinov, an armed mob stormed the British Embassy in Petrograd. The naval attache, Captain F.N.A. Cromie, was slain, but not before killing two of the invaders, and the embassy was sacked and its archives and documents taken. Cromie's body was dumped in the courtyard of the embassy church, and the remaining personnel were taken to the notorious prison in the Fortress of Peter and Paul. Even the Germans and Austrians vigorously protested these barbaric actions.[39]

As tensions grew and rumors abounded, Lockhart was arrested in Moscow on 3 September for "counterrevolutionary activities." On 6 September, the British arrested Litvinov and his staff, placed them in Brixton Prison without a formal accusation, and let it be known that they would stay there until all British subjects had left Russia. (This demand, of course, did not include British troops then fighting in northern Russia.)[40] Finally, on 15 September, negotiations began for an exchange of the hostages, but the talks got nowhere until the British government concluded that it would be impossible for its forces in northern Russia to reach Moscow by the coming winter and that, consequently, a compromise should be reached to obtain the release of as many Britons in Russia as possible.

The cabinet therefore summoned the leading advocate of compromise with Soviet Russia, Reginald Leeper,[41] and he proposed that, as a gesture of conciliation, the British should allow Litvinov and company to reach neutral soil before the Bolsheviks released the British internees. Understandably, the cabinet reversed this suggestion and said that the British must cross the Russian border before Litvinov and the others could leave Brixton. The cabinet then instructed Leeper to present this decision to Litvinov.[42] At Brixton, Leeper adamantly refused the prison governor's idea that an armed guard must accompany him into the "dangerous prisoner's cell," because Leeper believed that Litvinov had suffered enough indignity from British authorities, including a sign, Guest of His Majesty, hung over his cell door and the fact that he was allowed only a Bible to read.[43] Litvinov called the British proposal ridiculous and unacceptable, but he immediately suggested an alternative that quickly broke the deadlock. He proposed that he and the other Russians should be allowed to travel as far as Oslo before the British were allowed to cross the Finnish border but that he would give the British a written guarantee that he would return to England if Moscow refused to honor the agreement. The foreign secretary, Arthur James Balfour, thought that Litvinov's suggestion was quite fair and decided to proceed accordingly on his own authority.[44]

Ivan Maisky, however, claimed that Litvinov told him a somewhat different story. According to his version, Litvinov issued an ultimatum: Either the British government recognize him as the representative of the Soviet government and therefore release him, or they formally arrest him and not seek his help in securing the release of the prisoners in Russia.[45]

In any case, Litvinov and his associates left London in early October by a night train, and from Aberdeen, Litvinov telegraphed Chicherin that he was en route. As a concession on the Soviet side, thirty British subjects, including Lockhart, were released before Litvinov and his party reached Aberdeen. On the other hand, the Soviet government failed to honor Litvinov's pledge entirely and continued to hold forty-five Britons for over a year on the excuse that these people might be used in the ongoing British intervention because they were males between the ages of fifteen and forty-eight and deemed to be "bourgeois."[46] There is no evidence that the British asked Litvinov to return to England as he had promised he would do should his government not release all the hostages, probably because—as will be seen in the next chapter—the British did not want Litvinov back in their country for any reason.

Thus ended Litvinov's first diplomatic assignment, and it could hardly be termed a success, as the British government's already profound suspicion of the new regime in Moscow had been bolstered. Perhaps the British could have avoided some of the unfortunate events by simply granting diplomatic recognition to Litvinov. This move would have been very risky and politically difficult in the extreme, but it might have removed much of the basis for the Bolsheviks' violent anti-British propaganda. It certainly would have put Lenin in an awkward position and forced him to at least review an important part of his foreign policy.

For Litvinov personally, the experience was frustrating but probably exciting too. Litvinov apparently enjoyed the spotlight, even when his performance was not favorably reviewed, and in London he had certainly received a fair amount of attention from both the press and the state. But more important, Litvinov's days in London in 1917–1918 were his baptism in diplomacy. He had dealt with the representatives of a foreign power and had not done badly. He had had virtually to create and execute something that could be broadly called Soviet foreign policy toward Britain and had generally done so with restraint, patience, and persistence. As a complete novice, he could certainly have done much worse, and the fact that he left London in failure was owing largely to events beyond his control.

Three

KEEPING THE LINES OPEN

Litvinov and the West, 1918–1920

FROM 1918 TO 1920, the survival of the Soviet regime was constantly in question. Foreign troops landed with virtual impunity, and domestic anti-Bolshevik forces reached the height of their power. But the regime did survive, and although it is unquestionable that military might was its real savior, Litvinov's patient and persistent diplomacy certainly contributed to the grudging acceptance that Europe slowly accorded Soviet Russia. From late 1918 to the autumn of 1920, Litvinov was often, quite literally, the government's only official representative abroad. Faced with constant obstacles and snubs, Litvinov persevered and finally even achieved an agreement with Europe's dominant power, Great Britain.

The Soviet government had achieved a peace of sorts with Germany with the signing of the Brest-Litovsk Treaty in March 1918, but relations with the Entente (i.e., Britain and France) were still virtually nonexistent. In an effort to establish contacts with these powers and perhaps secure a basis for peace negotiations and economic talks, Litvinov, now a member of the Collegium of the Commissariat for Foreign Affairs, was sent to Stockholm in early December 1918. It is clear that Lenin attached some importance to this effort because following a meeting of the two men on 11 November, he dispatched a memorandum to all people's commissars asking them to give Litvinov any information and material that he might request in preparation for his mission. Three days earlier, the Soviet government had declared in a radio broadcast that it desired to talk peace with all states that were "waging war against Russia."[1]

31

One of Lenin's motivations clearly was fear of Anglo-French power as the war turned against Germany. Speaking before a mass rally in Moscow on 22 October, Lenin offered the obligatory thundering denunciations of "imperialists and multimillionaires" and asserted with complete confidence that "it is now clear that revolution is inevitable in all the belligerent countries." But he concluded on a more ominous note: "We have complete confidence that we will cope with the counter-revolution [which Lenin closely identified with the foreign intervention]. We know we have the forces but we also know that Anglo-French imperialism is stronger than we are." The solution, Lenin told his audience, was a tenfold increase in the size of the Red Army.[2]

But if the new regime was serious about Litvinov's peace mission, it is impossible to discern that fact from the contents of Foreign Commissar Georgii Chicherin's letter to President Woodrow Wilson of 24 October, which John Thompson has aptly described as "extremely caustic and insulting."[3] For example, Chicherin noted that Wilson's first gesture of "goodwill" toward Soviet Russia had been to give "every kind of assistance" to anti-Soviet forces on Russian soil. Instead of helping Russia have the chance to determine independently "her political development and her national policy," Wilson and his allies had sent "troops, to force on the Russian people the rule of . . . oppressing and exploiting classes." Asserting that the Soviet form of government "will soon be the universal form," Chicherin expressed his concern that "your post is not yet taken by Eugene Debs," the American socialist leader. Touching on the key element of Wilson's vision of a future world order, the League of Nations, Chicherin advised that "the League . . . be based on the expropriation of the capitalists in all countries."[4]

Accounting for a call for peace talks on the one hand and a personal attack on one of the leaders of the warring powers on the other is by no means an easy task. Maybe by the time of the 11 November meeting with Litvinov, which coincided with the signing of the Armistice, Lenin had decided that he must somehow deal with the Entente, or perhaps these acts were simply another manifestation of what E. H. Carr has aptly described a "dual policy" of seeking relations with the capitalist states while simultaneously promoting their overthrow. Or maybe there was simply confusion and division within the leadership over foreign policy. Whatever the case, there can be little doubt how Litvinov viewed this confusing "diplomacy," because a few weeks later, in a meeting in Stockholm with Wilson's unofficial envoy to the Bolsheviks, William H. Buckler, Litvinov said that he "personally deplored" Chicherin's remarks, calling them "propagandistic journalism . . . calculated to repel rather than conciliate."[5]

Once in Sweden, Litvinov, with only general instructions from his government, set out to improve Soviet Russia's international situation, and his actions suggest that he had learned in Britain that, as a diplomat, he must negotiate calmly and persistently with heads of state, not national constituencies of the international working class. On 23 December 1918, he addressed a note to the foreign ministers of the United States, Britain, France, and Italy. After an appropriately diplomatic introduction, Litvinov said that he was empowered by his government "to enter into preliminary peace negotiations . . . on all the outstanding questions which may give rise to a continuation of hostilities" if the respective governments were also prepared to do so.[6] Receiving no reply, the next day Litvinov sought to mend fences with President Wilson through direct correspondence.

Litvinov began his letter to Wilson with the interesting claim that the Soviet and U.S. public proposals for a European settlement had much in common, although he admitted that the Soviet concepts were "more extensive" (they included no annexations and no indemnities). Litvinov asserted that the "chief aim of the Soviets was to secure for the toiling majority of the Russian people economic liberty, without which political liberty is of no avail to them." He emphasized that the government's foremost need was for peace, which was unobtainable while foreign troops occupied Russian soil. If this intervention on the part of other powers was "successful," Litvinov predicted that there would follow "a restoration of the monarchy, leading to interminable revolutions and upheavals, and paralyzing . . . the country for long decades."[7]

Instead of that unfortunate scenario, Litvinov suggested that Wilson and the Allies should come to an understanding with the Soviet government that would involve a withdrawal of foreign troops and an end to the economic blockade. Such an arrangement would allow passions to subside, and then the other powers could help Russia rebuild the nation and participate in the exploitation of the country's "natural richness in the most effective way, for the benefit of all countries badly in need of foodstuffs and raw materials." He closed with an apology for the existence of the present dictatorship, claiming that it was not "an aim in itself, but the means of building up a new social system under which useful work and equal rights would be provided to all citizens. One may believe in this ideal or not, but it surely gives no justification for sending foreign troops to fight against it. I venture to appeal to your sense of justice and humanity."[8]

This remarkably diplomatic letter, following closely upon the shrill pronouncements signed by Chicherin, had some effect on Wilson, and it reflected two ideas that Litvinov was coming to embrace. First, his experience in London must have informed him of the dangers of attempting to deal with a traditional great power in an unorthodox way. It is very likely that Litvinov now wished that he had persisted in seeking formal contact with Lloyd George's government and had employed the conciliatory language he now used so skillfully with Wilson, although there certainly was no guarantee that this tactic would have met with success in London. Second, by early 1919 Litvinov had accepted the fact that Soviet Russia must forget about assistance from new socialist regimes for the foreseeable future. "The prospects for world revolution disappeared on November 11, 1918," was how he put it to Louis Fischer, a journalist and friend.[9] About the same time, Litvinov told Ludwig Meyer of the Norwegian Supreme Court that Soviet Russia needed "massive amounts" of foreign assistance. If an arrangement could be worked out, the Soviet government "would be willing to reconsider some of its decrees affecting financial obligations of Russia toward other countries" as long as doing so left intact the "cardinal principles of [Soviet] economic and financial policy." Specifically, Litvinov pledged that "special regard would be paid to the interest of small creditors abroad."[10]

Weak, disorganized, and badly mauled, Soviet Russia needed peace and help with reconstruction, and one did not obtain these aims by tweaking the British lion's tail or by insulting the U.S. president, regardless of one's personal feelings. The best hope, as Litvinov told his wife, was to seek good relations with the Allied powers, which he felt would redound to Russia's advantage both politically and economically.[11]

Litvinov must have been gratified by the response to his letter of 24 December. Wilson, who was already having doubts about the wisdom of intervention, showed the letter to Lloyd George, who was also deeply impressed, and only a few days after Christmas, Wilson suggested to the British prime minister that they formally and definitely ask Litvinov to elaborate on the Soviet government's proposal.[12] The British and Americans were now moving clearly toward the ill-fated Prinkipo plan, which provided that all "governments" in Russia should be heard before the great powers meeting in Paris settled on a Russian policy.[13]

The results of the Wilson–Lloyd George decision was a three-day conference between Litvinov and Buckler of the United States. At these confidential talks, Litvinov emphasized that the Soviet government fully supported the content of his letter to Wilson and was ready to "compromise on all points, including the Russian foreign debt, protection to existing foreign enterprises and the granting of new concessions in Russia." He insisted, however, that his government could not give details concerning future compromises until the Allied powers elaborated their claims and allowed the Soviet leadership sufficient time to assess whether it possessed the necessary resources to meet those claims. This proviso should be no great problem, he asserted, adding characteristically that the particulars could be worked out by a group of economic experts.[14] To bolster his argument, Litvinov then showed Buckler a telegram he had just received from Chicherin that confirmed the Soviets' willingness to conciliate on the question of the foreign debt.

Then Litvinov turned to the enticement of foreign concessions. He and his associates were fully aware "that for a long time Russia will need expert assistance and advice, especially in technical and financial matters" as well as foreign machinery and manufactured goods. Concerning the ever-sticky propaganda issue, Litvinov claimed that Soviet propaganda was directed primarily at the "militarist spirit of Germany," a country that was still in fact at war with Russia, "notwithstanding the nominal peace of Brest-Litovsk." In any event, the propaganda campaign would "cease as soon as the war stops," by which Litvinov also meant as soon as foreign troops were removed from Russia. He asserted that he had conducted no propaganda in Britain "except defense" of his government, and he urged Buckler to check this claim with the British Foreign Office. Litvinov added that his government fully realized that "in certain western countries, conditions were not favorable for a revolution of the Russian type. No amount of propaganda can produce such conditions."[15]

Beyond a revival of trade and an end to Communist propaganda, Litvinov extravagantly claimed that peace between Soviet Russia and the Allied powers would also mean the following: an amnesty to all Russian anti-Bolsheviks, who would be free to leave the country; an end to the Russian civil war, because the Bolsheviks' opponents would be helpless without foreign aid; and peace between Soviet Russia, on the one hand, and Poland, Finland, and the Ukraine, on the other. The source of the present conflict, Litvinov claimed, was the aid that the Allied powers were giving to the capitalists in those nations, who were virulently anti-Soviet. Moscow, in such a situation, felt "justified in supporting the working classes."

Litvinov admitted that his government had committed "many blunders," but he asserted that the system had worked well considering the enormous difficulties of the past year. And he reiterated that a restoration of the old regime would only lead to "more anarchy and starvation." He ended with the remark that if the new League of Nations could prevent war, "without encouraging reaction" and without interference in countries "supposed to be too advanced in their political and social aspirations," then "it can count on the support of the Soviet government," a truly remarkable statement when contrasted with the vituperation that Lenin and others heaped upon the League from its very inception.[16]

Evaluating the Soviet position, Buckler told Wilson that "the conciliatory attitude of the Soviet government is unquestionable." He believed, however, that not all Bolsheviks approved of this willingness to compromise, some actually wanting increased foreign intervention, which they believed would trigger revolutions in the intervening countries. Buckler added that prolonged intervention would certainly cause domestic unrest in the intervening countries and strengthen the hand of the extremists within Russia. Therefore, he felt that a policy of agreement with the Soviet regime—a policy that had some support within the Soviet leadership—was in the best interests of the major powers themselves.[17]

Litvinov's careful and impeccably diplomatic efforts to achieve a normalization of relations with those powers came close to bearing fruit. On 23 February, despite the grave misgivings of France, the Allied powers proposed that "every organized group that is now exercising or attempting to exercise political or military authority anywhere in Siberia, or within the boundaries of European Russia,

... send representatives" to a conference on the Island of Prinkipo in the Sea of Marmara. There they would meet with great-power diplomats, and everyone would confer "in the freest and frankest way" in order to facilitate a settlement both within Russia and between Russia and the rest of the world. The problem was that the execution of this whole proposal was contingent upon the attainment of a "truce of arms amongst the parties invited."[18]

Chicherin was highly suspicious of the offer,[19] but on 4 February, he communicated the Soviet government's acceptance of the Prinkipo plan. Reflecting Lenin's remarks concerning the superior power of the Allied countries, Chicherin outlined the impressive lengths to which the Soviet government would go to achieve peace with those countries, even including a willingness to discuss a partial annexation of Russian territory by those powers. He concluded, however, with the remark that the "scope of the concessions" depended upon "the military situation in relation to the Western powers," which Chicherin claimed rather prematurely was "improving every day."[20]

The Prinkipo plan, which Litvinov's patient diplomacy had done much to promote, was never implemented. If Britain and France had much confidence in the conference, which they ostensibly endorsed, their actions vis-à-vis the anti-Bolshevik forces did not reflect that fact. As John Thompson has pointed out, "from all sides the anti-Bolshevik governments received intimations that Allied aid would continue and that the Prinkipo plan would fail," and Admiral Aleksandr Kolchak, a leading anti-Bolshevik commander, put the matter even more succinctly: "While the British government advises an arrangement with the Bolsheviks, they continue to furnish me with generous supplies."[21] The plan, therefore, came to naught primarily because France and Britain apparently did not want it to work.

With Prinkipo a failure, President Wilson turned to William C. Bullitt, a friend of Wilson's trusted adviser, Colonel Edward House, and asked Bullitt to go to Russia and investigate conditions there.[22] Clearly, the U.S. president did not wish to close the door on the Bolsheviks, a feeling that was probably strengthened by Litvinov's letter of December 1918.

Bullitt carried with him an eight-point peace proposal, although it is by no means clear to what extent Wilson drafted or endorsed this plan, so the Soviet government was finally to receive something it had sought for some time. As recently as 10 January 1919, Litvinov and his assistant in Stockholm, V. V. Vorovskii, had asked Ludwig Meyer, then a counselor on the staff of the Supreme Allied Council, if he could ascertain exactly what it was that the Allies required for peace. The Russians said that because those powers were the aggressors, they must formulate and make known their demands. When that was done, the Soviet government would "not fail to state clearly and in unmistakable terms to what extent these demands could be satisfied." This statement, coupled with Litvinov's earlier talks with Buckler, demonstrates that the Soviet leadership was indeed desperate to at least begin talks with the intervening powers.[23]

On 8 March, Chicherin and Litvinov personally received Bullitt at the railroad station in Petrograd, a further indication of the seriousness with which the Bolsheviks viewed Bullitt's mission. Two days later, they left for the new capital, Moscow,[24] where Bullitt met with Litvinov and Chicherin for several days, later referring to the former as "practically the Assistant Secretary for Foreign Affairs."[25] The three men hammered out an agreement, and on 14 March, Lenin, accompanied by Chicherin and Litvinov, presented a draft of the agreement to a special plenum of the Central Committee.[26] The main points in summary were as follows:

1. All existing de facto governments on the territory of the former Russian Empire and Finland would remain in full control of the territories they occupied at the moment of the Armistice, the revision of frontiers to take place only by the self-determination of the inhabitants. Each government would agree not to use force against any of the others.

2. The blockade would be raised and normal trade relations reestablished between the Allies and the territories under control of the Soviet government.

3. The Soviet government would have the right of unhindered rail transit to the sea and the use of all former Russian and Finnish ports necessary for trade.

4. Soviet citizens would have the right of free entry into Allied countries and countries set up on former Russian territory, provided they did not interfere in the domestic politics of those countries. These rights would be reciprocated.

5. All governments on former Russian territory would grant a general amnesty to all political opponents, offenders, and

prisoners, and the Allied governments would do the same
with all Russian political prisoners whom they held. All
prisoners of war, including civil war prisoners on both sides,
would fall into this category.

6. All foreign troops would be withdrawn from Russia, and
foreign military assistance to anti-Soviet governments on the
territory of the former Russian Empire would cease. At the
same time, the Soviet government and all other governments
on this territory would demobilize their armies and reduce
their armaments to peacetime levels, which would be agreed
upon at the peace conference.

7. All governments set up on Russian territory would recognize
their share in the responsibility for the debts of the former
Russian Empire.[27]

Lenin needed all of his prestige to gain acceptance of the proposal,
although he could not prevent the addition by the plenum of certain
reservations—for example, when considering the issue of debts owed
to the Allies, the value of Russian gold and steamships seized by them
must be taken into account.[28] It was also added that the Soviet
government would accept these terms only if the Allies offered them
before 10 April. In view of the considerable territorial concessions
involved, the Bolsheviks could hardly propose the terms themselves.[29]

Indeed, the new regime viewed this agreement as another Brest-
Litovsk. The day before the plenum and after Lenin's last meeting
with Bullitt, Lenin had publicly gone beyond what he had pronounced
on 22 October in Moscow. He had conceded that Soviet Russia was
in circumstances very similar to those of the spring of 1918. The need
for retreat was clear, and there was no mention of the Red Army's
being able to save the new regime.[30] Bullitt later testified that he left
Russia convinced that Lenin, Chicherin, and Litvinov were all aware
of their country's need for peace and that the details of the draft
agreement could be successfully modified. On the other hand, he also
believed that what he carried back from Moscow "in the main . . .
represented the minimum terms that the Soviet government would
accept."[31]

Nothing ever came of the Bullitt mission. Wilson was plagued by
the issues regarding Germany, and Lloyd George had to contend with

a British press that was increasingly anti-Bolshevik. The French, of course, had never liked the idea of talks with the Bolsheviks in the first place. This unfavorable attitude toward Moscow received added weight with news of the rapid advance of the anti-Bolshevik, Admiral Kolchak—in Paris it was believed that he would take Moscow before the end of April.[32]

The years 1919 and 1920 were indeed dark days for the Russian people, virtually a second time of troubles, complete with a Polish invasion. But this period ended with a Bolshevik victory in the civil war and the collapse of the foreign intervention. By the end of 1920, it was clear to most observers that the Bolshevik regime and the great powers would all continue to exist indefinitely[33]—Litvinov had believed so for some time. In any case, in November 1919, Litvinov again left Russia for talks with an Allied power, Britain. This time the talks, which the British refused to hold in Moscow or London so they took place in Copenhagen, had a limited agenda—an exchange of prisoners still held in Russia and Britain.

The British proposed opening negotiations on a prisoner exchange because the families of the nearly 1,000 British subjects involved were clamoring for the repatriation of their relatives. The issue had first been raised in Stockholm, when Litvinov had replied that he would gladly discuss the matter,[34] but at that time, the British government had balked, accepting the assertion of the permanent undersecretary for foreign affairs, Lord Hardinge, that the Bolshevik price for an exchange would be the Allied "withdrawal from Siberia and Archangel" and that this price was "too heavy." By late 1919, with the tide turning against the Allied intervention, the notion of direct talks with Moscow was upgraded from "fatal" to merely "distasteful," although the Foreign Office adamantly resisted the notion that the new regime should receive diplomatic recognition.[35] Any talks would be limited strictly to the prisoner issue.

The Soviets, not surprisingly, never had any intention of limiting the talks or of expediting their conclusion, as the British fervently desired. Instead, Lenin wanted Litvinov to prolong the talks as long as possible and to attempt to encompass a whole range of foreign policy problems—and not just those with Britain. Litvinov later recalled that Lenin had given him these instructions because at the time, Soviet Russia still lacked formal diplomatic relations with any country and Litvinov would be the country's only official representative abroad.

Any nation that talked with Litvinov, it was argued, would therefore be in the position of granting de facto recognition of the new regime.[36]

Litvinov's departure was set for mid-November. During the preceding weeks, he met frequently with Chicherin and Lenin and selected his two assistants, Roza Zaretskaia and Liza Milanova. In his meetings with Lenin, Litvinov was instructed to distribute the Soviet peace proposal to all the embassies in the Danish capital, and Lenin reaffirmed his approval of the tactics that Litvinov had used in Stockholm: "Let everyone know that we want peace," he told Litvinov, but "rescue the prisoners without fail!" Lenin believed that the accomplishment of the latter task would be "both a foreign and domestic victory" for the Bolsheviks. In addition, Lenin authorized Litvinov to conduct negotiations with the new states that had recently been part of the Russian Empire and to open economic talks with all the Scandinavian countries.[37] As Louis Fischer has observed, Litvinov thus left Russia as "diplomat, humanitarian, and State merchant," but his overriding goal was to establish a modus vivendi between Soviet Russia and capitalist Europe.[38]

The Soviet historian, Valerii Shishkin, stresses the uniqueness of the Litvinov mission to Copenhagen. Soviet Russia was no longer offering one-sided territorial concessions and sacrifices from a position dictated by utter helplessness, as at Brest-Litovsk; instead, the Soviets wished to talk about "judicious compromise with the capitalist countries."[39] Shishkin may overstate the case, but clearly Soviet Russia's international position was finally improving.

In mid-November, the small Soviet delegation first arrived in the capital of Estonia. There they spent three days under heavy guard— Litvinov was not even allowed to go to the toilet unattended—because the Estonian authorities with whom he held talks emphasized that they could not guarantee his safety, and Litvinov himself expected some sort of violence from the anti-Bolsheviks, who he claimed had "swarmed into Estonia" before his arrival. His attempts to initiate peace talks with the Estonian officials were rebuffed, and there was nothing to do but proceed to Copenhagen.[40]

Following a three-day voyage on a British cruiser through the choppy waters of the Baltic Sea, the Bolsheviks reached their destination. They were very glad to be there, for on the journey they had been kept separated and refused permission to converse with the ship's crew. Upon alighting, Litvinov saw that seven "police spies" were waiting—curiously, they were all dressed the same. Like shadows, they were to be with Litvinov during his entire stay in Denmark.[41]

On 25 November 1919, after months of preparation, the actual talks began. Litvinov's counterpart was an Irishman, James O'Grady, an experienced trade unionist who had also been a member of Parliament but was hardly someone who could be called prominent in British political circles. Litvinov claimed that he got along well enough with O'Grady except for one occasion. Early in the talks, the latter said he might have trouble "finding a common language with the representative of a country that had exterminated its crowned head." Litvinov eyed O'Grady and said that unless his memory failed him, he believed that the English had sent a king to the executioner's block. According to Litvinov, O'Grady quickly changed the subject and became lost in a cloud of cigar smoke.[42]

Having cleared that issue aside, Litvinov soon placed the Soviet position before O'Grady. Obviously with an eye to prolonging the talks, Litvinov said that Russia, in return for the British prisoners, wanted the following:

1. Approximately 100 Russians recently taken prisoner by the retreating British at Archangel.
2. All Russians imprisoned by Britain in Turkey, Persia, Egypt, and all British colonies.
3. All Russians who had fled from German prison camps and who were presently scattered throughout western Europe.
4. Admission of a Soviet representative to the international commission dealing with the problem of Russian prisoners still in Germany.[43]

O'Grady was stunned, especially by the last request. He was not empowered to negotiate on behalf of the German government, whose permission presumably was needed for a Soviet representative to sit on the commission. The British foreign secretary, Lord Curzon, was also aghast, and in a clear effort to keep Soviet Russia out of European affairs as much as possible, he instructed O'Grady to offer Litvinov other inducements to reduce the demands—from offering "food and medical supplies to even the possibility of lifting the blockade."[44] While O'Grady communicated with London and Lord Curzon, Litvinov tried a tactic he had used in Stockholm a year earlier: He sent a message containing the peace resolution of the Seventh Congress of Soviets to all the embassies in Copenhagen. All his messages were returned unopened, as they had been in Stockholm.[45]

When the talks were resumed, Litvinov suggested that they go beyond talking about a prisoner exchange to discuss the establishment of a "real peace." O'Grady, however, adhered to his instructions, and on 12 February 1920, the two men signed an agreement on a prisoner exchange, which provided for the repatriation of virtually all prisoners, both civilian and military. With that matter settled, the British helped Litvinov obtain similar exchange treaties with the Scandinavian states, Austria, Hungary (where the Bolsheviks' ally, Bela Kun, had recently been deposed), Switzerland, Holland, Belgium, Italy, and even France. Even though Litvinov was unable to draw the British into more-comprehensive talks, he proudly believed that these agreements greatly increased the international prestige of Soviet Russia and were equivalent to de facto recognition.[46]

Of greater importance for the new regime was the historic decision of the Supreme Council of the Entente on 16 January 1920 to lift the blockade of Russia, although the council added that trade would be allowed only with the people, not with the Bolshevik regime. Arguably, this proviso betrayed a woeful ignorance on the part of the victorious powers, because one of the cardinal points of Bolshevik policy was a state monopoly of foreign trade. Certainly, the Soviet leadership found the council's statement amusing, and even the staid Chicherin could not suppress a chuckle years later when he thought of it.[47]

The Soviet government responded to the decision by presenting an existing Soviet institution *Tsentrosoiuz*, an acronym for the Central Trade Union, as the representative of the Russian people. As if to underline the absurdity of the affair from the Soviet point of view, some of the country's best-known diplomats, including Litvinov, were appointed to be "representatives" of *Tsentrosoiuz*. The British, however, flatly rejected the prospect of the recently expelled Litvinov returning to London for trade talks, and Litvinov advised Moscow that the economic needs of Russia were too great to have the talks delayed over the matter of his presence. Lenin agreed, and the Soviet trade delegation arrived in London without Litvinov.[48] Under the capable leadership of Leonid Krasin, the Soviet government obtained a trade agreement with Britain, and it was signed on 16 March 1921.[49]

Meanwhile, in Scandinavia, Litvinov met with more than just government agents. He established a modest salon where he received anyone who wished to know the Bolshevik version of what was happening in his country and what the new regime hoped to achieve— in other words, Litvinov limited discussions to events within Russia. In this way, he rather immodestly reported, he "won a considerable number of friends" for the new government.[50] Of more tangible consequence, Litvinov also had discussions with various European businessmen, including Swedish industrialists and Italian and Danish merchants, and he contracted with a Danish firm for the purchase of a large amount of grain seed, something the Russians desperately needed.[51] His negotiations with these capitalists were not without certain temptations. Ivy recalled that often a visitor "left" something after their talks, for example, a box of fine cigars, but Litvinov always returned this "forgotten" property. He said such items were "trifles" rather than bribes, telling Ivy with disgust: "Bribes! Do you realize that I could be rolling in gold if I liked?"[52]

As noted, the center of Russia's formal diplomatic activity was shifting to the trade talks in London. In the early summer of 1920, Litvinov's wife, their son Mikhail, and their new daughter, Tatiana, had joined him in Copenhagen, and in a last chat with O'Grady, the Irishman asked Litvinov if his family had left England with the intention of returning with him to Russia. Litvinov replied in the affirmative. "For how long?" asked O'Grady. "For good," was Litvinov's reply. In September 1920, they sailed for Petrograd.[53]

In these early years of the Soviet regime some important aspects of Litvinov's diplomacy emerged. His determination to normalize relations with the capitalist powers can be clearly discerned in his letter to Wilson and in his condemnation of Chicherin's abusive letter to the president. Eventually, Lenin accepted a policy of conciliation that was much closer to Litvinov's position than to that of Chicherin, although nothing ever came of this policy after the failure of the Prinkipo plan. On a more positive note, Litvinov held his own in the one-on-one negotiations with O'Grady. It is true that he was unable to achieve Lenin's maximum program, but he did establish contacts with several European states and signed agreements for prisoner exchanges with them. And in this task he was able to obtain British assistance, no mean accomplishment given London's animosity toward Soviet Russia.

None of the above, however, should obscure the basic fact that hostile recrimination remained the norm in relations between Soviet Russia and the great powers throughout most of the 1920s. But it was becoming increasingly clear to many non-Russians that some type of broad settlement, especially economic, must be reached with Moscow, and the new revolutionary regime and the other powers did finally meet at the diplomatic table. It was not an edifying experience for either side.

Four

THE CONFERENCES AT GENOA
AND THE HAGUE

IN 1921 AND 1922, Litvinov, now a deputy commissar for foreign affairs, continued his efforts to achieve a modus vivendi with the capitalist powers. He made a public overture to the United States and, in a truly spectacular move, tried to change Soviet policy on the crucial issues of imperial debts, confiscated foreign properties, and foreign credits for the new regime. Indeed, when Litvinov was free to act without the restraining presence of Foreign Commissar Chicherin, he went so far in his concessions to the capitalist powers that his own government publicly disavowed his actions.

In December 1920, Litvinov was named deputy commissar of foreign affairs and given direct supervision of all organizational work—including, presumably, a strong voice in diplomatic appointments—and the Western Section of the Foreign Commissariat. Chicherin, unique among the Bolsheviks in that he had served briefly in the imperial diplomatic service, took protocol and the Eastern Section. This division of authority, however, was not hermetic, and important policy matters were reviewed by both men. But according to two highly knowledgeable observers, Litvinov gave special attention to Europe,[1] which was only natural, given his familiarity with the region and, in the case of Britain, his personal high regard for that pivotal nation. At first, however, Litvinov had to wait until the western countries were again ready to talk with Soviet Russia; that was to occur at the Genoa Conference in April 1922.

Litvinov also devoted much of his time to the organization of the Soviet diplomatic corps,[2] and fiscal discipline within that sometimes profligate commissariat particularly concerned him. Since his early party days, Litvinov had been recognized as a capable and rather

47

tightfisted individual when it came to party funds;[3] he was the same
with government funds. In late 1921, Litvinov wrote to Lenin that
upon study, it had been discovered that many Soviet representatives
abroad were holding large sums of government money in their personal
bank accounts. In one case, the Soviet representative in Revel, Estonia,
a man named Gukovskii, had died, and Litvinov's efforts to obtain the
government funds deposited in his name had proved unsuccessful.
Litvinov proposed, therefore, that all sums held abroad be placed at
once into Soviet government accounts. This eminently sensible and
urgently needed measure was promptly approved by Lenin and the
Council of People's Commissars (Sovnarkom).[4]

This organizational work was interrupted in the summer of 1921
when Litvinov was again called upon to leave the country to negotiate
with a capitalist power. As in the past, Litvinov saw an opportunity
to establish some sort of permanent relations, but this time, the issue
was not peace, debts, or prisoners but literally life or death for millions
of Russians, especially children. Once again, Russia was facing its
distressingly frequent historical problem—famine—and this time, the
disaster was aggravated by years of war and turmoil. Indeed, by mid-
1921, it was already clear that the main grain-producing regions would
be particularly hard hit; Russia was again on the verge of complete
collapse.

Soon after writer Maxim Gorky's famous appeal "To All Honest
People" to help the Russians in their fight against starvation, Litvinov
went to Riga and negotiated a relief agreement with Walter L. Brown,
the European director of the American Relief Administration. But
reaching an agreement was no easy matter. When Litvinov told Lenin
during the talks that the United States insisted on the right to select
the area where the relief would be distributed, Lenin exploded,
privately referring to the "baseness" of the Americans. After reflection,
however, Lenin calmed down and merely instructed Litvinov not to
let the United States be "insolent."[5]

Litvinov remained for the most part businesslike. He announced
simply that the Soviet government would not allow a foreign power
to use famine conditions in order to circumvent the new regime and
deal directly with the Russian people. A brief stalemate ensued until
Herbert Hoover, director of the American Relief Administration and
hardly a friend of Soviet communism, decided to compromise. His
primary interest, Hoover said, was "simply to save the lives of children."

Specifically, Hoover allowed the Soviet government some measure of control over the selection of relief personnel to be sent into the country and the areas where food and supplies would be distributed. But Litvinov insisted that his government must have the right to expel anyone it judged guilty of pursuing political or commercial activities, contending that such a provision was necessary to preserve the appearance of Soviet sovereignty in relation to the relief mission. Indeed, the affair had become something of a matter of national pride for Litvinov. In the midst of the negotiations, Ivy said, "How sad we have to appeal to Americans to help," and Litvinov pointedly replied, "Ah, you too feel for the honor of Russia."[6] In the end, Hoover agreed to the Soviet conditions.[7]

At the ceremonial signing of the relief agreement in Riga, Litvinov seized the opportunity to renew his bid for the establishment of diplomatic relations with the United States, which he had initiated earlier in London, by praising the negotiations as a potential stepping-stone to a "more extended treaty" between the two governments. Brown was caught off guard by this injection of politics into the ceremony and did not respond directly to Litvinov's remarks.[8] Nonetheless, Litvinov's service to his nation at these talks can be viewed as one of his most praiseworthy achievements.

About a month later, Litvinov characterized the talks in a remarkably frank matter to a correspondent of the *New York Tribune.* Taking a slap at both Lenin and Hoover, Litvinov declared: "The trouble is that there has been too much suspicion on the one side and lack of confidence on the other. If you apply my remark to either side you will not be incorrect."[9] This observation was perhaps true enough, but it should be noted that once the actual talks began, the two men in Riga took only a little more than a week to reach an agreement. This remarkable diplomatic celerity clearly reflected the gravity of the issue with which the men were grappling, but it was also a tribute to their own efficiency and reasonableness.

With the conclusion of famine relief talks, Litvinov turned to a diplomatic offensive for broader economic aid. In late October he publicly acknowledged that Russia had been "obliged to establish a *modus vivendi*" between it and the "capitalists systems" and said that Moscow was "willing to recognize all debts. It is not merely a question of paying but of finding a way of paying those debts." To solve this problem, Litvinov suggested a "joint conference between the Soviet government and the Western powers."[10] A couple of weeks later, Litvinov told the Swedish press that the New Economic Policy, which loosened government control of the economy, was evidence of Moscow's desire to bring "order and system into Russia's economic life." He added, however, that his country could "not pull itself up by its own bootstraps and therefore appeals to Western Europe and to America" for help. With the establishment of mutually advantageous trade relations based on Soviet "raw materials and potential" and western "industry," Russia would be able to "a certain extent to compensate her old creditors." But he repeated that to achieve this, an international conference should be convened. He added enticingly that if such a meeting were held and a "definite settlement of the entire Russian problem" achieved, then the Soviet government "would undoubtedly be prepared to go beyond" its previous proposals on the debt issue.[11]

While Litvinov was on the diplomatic stump for a general European settlement, the rest of Europe was having its own problems, a fact clearly acknowledged in the Allied Supreme Council's Cannes Resolution of January 1922. Its call for a European conference to address the issue of economic recovery led to the Genoa Conference of April 1922 and Soviet Russia's first appearance at a diplomatic gathering with the other European powers.[12] The two immediate problems that were disrupting Europe's postwar restoration were German reparations and Russia's repudiated debts. As long as these issues remained unresolved, economic stability was virtually impossible. The reparations issue never was really settled, despite the Young and Dawes plans, and the problem of Russia's debts met the same fate, despite the Genoa and Hague conferences of 1922.

Beyond the specific economic issues, however, was a more basic problem. Britain and France had not yet allowed either Germany or Soviet Russia to return to the European community as full partners. France, with some justification, wanted Germany to be a financial account to be drawn upon virtually at will, and all western countries generally took the position that repudiated debts had to be paid and nationalized properties returned or suitable compensation given. The Russians were willing to discuss such a policy but would seriously consider it only in return for substantial credits or loans. The French government, however, publicly proposed in February 1922 that its erstwhile Russian ally actually should accept a "system of capitulations" similar to that existing in China and Turkey before the war. This idea, which seems preposterous in hindsight, appeared in the London Memorandum of March 1922, signed jointly by France, Britain, Italy, Belgium and Japan. A typical provision held that no foreigner would be arrested in Russia without the permission of the concerned nation's consul![13] It is not difficult to understand why the Soviet government scrambled subsequently for an agreement with Germany on the eve of the Genoa Conference. If such terms were the price for economic reintegration into Europe, then Lenin and the Bolsheviks would look elsewhere.

Initially, however, the Soviet government placed great importance on the Genoa Conference, judging by the rather heated internal policy debates that occurred in early February 1922. On 5 February 1922, the Politburo appointed a special commission to study the issues that were likely to arise at Genoa. Chicherin chaired the commission, and its leading members were Litvinov; N. N. Krestinskii, an old Bolshevik and later Soviet *polpred* to Germany; A. A. Ioffe, the Soviet *polpred* to Germany immediately after the Brest-Litovsk Treaty; and the capable negotiator Leonid Krasin.[14] These men were hardly unanimous in their opinions.

All agreed that Soviet Russia must not allow its sovereignty to be subordinated to the capitalist powers, but they sharply disagreed concerning the policy goals and the tactics to be employed at the conference.[15] At one extreme stood Ioffe, who argued that Genoa should primarily be used as a platform for revolutionary propaganda, but he was practically alone in his opinion and out of tune with the dominant policy of retreat from revolutionary internationalism embodied in the New Economic Policy. In marked contrast, the former businessman Leonid Krasin asserted that the country's transportation, agricultural, and industrial systems were in such disarray that not only should the Bolsheviks recognize the imperial debts but they should also be prepared to compensate foreign investors for their losses. Otherwise, the new regime should expect no assistance in the formidable task of reconstruction.[16]

Litvinov also rejected the notion of using Genoa as a propaganda forum. Writing without knowledge of the harsh French-sponsored plans for Soviet Russia, Litvinov asserted that the Soviet delegation should use the Cannes Resolution as a basis for an economic agreement and he hoped that it would pave the way for eventual de jure recognition.[17] Litvinov knew that although this resolution conceded the troubled state of the European economy, it also laid down certain principles for Europe's recovery. Most important, it would guarantee the right of each state to order its own economy and government as it saw fit, but the resolution added that all states "must recognize all public debts and obligations and compensate foreign interests for confiscated property." In this latter context, Soviet Russia was specifically named.[18] By urging acceptance of these terms, Litvinov was clearly aligning himself with Krasin against those people who wished to propagandize for Marxist revolution at Genoa.

Litvinov was nonetheless rather pessimistic, even at this early date, as he did not expect that either de jure recognition or any substantial loans on an acceptable basis would be granted at the actual conference. Indeed, he believed that Russia possibly faced another military intervention, this time from Poland, Finland, and Romania, with French approval. If events reached such a dire crisis, Litvinov felt the Soviets should turn to Britain with a request for aid, although he conceded frankly that this proposal had only a slight chance of success.[19] Litvinov believed that the more likely result would be a failure at Genoa and a superficial increase in European anti-Bolshevik sentiment. But he accurately predicted that such a situation would not last because of the economic crisis, especially unemployment, in Europe. Soon, he believed, individual states would be forced into agreements with Moscow, which might even entail formal recognition, the plum that Litvinov desired from Britain with almost obsessive zeal.[20]

Members of the Politburo may well have wondered why Litvinov placed such emphasis on Britain, the land of imperialism par excellence, but Litvinov's Soviet biographer Z. S. Sheinis has noted that the deputy commissar's emphasis was quite justified. Some of the reasons he cites are: "Significant circles of the British bourgeoisie were striving for trade and economic relations with Soviet Russia. Lloyd George was prepared to extend recognition; and the British working class was the most active of the European proletariat in opposing the [earlier] intervention." Sheinis adds that all these factors were in sharp contrast to France, which was the leader of anti-Soviet feeling in Europe. Therefore, Litvinov bluntly stated, "In European issues we should orient ourselves toward Britain."[21]

Despite Litvinov's understandable pessimism concerning the Genoa Conference, he felt that the Soviet delegation should arrive there with a detailed program for reestablishing a European status quo. Accordingly, he suggested that the Soviets propose the following: a mutual annulment of all debts and claims; disarmament; stabilization of the international monetary system; general but partial devaluation of paper money in the impoverished states; and an abolition of tariff barriers that impeded commercial relations. This plan has been succinctly described as, "not communist propaganda, but a palliative which could be accomplished" with the bourgeois world.[22]

Sheinis concludes his archival-based account of Litvinov's early pro-British proposals to the supreme authorities of Soviet Russia with the remark that Litvinov also "gave great significance to relations and an agreement with the German government." He claims further that Litvinov "discussed this in his letter to the Politburo," but he offers no direct quotations.[23] The fact that Sheinis is comparatively silent on Litvinov's allegedly strong feelings in favor of an agreement with Germany (and which eventually came about as the result of the Treaty of Rapallo) is probably because Litvinov only grudgingly accepted such a policy, having regarded Germany with great suspicion since the days of Brest-Litovsk. Gustav Hilger, a German diplomat intimately involved in Soviet-German relations between the two world wars, asserted that "for Chicherin, Rapallo was one of the main pillars of Soviet foreign policy. In Litvinov's eyes, however, Rapallo was a political expedient just as any other measure was."[24] A higher-level German diplomat of the same era was more blunt. Herbert von Dirksen declared that Litvinov's "sympathies were with Great Britain. [He] had to be earnestly admonished from time to time when he was disposed to deviate from the correct faith to the Western heresy."[25] Finally, the German historian, Martin Walsdorff, a specialist on German-Soviet relations in the 1920s, has observed that Litvinov's years in exile had given him a very different outlook on Europe from that of Chicherin and that he totally lacked Chicherin's "hatred of England."[26] In the face of this evidence, it seems unlikely that Adam Ulam is correct in his statement that Litvinov's pro-Western reputation is "a legend."[27]

None of this discussion, however, is intended to suggest that Litvinov's inclinations were the result of anything but hardheaded realism. He simply believed that Britain, if handled properly, had potentially the most to offer Soviet Russia and that Germany would always be a potential enemy. Still, his hopes for better, and even cordial, relations with London were never realized, and although

Litvinov can hardly be blamed for that fact, it was certainly one of his great professional disappointments.

Many of Litvinov's proposals were incorporated into the final Soviet position at Genoa,[28] but because of the influence of Chicherin, the Soviet program's first point was the idea that "African and other colonial peoples [be allowed] to participate, on an equal footing, with the European peoples in conferences and commissions."[29] This point may have been a noble and laudable sentiment in principle, but in the context of the times, it amounted to little more than a gratuitous slap at the British and French. Again, the dual nature of Soviet policy is evident.

With the program settled, the Soviet delegation, headed by Chicherin, arrived in Genoa in April 1922, but only after a stopover in Berlin where Chicherin sought to reach an agreement with the German government that could be presented as a fait accompli to the other countries. The Germans, however, refused to sign the proposed treaty, largely because of objections on the part of Foreign Minister Walter Rathenau, a man who deeply desired accommodation with the western powers. President Friedrich Ebert supported that position.[30]

En route, Litvinov informed Moscow on 5 April of the virtual impossibility of achieving anything constructive at Genoa with the capitalist powers. He had learned that

> France has decided to blow up the conference no matter what
> the costs. Lloyd George remains in power by the favor of his
> Conservative colleagues in the cabinet. Lloyd George has
> struggled against a limitation of his authority, but in the Russian
> matter he still runs into serious opposition from the
> Conservative members of his cabinet and his friend Churchill.[31]

Clearly, Litvinov understood now that Russia could expect nothing from the Allied powers. Accordingly, he accepted the need for a treaty with Germany, despite his personal inclinations.[32] Indeed, there existed no other choice.

With little hope for a Soviet-British rapprochement at Genoa, it is not surprising that Litvinov kept an unusually low profile. After the initial speeches, during which Franco-Soviet hostility received a distressingly clear airing,[33] Lloyd George proposed that the British and the Russians get together informally to discuss mutual financial claims, that seemingly insurmountable block between Soviet Russia and the capitalist countries. At the first of these meetings, Litvinov gave Soviet figures for damage inflicted by foreign troops during the 1918–1920 intervention. His heart, however, clearly was not in his task. One observer noted that Litvinov spoke "in a kind of impassive, expressionless tone";[34] clearly, he was bored. But the total bill he presented (about 50 billion gold rubles) did not in the least bore the British prime minister, who called the amount "absolutely incomprehensible." Lloyd George insisted that the Russians must take into account all the aid Russia had received during the war.[35]

That remark was more than the knowledgeable and recognized Anglophobe Chicherin could endure. Normally a quite composed negotiator, he rather lost control of himself, shouting, "What did Russia gain from the war? We lost 20 billion gold rubles and lives to match. These things have freed the new Russia from any obligations to the Entente."[36] To that problem, one must add the French and Belgian insistence on the immediate return of all nationalized properties or appropriate compensation as the precondition for further negotiation.[37]

The Germans, however, were kept in the dark about the true nature of these stormy informal talks between the Soviets and the capitalist powers, and Berlin's greatest nightmare was the prospect that Russia would come out of the talks with an agreement at German expense: a settlement wherein Russia would be allowed to demand reparations from Germany on the basis of Article 116 of the Treaty of Versailles. Utterly ignorant of the facts, but fearing the worst, the German delegation received a now-famous predawn telephone call from the Russians on 16 April. The latter made no mention of the difficulties being encountered at the conference and asked the Germans if they would now like to sign the treaty drafted in Berlin. Rathenau, almost in a panic, made repeated efforts to reach Lloyd George but was told the prime minister was asleep and could not be disturbed. It seemed clear that Britain had abandoned the idea of a suitable settlement with Germany. Rathenau and the Germans capitulated, and in signing the Treaty of Rapallo, Germany and Russia renounced all mutual claims, and Germany promised to give all possible support to private German firms operating in Russia.[38] Thanks to the almost incomprehensible behavior of the British, Chicherin gained the crowning glory of his diplomatic career.

Rathenau was crushed by the turn of events, writing that "this period . . . is nothing else than a farewell to everything." Within two months he would be dead, murdered by young Nazis.[39] Litvinov, despite the failure of his own plans, derived a certain grim pleasure from the Germans' predicament. He wrote to Moscow that "our semiprivate talks with the Supreme Council inspired alarm in the hearts of the Germans. Rathenau, neither alive nor dead, came running to us yesterday and offered . . . to sign the very same agreement which he had rejected during our stay in Berlin."[40] Ten years later at Geneva, Litvinov, speaking publicly about the Treaty of Rapallo, was more politic. He said that although the war had been over four years, "there was no real peace among the Soviet Union, Germany, and the other powers. Germany and Russia were both isolated. [They were] even hostile to each other but overcame that to lay aside the recent difficult past. This was dictated by a correct understanding of each nation's own interests."[41]

After the signing of the Treaty of Rapallo, the Genoa Conference dragged on for a few more weeks but without results. With biting sarcasm, Litvinov wrote that the only accomplishment of Genoa was Rapallo, but that in an effort to save himself from political disgrace, Lloyd George arranged for the Hague Conference to take place that summer. There the "Russian question" could be considered anew.[42]

Chicherin, satisfied with the new Soviet-German rapprochement, had no desire to argue further with the capitalist powers about repudiated debts and nationalized properties. Exhausted after the intense diplomatic activity of the spring, Chicherin, whose health was never robust, went to Berlin and other parts of Germany to "take a well-deserved rest."[43] It was left to Litvinov to head the Soviet delegation in the Hague.

Upon arriving, in June 1922, Litvinov addressed a large press conference and took a hard line. He insisted that the Russians "have come to hear what other nations have to offer in the way of credits" and that they would drop their counterclaim of 50 million gold rubles only in return for such credits.[44] However, almost simultaneously, Litvinov led the Dutch foreign minister to believe that his tough talk was "bluff imposed on the delegation by Moscow" and that once the bluff was called, Litvinov would seek fresh instructions because "Russia couldn't afford to come empty-handed" from the Hague.[45]

The history of the ensuing futile negotiations in the Hague can be followed in detail in the British Foreign Office papers, and there is a certain unreality to the proceedings. The French and Belgians were unwilling to admit the proposition that "countries were entitled to nationalize property and to disregard the rights of previous owners," and the British supported this position.[46] Yet the Soviet leadership clearly felt that the return of nationalized properties was unacceptable, even a betrayal of revolutionary principles that could have disastrous domestic consequences.[47] Litvinov, therefore, was caught between two irreconcilable positions on this fundamental issue. He thrashed about seeking compromise but to no avail.

During the talks, Litvinov met privately with the British representative, Sir Philip Lloyd-Greame, for a frank conversation. Litvinov bemoaned his own ignorance about the details of financial and industrial issues and complained of a lack of technical help from Moscow. He doubted if there could be any restoration of foreign property, but Lloyd-Greame emphasized the importance of settling this issue if the Russians wanted assistance. Litvinov asserted that a "certain number of people" in Russia believed that recovery was possible purely on the basis of domestic resources, but he added gloomily that Russia without foreign assistance would be a "very primitive affair." He therefore wanted to "explore every avenue," and he emphasized that Moscow "had to make up [its] mind whether it was worthwhile to pay the price for assistance."[48] By 10 July, the conference had reached a critical stage. It was clear that Russia would have to back down on the retention of nationalized foreign properties because the French and Belgians refused to compromise and they had British support.[49] On 18 July, Litvinov told Moscow that little could be expected from the conference, mainly because Lloyd George so desperately wanted French help with German problems that he would meet Paris's demands in regard to Russian policy. He then added that the properties issue had eluded a settlement.[50]

What is interesting about this letter to Moscow as published is that it makes no mention of the diplomatic initiative Litvinov launched the next day. At the session on 19 July, he created quite a stir when he set forth a four-point program that went well beyond the line followed at Genoa. Litvinov asserted that he was prepared to ask his government to continue the negotiations on the basis of a "recognition in principle" of the prewar imperial debts and Soviet compensation for nationalized properties. Significant for its absence was the Soviet quid pro quo that these concessions necessitated extensive European credits or loans to Moscow. To the amazement of the other delegates, Litvinov said he would recommend to his government that this familiar proviso be dropped, but, in return, the other countries must open negotiations for a de jure recognition of the Soviet government, which, he asserted, would make possible acquisition of the desperately needed credits from private sources. Lloyd-Greame called Litvinov's initiative "extremely important," but the talks still broke down.[51] At lunch, Lloyd-Greame told Litvinov that de jure recognition was out of the question. This information left Litvinov "evidently disturbed," and he was "doubtful about referring the question to Moscow at all after what was said."[52] Moreover, the French and Belgians, with U.S. support, would accept nothing less than full and unconditional restitution of nationalized properties.[53] Isolated, Lloyd George retreated.

With Litvinov's failure in the Hague, the Soviet government formally recognized the freeze in relations with the capitalist countries. On 16 August, Lev Karakhan, another deputy foreign commissar, told the British that Litvinov's proposal of 19 July had been "put forward on his own initiative, *ad referendum* to his government and that the latter could not be held to have endorsed it."[54] It is easy to imagine that the leadership used less diplomatic language in the Kremlin discussions that surely took place after Litvinov's return from the Hague.

Thus ended Soviet Russia's first round of formal discussions with the European powers. The effort had achieved its most important success in the Treaty of Rapallo, which had indisputably placed a great obstacle in the path of any effort to create an anti-Soviet bloc among the European powers. Much, very much, remained to be done, but the Soviet government could, with justification, consider that at least the first steps had been taken toward reintegration into the European community. As will be seen, Chicherin's pro-German policy had its limitations and never resulted in all the advantages he had expected.

Five

LITVINOV AND THE ORIGINS OF SOVIET DISARMAMENT POLICY

The Moscow Conference of 1922

LITVINOV HAD FARED rather poorly at Genoa and the Hague, and Chicherin and the German orientation had triumphed despite Litvinov's considerable efforts to the contrary. Litvinov, however, was never given to idleness, and even while the Hague talks were in session, he was planning a new diplomatic maneuver—a disarmament conference in Moscow. Such a gathering would necessarily be small, since there was no hope of obtaining the participation of the great capitalist countries. However, a conference that included Russia and its immediate neighbors might serve as a forum to promote the country's prestige in eastern Europe and thereby reduce what Moscow believed was Poland's virtual dominance in the region. Poland did manage to put itself in an embarrassing position at the conference, but Litvinov was unable to derive any lasting advantage from that fact. It is also important to note that at the Moscow Conference, Litvinov again got rather carried away in his search for a diplomatic compromise, although this time he left himself an avenue for retreat. In short, he made political concessions more sweeping than anything the Soviet government would accept subsequently—and probably received another official reprimand, but not a public one.

As the Hague Conference was reaching its dismal conclusion, Litvinov's anger was virtually boundless. Speaking with reporters after the capitalist powers had rejected his 19 July proposal as a basis for further negotiations, Litvinov asserted that "Russia will attend no more conferences. Genoa and the Hague have been enough for us."[1]

Most likely, great bitterness inspired this statement; veracity certainly did not, because more than a month before Litvinov made this remark, the Soviets had proposed to Latvia, Poland, Finland, and Estonia that those nations and Soviet Russia hold a conference for the reduction of armaments.[2] That invitation resulted in the Moscow Disarmament Conference of December 1922, but before examining the background, proceedings, and results of this conference, over which Litvinov presided, it would be useful to discuss briefly the attitudes of the Soviet leaders and government toward the general issue of disarmament.

During the revolutionary struggles before October 1917, Lenin had nothing but contempt for disarmament and "pacifism," and writing in the early days of World War I, he declared that "disarming is emasculation. Disarming is a reactionary-Christian jeremiad. Disarming is not a struggle against the imperialist reality but a flight *from* it into the beautiful future *after* the victorious socialist revolution!"[3] By "victorious socialist revolution," Lenin was, of course, thinking in global terms. He did not therefore believe that disarmament was feasible as long as socialism and capitalism existed side by side.[4]

When Lenin came to power, his views did not immediately change. In March 1919, the Soviet government established the Communist International, and in 1920, that organization adopted the Twenty-One Conditions for admission of Communist parties to its Second Congress. Of the twenty-one points, number six dealt with disarmament in the following fashion:

> Every party . . . is obliged to renounce not only open social patriotism, but also the false and hypocritical social-pacifism: [each party] must demonstrate systematically to the working class that without a revolutionary overthrow of capitalism, no international arbitrator, no treaty for the reduction of armaments, no "democratic" reorganization of the League of Nations can save mankind from a new imperialist war.[5]

It must be noted that Lenin personally wrote or specifically approved each article of this document.[6]

This Soviet position, however, must be seen against the background of civil war, foreign intervention, and invasion by Poland, as in such a situation, talk of disarmament would hardly have made sense.[7] By 1921, the internal situation had improved from Moscow's perspective: The nation was still terribly impoverished, but the Bolsheviks had achieved some internal domestic stability.[8] In March 1921, the New Economic Policy, providing for significant relaxation of central control and coercion in the national economy, was approved by the Tenth Party Congress,[9] and as the domestic situation continued to stabilize, Lenin and the rest of the leadership apparently felt that they could now resume the drive for normalizing relations with the outside world, which meant some tentative accommodation on the issue of disarmament. Moreover, the Bolsheviks desperately needed all their funds for domestic reconstruction, and a successful disarmament program could promote both goals.

In any case, Chicherin gave formal notice of a policy change vis-à-vis disarmament in a July 1921 radio broadcast addressed to Britain, the United States, France, China, and Japan.[10] He expressed "extreme astonishment" that the forthcoming Washington Conference would not include Soviet Russia, despite recent press reports that revealed the other powers "fully recognized" the right of that country to participate in a conference convened to discuss issues connected with the Pacific Ocean. Chicherin found it wholly inadequate that the other powers had promised to "take Russian interests into account," and declared that "the decisions of this conference will remain ineffective and devoid of all significance" as far as Russia was concerned.[11] Chicherin then announced the new policy:

> It has likewise come to the knowledge of the Russian
> government that a more general question, the question of
> disarmament, or at least naval disarmament, is to be discussed.
> The Russian government can only give a warm welcome to
> disarmament of any kind or to the decrease in military
> expenditures, under which the workers of *all* countries are
> prostrated. But it regards as indispensable the need to settle
> beforehand the guarantees which are to be given to ensure the
> disarmament will really take place, bearing in mind that the
> possibility of such guarantees at the present time appears to be
> rather doubtful. Nevertheless, the very idea of disarmament
> cannot be regarded as anything but worthy of support.[12]

He concluded with a reiteration that because Soviet Russia would not be present, it would not feel bound by any disarmament decisions.

There is no evidence that any of the powers responded to Chicherin's radio message.

In the spring of 1922, the first concrete step toward holding the December conference was taken at Riga, where representatives of Russia, Poland, Estonia, and Latvia met informally to discuss the possibility of an arms limitation agreement and a demilitarization of their frontier zones.[13] The need to normalize the situation among the countries was clear, and Litvinov probably thought he could seize this opportunity to reassert his country's leading position in the region.

In the invitation to the Riga meeting, Litvinov quite predictably condemned the Genoa Conference, charging that it "had not justified the hopes placed in it by the broad masses of Europe" and that it had

> devoted almost all its attention to defense of the material interests of a relatively insignificant group of people who had suffered losses as a result of the European war, the revolution, and the intervention of Russia and avoided such decisions of the problems before it that might actually have eliminated, to a significant degree, the causes of the economic crisis in Europe and elsewhere.[14]

Litvinov then asserted that "one of the chief causes of the economic crisis and the political instability of Europe is its extraordinary level of armaments." He claimed that the initiators of the Genoa Conference knew this fact, but "nonetheless, in deference to the self-interests of a few countries, [they] excluded from the agenda of the conference the issue not only of complete disarmament but even of a partial limitation of armaments." With biting sarcasm, Litvinov said that such had been the position on disarmament of a conference "for the consolidation of peace and the economic restoration of Europe."[15]

Despite the poor reception the idea of disarmament had received in Genoa, Litvinov announced that the Soviet government had decided to invite Latvia, Poland, Finland, and Estonia to a conference for "mutual discussions with Russia of the issue of a proportional reduction of armed forces." The conference would not necessarily be limited to the invited states; it would also be open to countries with whom Russia "still has unresolved territorial or other problems," a clear allusion to Romania and the continuing argument over Bessarabia.[16]

Litvinov concluded with a request that the invited parties express their opinion concerning the best time and place for the conference.

Soon the replies arrived in Moscow. On 29 June, the Finnish government announced that "because it sincerely loved peace and desired the safe development of an independent Finland . . . it accepted participation in the proposed conference." The Finns, however, did express reservations, mainly the opinion that a conference of only Russia, on the one hand, and Estonia, Finland, Latvia, and Poland, on the other, "will not be able to produce the results which the Russian government has in mind."[17] Moreover, the Finns pointed out that their October 1920 treaty with Russia already contained "directions relative to the means for a decrease of military forces in the future, especially naval forces." Such an arrangement, however, could only be achieved through discussion involving all the interested [i.e., Baltic] powers.[18]

On 19 August, Litvinov responded to the Finnish note. He freely admitted that a conference as limited as the one he had proposed would not solve all of Europe's problems, but he thought it might alleviate tensions in eastern Europe. He, too, favored a broader conference, but he went on to say that "the principle of disarmament as a path to peace should not be rejected because it has not been accepted by all states."[19]

There is little evidence that anyone had much hope for the Moscow Conference. Certainly, it was plain that such chances would be reduced to nil if the Poles refused to attend, and their initial response was not encouraging. The Polish Foreign Ministry observed that disarmament talks were already going on at the League of Nations and that, although agreeing in principle to Litvinov's proposal, Poland felt that the conference should be postponed until the conclusion of the League's disarmament discussions.[20] At the rate with which those talks were progressing, the Polish response amounted to a rejection, and Litvinov's reply to the Poles certainly characterized their response as such. In the reply, Litvinov observed that a regional reduction of arms should in no way hinder the work of the "so-called League of Nations," and pointed out that Finland, Latvia, and Estonia had accepted the principle of a regional disarmament conference despite their various reservations.[21]

On 29 August, the Polish government again addressed itself to Litvinov's invitation, and this time, the Poles reversed their position without explanation, saying that they had "willingly agreed to participate in the conference" all along.[22] It is most likely that the Poles, seeing that a conference was about to take place, decided it would not be wise for them to be absent.

On the eve of the meeting, *Pravda* published an interview with Litvinov in which he said that Russia viewed the impending conference with "utmost seriousness" and that the Soviet delegation had decided to place before the conferees only one issue—the reduction of land forces. The discussions, of course, would also touch on matters of a technical nature, for example, military budgets, but the Soviet government was opposed to bringing in any issues that did not have a "direct relationship to genuine disarmament."[23] In concluding, Litvinov hinted at the broader purpose he had in mind in summoning the conference; not surprisingly, it was aimed at the capitalist powers. He said that "Britain and France especially have great significance for the questions that will be placed before the conference," and he hoped that if "brave and serious decisions" were made at Moscow, they might "become the point of departure for a general European movement on behalf of genuine disarmament."[24]

This gesture toward the larger powers without doubt was aimed at public opinion in those countries; Litvinov almost never tired of trying to minimize tensions with them. Among Soviet government officials, Litvinov perhaps understood best the importance of public opinion in the democracies of western Europe. (It must be remembered that in 1920, British dockworkers had refused to load weapons and munitions bound for Poland, then at war with Russia.)[25] Stepping forward as an advocate of "genuine disarmament" was an excellent way to favorably influence western opinion. Of course, appealing to public opinion there was not without risks—it could, and often did, irritate Western politicians—but after the fiascoes of Genoa and the Hague, Litvinov may well have reasoned that he had nothing to lose.

Certainly, disarmament was a very popular cause. Francis P. Walters, former deputy secretary-general of the League, observed that since the end of World War I, "public opinion had demanded . . . an end to the burden and danger of great national armaments."[26] Of course, the focus was on the League to accomplish this formidable task, but the initial sessions of the League's Preparatory Commission for the League's Disarmament Conference did not even convene until May 1926, after seven years of mostly fruitless argument.[27] The Moscow Conference may be viewed as Litvinov's attempt to shift the focus of progress in reducing arms to Moscow. As Louis Fischer wrote, Litvinov "wanted Moscow to appear on the world stage," and he "endeavored to enhance Moscow's prestige by Soviet participation in conferences, pacts, and agreements." Fischer added that disarmament was Litvinov's "baby," and that "Chicherin never liked it."[28] If the Soviet disarmament campaign was indeed Litvinov's "baby," then he became a "father" in December 1922.

E. H. Carr has observed that the Moscow Disarmament Conference "was in itself totally unproductive."[29] In fact, it was probably doomed as early as the first days of August when military representatives from Poland, Finland, Latvia, and Estonia met in Revel [Tallinn] to coordinate their policies. A subsequent conference, this time including Romania, met in Warsaw in September, and the concluding secret protocol agreed upon at these talks asserted: "Whatever the proposals that will doubtless be advanced . . . by Russia, they will assuredly envisage a significant reduction of the armed forces [of the conferees]. Such proposals ought to be recognized as unacceptable."[30] Such an attitude certainly gives credence to Litvinov's postconference assertion that the non-Russian delegates never intended to discuss disarmament seriously and only came to Moscow because of domestic political pressures.[31]

The Moscow Disarmament Conference finally convened in the Kremlin on 2 December 1922. In his opening remarks, Litvinov reiterated a point he had made in the *Pravda* interview: "As regards the . . . agenda of the conference, the Russian government believes that [it] should be limited only to the one issue of a limitation of arms on a basis acceptable to all the participants."[32] This Russian insistence that the conference limit itself to disarmament proved to be a serious obstacle in the initial sessions. Moving to his first (and maximum) proposals, Litvinov said that the Soviet government desired

> a precise plan for mutual reduction of land forces, based on a
> decrease over the course of the next year and a half to two years
> of the present Soviet army to one quarter its present size, i.e., to
> 200,000 men, and a corresponding reduction of the land forces
> of Russia's western neighbors. The Russian government
> understands that the establishment of precise numbers, time
> periods, and other details of such an arrangement may follow
> only after the detailed consideration of all these issues by special

commissions. The Russian government, however, considers it necessary to emphasize that in all points of its proposal it will proceed from the principle of full reciprocity and an impartial calculation of all conditions which each country must make for support of its armed forces at this or another level. The Russian government is confident that these conditions will convince the whole world of the peacefulness of Russia and its lack of aggressive intentions.[33]

Having proposed a 75 percent reduction, Litvinov next urged limitations on military budgets, preferably set at a certain amount per soldier to be worked out specifically in subsequent discussions. He then called for the "elimination of all military units of an irregular character found within the contracting powers" and a "mutual neutralization of frontier zones," using as a model for the latter idea the June 1922 Soviet-Finnish agreement.[34] Litvinov concluded with the scarcely veiled warning that his plan was "concrete and feasible and can not be replaced by any talk of so-called 'moral disarmament' which is so often heard at international conferences, when the participants desire . . . to evade the issue of disarmament."[35]

When Litvinov returned to his seat, "a buzz of astonishment" filled the long hall.[36] He had placed the other delegates in an awkward position, to say the least. His proposal for a 75 percent reduction in each nation's army would definitely appeal to public opinion, but to the politicians present it seemed (and was) utterly fantastic. As Walter Clemens has pointed out, Russia's real fears at this time were centered around the other great powers, and as long as their armaments policies remained unchanged, it was absurd to believe Russia would cut its army by three-fourths.[37] This point was certainly true, but also the offer was not the Russians' final one.

The unenviable task of giving the first response fell to the Estonian representative, and he set the stage for subsequent frustrated speeches when he claimed that "material disarmament must be preceded and accompanied by political disarmament."[38] The views of the other non-Russian delegations were similar and stressed the need to create a "situation of security and tranquility" before any specific arms reductions.[39]

The rest of the day was spent quarreling. Litvinov argued for open plenary sessions to seek a modus operandi, claiming that the conference's work should be conducted in public so "that the rest of the world" could be kept "fully informed." The other powers wanted the conference to work in closed committees. The final compromise was to appoint a "chief committee," consisting of the heads of the delegations, to frame a working agenda for various subcommittees, and the results of their work would be revealed in regular, open, plenary sessions.[40]

The *New York Times* reporter at the conference perhaps served as a conduit for Litvinov to make yet another gesture toward the United States. The correspondent wrote that a "member of the Russian delegation" told him that the Soviet Union hoped its neighbors would grasp the opportunity to reduce the general arms burden, "but we realize that America is the only power besides Russia genuinely willing—and able by virtue of her strong position—to advance the cause of world disarmament."[41] The reporter did not identify Litvinov as his source, but the remark certainly reflected Litvinov's conciliatory attitude toward the United States.

On 4 December, public deliberations resumed, and Litvinov immediately attacked proposals for "political or moral disarmament." He said that nothing could reveal and demonstrate better a government's rejection of aggressive intentions than a "clear, open expression of a willingness to reduce its arms and its military budgets. The touchstone with regard to the so-called moral disarmament is the degree of preparedness to accept material disarmament"—and the Soviet government had shown its willingness to disarm materially.[42]

Litvinov then used the story of the tragic summer of 1914 to drive home his point. To counter the talk of political treaties as a substitute for material disarmament, Litvinov raised the example of Belgium, because the wartime experience of that unfortunate nation revealed the worthlessness of treaties and guarantees when the

> interested sides embellish these guarantees with military competition, continuously growing levels of arms and increasing military expenditures. Consequently, it is sufficiently clear that arbitration courts, diplomatic agreements and so forth will not become a trap for the masses only if the basis of these institutions is a definite, concrete, and precisely worked-out program of material disarmament.

> Thus, the Russian government can consider acceptable the
> principle of arbitration only if there is simultaneous material
> disarmament.[43]

In this declaration then, Litvinov revealed the essence of the 1922
Soviet position on disarmament. Political or moral disarmament and
treaties of arbitration were fine as long as they were accompanied by a
concrete disarmament agreement. Or, as Litvinov put it in his speech
of 5 December, the Soviet government was prepared "to sign ten
times, a nonaggression treaty, it was prepared also to recognize the
principle of arbitration. But the Russian delegation can not allow such
a document to alter the business for which the conference was assembled." To sign such agreements, without "radical measures for reduction of arms," would be to "delude the people of Russia and other
countries with a fiction, a substitute of words for deeds."[44]

The Poles responded that they had come to Moscow in good
faith, but they insisted that an agreement on nonaggression and
arbitration was a prerequisite "to create an atmosphere of mutual trust
and security, necessary for the practical, positive resolution of the
issues of technical disarmament." The other non-Russian delegates
adhered to Poland's position.[45]

Seeing himself outnumbered, Litvinov retreated and later accepted a provisional treaty of nonaggression and arbitration hammered
out by the Bureau of the Moscow Conference between 6 and 8
December. This remarkable document constitutes the first and only
time Soviet Russia agreed to the arbitration of a political dispute with
another country.[46] Article 5 stated that if one of the contracting parties
found itself in a dispute with one of its counterparts that could not be
settled by diplomatic means, "the issue will be handed over to an
arbitration commission. The details of the application of this article
will be defined by subsequent agreement."[47]

It seems clear that either the Soviet government really desired an
arms reduction agreement or Litvinov was sticking his neck out again
as he had done in the Hague. Of course, this time he had an escape
hatch ready: Litvinov had made it obvious that the treaty would not
be ratified without a corresponding arms reduction agreement.

With the treaty drafted, Litvinov left matters in the hands of his
assistant Viktor Kopp, who endured several days of futile wrangling
with the other delegates over the specifics of arms reduction. Kopp

proposed a 25 percent reduction in land forces, which would reduce the Red Army to about 600,000 effective participants, and the Poles seemed agreeable, saying a similar reduction would bring their forces down to about 280,000.[48]

Then on 11 December, Litvinov returned to drop the bombshell of the conference. Rising to his feet, he "blandly announced" that in June 1922, the Polish government had told the League of Nations that its armed forces totaled 293,744 men. A reduction to 280,000 therefore constituted a mere drop of 4 percent and was meaningless. Prince Janus Radizwill of Poland was, to say the least, in an embarrassing situation.[49] Exasperated and apparently thinking none too clearly, the prince said that he "refused to discuss the numbers of the Polish budget [?] for the current year."[50] The unmistakable death rattles of the conference could be heard in Radizwill's remarks.

Litvinov recognized that yet another conference was about to end in failure for him. On the same day that he exposed the inconsistency in the Polish figures, he telegraphed Chicherin, who was at the Lausanne Conference, that he had agreed to a treaty of nonaggression and arbitration but that "we are prepared to sign it only after the inclusion of an article on arms reduction." He then related the problem with Poland's army figures and concluded with the understatement that "this threatens the breakdown of the conference."[51]

The next day Litvinov admitted the obvious. Speaking before the military-technical commission, he said that the conferees had agreed to come to a conference on arms reduction but had then refused to discuss that issue seriously. He, of course, came down hard on Poland, but he also declared that on the general issue of disarmament, France was the real culprit. That nation (with which Poland had a military alliance) "is not merely not reducing its armaments, but is continuing to increase them" while "playing around" with the formula of "moral disarmament." He concluded bitterly that he would leave it to public opinion to decide who should be blamed for the failure in Moscow.[52]

In view of the failure of this conference, a pertinent question is, Did the Soviet government really desire a reduction of arms? It appears that it had no real choice. On 27 December, the All-Russian Congress of Soviets announced "to all the peoples of the world" that Russia intended to reduce its army from 800,000 to 600,000 men.[53] Litvinov told journalist Walter Duranty that Russia had been forced into this decision because it needed the money for reconstruction. However, he had believed that the same was true as far as the other countries at the conference were concerned.[54]

In evaluating this first international conference held inside Soviet Russia, it must be repeated that the initial Soviet proposal for a 75 percent reduction was clearly intended for propaganda purposes (later, Litvinov was to try the same ploy at Geneva with a proposal for a "complete and general" disarmament). But in Moscow, Litvinov quickly backed down from this maximum position and was ready to accept a 25 percent reduction along with an extraordinarily extensive treaty for nonaggression and arbitration. If this final position was purely propaganda, it was certainly of the most elaborate kind. The Russians were about to reduce their land forces significantly, and Litvinov's assignment was, in all likelihood, to attempt to secure similar reductions from Russia's immediate neighbors. It seems plausible to argue, in retrospect, that acceptance of Litvinov's final position would have done no harm to international relations in eastern Europe. France would probably have been infuriated, but not to the point of repudiating its military alliance with Poland. The Poles and Lithuanians would still have been at odds over Vilna, just as the Russians and Romanians were over Bessarabia, but if Litvinov's plan had been accepted by all parties, the Moscow Conference might have been a first step toward reducing some of the tensions in an exhausted and bewildered part of the world.

Six

YEARS OF DRIFT AND WAITING

1923-1927

FROM THE END OF 1922 until 1927, when the Soviet Union appeared at the disarmament talks in Geneva, Soviet foreign policy moved from crisis to crisis. Soviet diplomats were usually on the defensive as internationalist elements within the Soviet Communist Party were able to push for an aggressive policy in China, Germany, and, to a lesser extent, Britain. In the case of the last nation, the actions of the Soviet trade unions in giving aid to striking British workers made a cruel mockery of Litvinov's public call for normal diplomatic contacts. The aborted Communist uprising in Germany and the Soviet adventure in Chinese affairs were matters in which Litvinov played no role, but he could only have been distressed by such pointless ventures. Because he opposed the Soviet leadership's initiatives during this period, it is not surprising that he played a clearly secondary role to Chicherin.[1]

However, the commissar for foreign affairs had his troubles, too, in the mid-1920s, as the Treaty of Rapallo received a serious blow when Germany signed the Locarno Pact and even joined the League of Nations. Despite assurances from Berlin, it became increasingly clear that the Soviet Union could no longer view with complacency its relations with Germany.

Although Litvinov stayed in the background, he was not inactive. He made specific efforts to improve relations with Britain and France, but he was unable to achieve a change in Soviet policy on the old issues of debts and claims. He continued to pursue a conciliatory line toward the United States but, again, to no avail. About all Litvinov could do was to wait while Chicherin's health deteriorated and his policies came unraveled.

It must be clearly understood, however, that from 1923 to 1927, domestic events in the Soviet Union completely overshadowed foreign policy. In May 1922, Lenin suffered the first of a series of strokes that eventually ended his life in January 1924, and an intense power struggle ensued and lasted until 1929, when Stalin defeated all overt opposition. Litvinov made a conscious attempt to stay out of this struggle. In 1924, he had a long conversation in England with the radical U.S. writer Max Eastman and his wife, Eliena Krylenko, who was Litvinov's secretary. According to Eastman, even in the very first days of the domestic power struggle following Lenin's death, Litvinov was disgusted. He told them

> the whole story of his political life. He was in my opinion and Eliena's, disillusioned to the point of cynicism about the outcome of the revolution. He took no part in intraparty disputes; he advised Eliena not to join the party, when she feared it would be necessary to hold her job. "Why waste your time in those futile squabbles?" he said. He had lived long enough in England, out of the jurisdiction of German metaphysics—which dominated the whole Russian intelligentsia—to acquire an unclouded sense of fact, realistic and potentially cynical.[2]

Eastman concludes his remarkably revealing glimpse of Litvinov with the observation that he was a man "with very simple common sense" and void of the "pious logic of the Hegelian-Marxian religion."

Litvinov had lost his hope for world revolution in 1918, and upon Lenin's death, it seems he lost his faith in the party's ability to save Russia. Why then did he continue to serve? One can only speculate, especially as long as Litvinov's papers remain unavailable to foreign scholars. It seems certain that even though Litvinov had become disenchanted with the Communist Party, he still retained a belief in socialism as an ideal. Perhaps he thought that in the future the party might return to his socialist vision. But it also seems clear that Litvinov had developed definite ideas on the direction that Soviet foreign policy should take and he wished to see them implemented.

As has been shown, Litvinov had a strong pro-British orientation, but by the mid-1920s, his views on international relations had matured conceptually. Two ideas in particular emerged in an obscure, but public, speech Litvinov made in 1925 in the relatively free era before Stalin's ascendancy. Addressing an audience of peasant-administrators, Litvinov first advanced his notion that "peace is indivisible." Soviet diplomacy, he said, aimed at the establishment of peace not only between the USSR and the rest of the world but "among the bourgeois states" because "history shows that war rarely remains isolated, exclusive." Instead, "wars between two peoples . . . spread further and become a general war. Therefore any war may draw in our union. Thus we are interested in a struggle with the idea of war and promote peace among all nations."[3]

Litvinov also made a second point that would become prominent in his diplomacy of the 1930s: It is not a country's domestic ideology and actions that are paramount but its specific foreign policy goals and actions. Thus, he noted that although Italy had "fascist, reactionary government," it nonetheless had a "weak economy and heavy debts" and "therefore looked for friends." Moscow was glad to establish normal relations with such a government.[4] In the 1930s, Litvinov repeatedly said that domestic fascism was not the real issue; the expansionist ideas expressed in Mein Kampf were another matter altogether.

In these years, however, Chicherin retained his control over Narkomindel. Good relations with Weimar Germany remained his paramount concern—no mean task after the twin shocks of the 1923 Communist uprising in Germany and the 1925 Locarno Pact among Germany, France, Britain, Belgium, and Italy. The abortive 1923 revolution was the last violent attempt the German Communists made against the Weimar Republic.[5] The fact that it was inspired and funded by Moscow was no secret to German Chancellor Gustav Stresemann,[6] but the German government lodged only the "most perfunctory protests" in Moscow,[7] eloquent testimony to Stresemann's iron determination to maintain connections with the Soviet Union.

If the failed 1923 Communist uprising angered Stresemann, the Locarno Pact horrified the Soviets, Litvinov included. This pact guaranteed Germany's western borders as set forth by the Treaty of Versailles, left the eastern borders an open issue, and, most alarming for the Soviets, provided for Germany's entrance into the League of

Nations. As Gerald Freund has observed, "The heyday of Rapallo had long since passed; the Russo-German alliance was now simply one in a network of many."[8] Nonetheless, Soviet-German relations after Locarno continued to exhibit the same "chronic instability and remarkable longevity"[9] that had characterized much of the period before 1925. Locarno did represent an effort to ostracize the Soviet Union,[10] but Stresemann never intended to sever his country's Soviet connection for a purely western orientation.[11]

Although *Narkomindel* continued to look on Germany as the Soviet Union's only friend in Europe, a perceptible shift of Soviet policy toward Asia occurred in the mid-1920s, one that further reduced Litvinov's overall importance. Revolutionary movements began to flourish in China just at the time when the Soviet Union suffered the 1923 debacle in Germany and Anglo-Soviet relations deteriorated after the "Zinoviev letter" incident of 1924.[12] The conjuncture of events led Chicherin in March 1925 to tell Count Ulrich von Brockdorff-Rantzau, the German ambassador in Moscow, that "at present the Soviet Union finds herself compelled to become active in Asia . . . where she finds herself colliding everywhere with English interests."[13] Litvinov had no sympathy with such policy. Speaking with Louis Fischer in 1929 after Soviet policy in the east had met with disaster, Litvinov said, "I think an agreement with England . . . about the East, generally is possible, but the government takes a different view."[14] Clearly, Litvinov played no role in Asian affairs and even disagreed with his government's policy there. He was active elsewhere, however.

In early 1924, Britain extended de jure recognition to the Soviet Union. This change was wholly the result of British initiative; Soviet policy on the crucial debt issue remained unchanged.[15] Nonetheless, Litvinov had long favored good relations with Britain, and it was one of the high points of his career when he personally received the official news of recognition from Sir Robert Hodgson. Litvinov expressed "his profound satisfaction" and said that he hoped the British move would "result in a real and permanent improvement in the relations between the two countries."[16] On 2 February, Litvinov appeared before the Congress of Soviets to announce British recognition.[17] In a later meeting with Hodgson, Chicherin was more hesitant. He expressed "some nervousness" with the British text, feeling that it was too "ambiguous," but Hodgson assured the commissar that British policy was "to accord full recognition . . . at once." Even Chicherin could not conceal his satisfaction.[18]

Almost immediately, however, it became apparent that only a superficial calm had descended upon Anglo-Soviet relations. The old antagonisms remained—repudiated debts, nationalized properties, Soviet counterclaims and demands for credits, and, of course, the Comintern's guiding relationship with regard to the British Communist Party—and the extent of these fundamental Anglo-Soviet conflicts became abundantly clear in April 1924, when an Anglo-Soviet conference opened in London to work out a general treaty between the two states. At the outset, Prime Minister J. Ramsay MacDonald, following the wishes of London's leading bankers,[19] informed the Russians that "intergovernmental obligations, the claims of British holders of Russian bonds and of British subjects who have had their properties taken away from them," must be satisfied before the extension of credits could even be discussed.[20]

The head of the Soviet delegation, Khristian Rakovskii, responded that the conference should concern itself with promoting "a close collaboration between our two countries in the fields of commerce, industry, and finance," and he added that British and Soviet economic assets were complementary. Britain possessed "industry, finance, and shipping," and the Soviet Union had "a population of 130 million in possession of enormous potential riches, which requires for its development large quantities of industrial products and credits."[21] Finally, facing the issue of "prewar debts and private claims," Rakovskii said these could be resolved, but, more important, he claimed that in recent years "this question [sic] had lost the exceptional importance" once attached to it.[22] An impasse in Anglo-Soviet relations again loomed.

The Soviet government was so alarmed the talks might collapse that Litvinov was sent to London. In direct talks with MacDonald, the prime minister tried to draw the Russians "away from their usual ground of a loan first, then a settlement" by proposing that Moscow "come to an agreement . . . with the bondholders [and] to settle up all outstanding points with us, making it clear throughout if they so wished that they would sign nothing unless a loan was forthcoming." If Litvinov would agree to these terms, MacDonald promised "to do his best with the City," but he warned Litvinov that he "must not expect large sums" until there was a "re-establishment of confidence" in the Soviets.[23]

It seems that Litvinov regarded this proposal favorably; at least MacDonald had that impression.[24] If such was the case, however, Litvinov was unable to convince Moscow to accept the British offer, and Litvinov left for Berlin "on doctor's orders." There he announced that henceforth, it was up to the British to come up with a clear and positive decision on the loan issue.[25] These words constituted Litvinov's last statement on the Anglo-Soviet talks. The negotiations dragged on through the summer with seemingly endless wrangling over financial compensation and government credits, but finally, on 8 August, a treaty was signed. The Soviets promised to settle with British claimants, at which time the British government would make a loan to the USSR.[26]

The treaty, of course, required Parliament's approval, but the "Zinoviev letter" affair burst on the scene in October 1924 and contributed to the fall of the MacDonald government. Its successor, headed by Stanley Baldwin, took a firm (or intransigent) position toward the Soviets, demanding that they cease interfering in British internal affairs. Given the atmosphere, a loan was unthinkable,[27] and the pattern was set for the course of future negotiations.[28]

Litvinov recognized the continuing decline in Anglo-Soviet relations and attempted without success to improve the atmosphere. In a dispatch to the Soviet chargé in London, dated 13 January 1926, he noted that the British had refused to afford "embassy status" to the Soviet mission in London and even had rejected such status for their mission in Moscow. Litvinov found this situation absurd and urged the chargé to give his "serious attention" to a clarification of the matter. Litvinov believed that such a change might help improve the existing poor relations.[29] Of course, the cause for the Anglo-Soviet hostility went much deeper than the mere status of each nation's representatives.

In April 1926, in speaking about relations with Britain before the party's Central Committee, Litvinov tried publicly to suggest a way out of the diplomatic stalemate. He said that "recently . . . it has been possible to detect some signs of a certain shift in our favor even in England" (he had in mind the fact that the government's majority in the House of Commons had been significantly reduced).[30] Nonetheless, Litvinov emphasized that the Soviet government would make no promises on the debt issue as a preliminary to reopening the negotiations. "We think it in the highest degree desirable that businesslike negotiations should be opened with the English government to settle questions in dispute. The first step would be an exchange of suggestions in a normal manner through diplomatic representatives."[31]

Litvinov's public and private efforts to mend fences with Britain came to naught, and soon relations were to change from frozen and hostile to an open breach. The Soviet trade unions' support for the British strikers during the 1926 general strike made a mockery of Litvinov's public call for normal discussions through diplomatic channels,[32] and as a result of Soviet actions, Austen Chamberlain, Stanley Baldwin's foreign secretary, was scarcely able to prevent a complete diplomatic rupture in early 1927. He carried the day with the argument that the lack of some incident analogous to the Zinoviev letter made a breach unjustifiable,[33] but it was not long before the anti-Soviet forces in Britain did receive just such ammunition. On 12 May, the building used by both the Russian Co-operative Societies (Arcos) and the Soviet Trade Delegation was raided by the London police searching for a missing War Office document.[34] This intrusion violated Article 5 of the 1921 trade agreement, but it apparently caused the British government little alarm.

Litvinov waited until 17 May to protest officially, giving the British time to explain and thereby avoid an otherwise almost inevitable rupture. Litvinov's note roundly condemned the raid as a violation of the trade agreement but said its implications were even broader. Politically speaking, the raid was "a most serious hostile act, without doubt jeopardizing the further maintenance of relations."[35]

Litvinov was certainly correct. On 24 May, Baldwin asked Parliament to approve the government's decision to break relations with Moscow, although in a cabinet meeting it was recognized that the materials seized did not warrant such a drastic move. Nevertheless, documents collected elsewhere that related to Soviet activities in China were brought forward, and Chamberlain reviled the Soviets before Parliament as "incorrigible." The breach of diplomatic relations was approved by a hearty 357 to 111 votes and remained in effect until late 1929.[36] In his response, Litvinov said that the rupture was no surprise and that his country was taking measures to ensure its defense.[37] Thus began in earnest the "war scare" of 1927.[38]

Once again, Litvinov's efforts to construct a working relationship with Britain had foundered. In 1922, he had done his best to orient Soviet policy toward a rapprochement with London, and the extension of de jure recognition had seemed to augur a new and happier phase in Anglo-Soviet relations. But forces and events beyond Litvinov's control, particularly "internationalist" elements in the Soviet Union and confirmed anti-Soviet attitudes on the part of Conservatives in Britain, frustrated his efforts. He continued, however, to fight his losing battle into the 1930s, doggedly bucking the odds in a cause he must have felt was a vital necessity for his country.

During the mid-1920s, the stormy relations with Britain occupied much of Litvinov's time, but relations with Germany loomed larger in overall Soviet foreign policy. It must be reiterated, however, that Rapallo and relations with Berlin were Chicherin's special preserve, even after the shocks of the Locarno Pact in 1925 and Germany's entrance into the League in 1926.[39]

With hindsight, it is clear that Locarno was, to a great extent, simply a logical political consequence of the Dawes Plan, which Germany had accepted in 1924 to stabilize its ghastly economic situation through foreign aid.[40] Logical or not, the Soviet leadership, Litvinov included, was thoroughly horrified at the prospect of a German orientation toward the west, leaving the Treaty of Rapallo a dead letter and the Soviet Union isolated.

On 17 October 1924, Litvinov met with the German chargé, Radowitz, to denounce press reports that asserted the Soviet Union had not only changed its attitude toward the League but was even contemplating membership. With words that could have come from Chicherin, Litvinov said that to entertain such an idea "after we have attempted by friendly advice and warnings to restrain you from such a step means that absolutely no one understands our policy, which absolutely excludes the possibility of such perfidy." Litvinov then proposed that both states conclude an agreement wherein each would agree not to enter the League without the concurrence of the other.[41] Radowitz promised to telegraph Litvinov's statement immediately and expressed his joy that Litvinov's remarks would strengthen the hand of opponents to League membership within the German government.[42]

Radowitz's communiqué to Stresemann had little, if any, effect, and on 8 April 1925, Litvinov issued another warning to the Germans. He told Ambassador Brockdorff-Rantzau that although he, Litvinov, did not doubt that the German government desired to maintain friendly relations with the Soviet Union despite Berlin's "reorientation" of policy, he felt it would be extremely difficult to do so. Germany, he said, has turned into "an arm of British diplomacy"—a very serious charge when Anglo-Soviet relations were at such a low point—and he added that in the League, where Germany "has no friends," it will be forced "to lean on Britain." The situation would amount to a German "crossover to the camp of our enemies," and Litvinov revealed the Russians' deepest fears when he exclaimed that Stresemann would be forced to accept and abide by Article 16 of the League Covenant.[43] If that were the case, Germany could be forced to participate in a League-sponsored crusade against the Soviet Union.

Addressing these fears, Stresemann denied that Germany must choose between east and west. Indeed, he wanted foremost not to have to make such a decision at all.[44] As Gerald Freund succinctly wrote: "Stresemann did not want to become embroiled in a Western crusade against the Bolsheviks any more than he would allow the Soviet government to impose an exclusive alliance with Germany. The object of his policies . . . was to revive German power and gain an independent middle position in Europe."[45] When it became clear that Stresemann intended to accept a security arrangement with the west and League membership,[46] Chicherin, despite his poor health, personally launched a campaign to maintain the exclusive Soviet-German relationship. On 13 July 1925, he presented Brockdorff-Rantzau with a preamble of a political treaty, the most important provision of which was that both states "mutually oblige themselves not to commit . . . any type of unfriendly act toward each other and not to enter into any type of political or economic blocs, treaties, agreements, or combinations with third powers against the other government."[47] Since the Soviet government in 1925 clearly considered the League a "bloc" or "combination" aimed at the Soviet Union, the meaning of the proposal was clear. Stresemann rejected it, and the impression was growing in Germany that "Russia was less interested in Germany's good will to collaborate than in compromising Germany with the West."[48]

Nonetheless, there was strong feeling in the Reichstag that good relations with the Soviet Union must be preserved, and in late February 1926, the Germans presented a formal treaty to Moscow.[49] This proposal, which later became the Berlin Treaty, contained four short articles and an appended protocol. The basic points of the treaty were a reaffirmation of the Treaty of Rapallo as the foundation of German-Soviet relations; a provision for neutrality in the event that one of the countries came into an unprovoked conflict with a third party; and a proscription of participation of one of the signatories in an economic or a financial boycott against the other. The most significant parts of the appended protocol asserted that Germany would take part in League sanctions against the USSR only if the latter were the aggressor and that to designate Russia as such would require German agreement. In this way, Stresemann argued, Germany would be in a position to block League actions against the Soviet Union,[50] so "Germany's friendly relations with Russia" would be maintained, despite the change in German policy initiated by Stresemann.[51]

Speaking on foreign affairs before the Central Committee on 24 April 1926, Litvinov appraised the Berlin Treaty as "an appendix to, or rather an amplification of, the Rapallo Treaty." The Soviet Union in 1926 was still "somewhat threatened, and the enmity towards it on the part of the Western non-Soviet world" continued to exist, so the possibility of "a general or collective attack" against the USSR could not be excluded. "The object of Soviet diplomacy is therefore to lessen the danger of the formation of anti-Soviet blocs and combined attacks."[52] Litvinov believed that the Berlin Treaty promoted this policy goal.

It seems clear that Litvinov and Chicherin were united in their alarm over the possibility of losing the Soviet Union's only friend in Europe and that both gave their full support to the Berlin Treaty in the hope of making the best of a bad situation. Nonetheless, the Locarno Pact was a definite setback for Chicherin and doubtless started Litvinov thinking about ways to exploit his superior's predicament. One way to chip away at Chicherin's authority would be to better relations with France.

In 1924, the French were ready to establish normal relations with the Soviet Union but not much else. Since 1914, France had experienced four and a half years of war with Germany and then over four more years of continued tension with Berlin, aggravated by increasingly poor relations with Britain. It was time for a change, and the opportunity came in May 1924 with the election of Edouard Herriot and a government of radicals and socialists, the Cartel des Gauches.[53]

Herriot had been an outspoken advocate of de jure recognition by France of the Soviet Union even though such a step, without Soviet recognition of imperial debts and compensation for nationalized French properties, was fraught with difficulty because of the vast size of the debt and the former French holdings.[54] Nonetheless, Herriot, despite considerable opposition, pressed forward and on 28 October 1924 notified the Soviet government of France's unconditional de jure recognition.[55] In November, Krasin was appointed *polpred* to France, while remaining commissar for foreign trade, and Herriot selected Jean Herbette, a prominent journalist, to represent France.[56]

Thus ended four years of open hostility between France and the Soviet Union. However, from the very beginning, Herriot, like MacDonald, made it plain that an economic settlement was an indispensable prerequisite for friendly relations.[57] Because a settlement with France could provide a dangerous precedent for the Soviet Union's dealings with other states, it is hardly surprising that the economic talks made no headway.[58] Finally, after the Conservative government came to power in Britain, France agreed in December 1924 to coordinate its Russian policy with London. In this way, a deadlock between Paris and Moscow was ensured,[59] and French-Soviet relations went back virtually to square one.[60]

Litvinov, however, went to great lengths to explain the Soviet position precisely and what France must do to meet the Russians half way, because an acceptable settlement with France would be a great achievement and Litvinov was willing to go after one with determination. In a long meeting with Herbette, he outlined in detail the causes of the skepticism of the Soviet "ruling circles" toward meeting French demands, but first, Litvinov explained that what he had to say was something the leadership "cannot write publicly."

First of all, Litvinov said, the Soviet people increasingly had come to believe that one of the most valuable gains of the revolution was the annulment of the imperial debts, and the French had not strengthened their case for payment by their well-known support for counterrevolutionary forces. These facts made it doubly difficult to reach a settlement with Paris, but there was yet another formidable obstacle. Any repayment would diminish the prestige of the Soviet government in the eyes of western working classes, "on whose support we must depend in our defensive struggle with a capitalist world that remains hostile." And beyond these problems is the "great material sacrifice" a settlement would entail,[61] which raised the question, "What can we expect as a reward for these sacrifices? Would France help the Soviet Union with economic reconstruction; will there be loans, credits, etc.?" Litvinov said the Soviet "ruling circles" were more and more asking themselves these questions.[62]

Still, Litvinov also tried to inject a more positive note. He said that "no decision has been taken; exchanges of opinion continue; we are trying to convince each other." However, he warned that the situation did not look good and said that matters had not been helped when Herriot asserted before the Chamber of Deputies that France must support unity among Poland and the Baltic states because those nations lived in fear of the Soviet Union. Litvinov said this policy was clear support by France of Poland's "intrigues" against his country.[63] Herbette replied blandly that French policy recognized the genuine "terror" felt by the Baltic states and viewed it as the source of their efforts to unify against the Soviets.[64]

Thus, economic and political interests kept the Soviet Union and France separated in the relatively peaceful period between Locarno and the Great Depression, even though Litvinov did his best to clarify the Soviet position in the obvious hope that France would change its policy. Instead, France took a different approach, and on 10 June 1926 a treaty of friendship between France and Romania was signed in Paris.[65] Herbette assured Litvinov that Russia had nothing to fear from the treaty; indeed, it might give France leverage with the Bucharest government "to push" it toward a settlement with the Soviets over Bessarabia. Litvinov replied, with bitter sarcasm, that such "logic" would have led France before 1914 to welcome additional states reaching agreements with Germany because then they could "pressure" Germany to return Alsace-Lorraine.[66] The Mutual Assistance Pact of 1935 between France and the USSR could hardly have been predicted in 1926!

Rebuffed by Britain and France, Litvinov met much the same fate with the United States. But despite the open hostility of the U.S. government toward the Soviet Union in the 1920s,[67] Litvinov continued to seize any opportunity to maintain at least a dialogue with that country, despite his deep pessimism that any good would come of it.[68]

For example, on 6 June 1923, Litvinov had a long meeting with the president of the New York Chamber of Commerce, one Mr. Bush. Litvinov told Bush that the Soviet government welcomed such visits as his, although of course it would prefer official contacts. Bush replied that exchanges of official representatives were blocked by Soviet censorship of foreign journalists, by the activities of the Comintern, and, most important, by the confiscation without compensation of U.S.-owned properties and the Soviet refusal to pay individual creditors. Bush said that the annulment of state debts was "understandable and forgivable."[69]

Litvinov replied that his government was "forced" to impose censorship because the "sources which American correspondents draw upon for their information" made it impossible for them to give an accurate picture. Probably realizing the weakness of this argument, Litvinov immediately switched to an attack on the "unfettered propaganda" allowed to "whites and counterrevolutionaries" in the United States while U.S. sympathizers of the Soviet regime were stigmatized as "Bolsheviks."[70] Moving to the next point, Litvinov recorded laconically that "relative to the Comintern I gave him the usual explanation."[71] Litvinov apparently was not overly anxious to discuss that organization.

On the debt and property issue, Litvinov said that the Soviet position was the same: "We agree to recognize all debts in the event of recognition of our counterclaims." He added that he was ready to discuss the possibility of the formation of a "mixed commission to review the claims of both sides." Bush thanked Litvinov for his views and promised to report to President Harding,[72] but nothing ever came of the matter.

On 20 February 1926, Litvinov made another attempt at a dialogue with the United States. He told Khristian Rakovskii, the new Soviet *polpred* in Paris, that Moscow had received a letter from the U.S. politician and banker James P. Goodrich[73] inquiring about the chance of Soviet-U.S. talks using a U.S. ambassador as intermediary. The basis for the talks would be U.S. recognition of the Soviet Union "based on Russia's recognition of the Kerenskii debts and restitution or compensation for confiscated American property." There would also be discussion of Soviet claims against the United States (presumably arising from the intervention), and this amount would also receive a final settlement. Lastly, both sides would give assurances to refrain from propaganda. Goodrich believed that such a formula had an excellent chance to facilitate the establishment of normal relations.[74]

Litvinov jumped at this unofficial offer. He instructed Rakovskii to tell the U.S. ambassador in Paris that the Soviet government had all along wanted normal relations with "the great American people." There was no reason such relations could not be accomplished, because "the interests of both peoples clash nowhere, neither in political nor economic areas." Moreover, "in a whole series of international issues the tasks and efforts of both countries coincide. The reestablishment of relations would not only serve the interests of both countries but to a significant measure promote the reestablishment of the whole European economy and a general disarmament."[75] Having made this rather effusive evaluation of the benefits of normalized Soviet-U.S. relations, Litvinov told Rakovskii to ask the U.S. ambassador if Goodrich's proposals, or "some other path" to official negotiations, might be pursued to remove the obstacles the United States felt were blocking regularization of relations. Litvinov even said that although official talks were preferred, the Soviet government would accept an unofficial U.S. delegation.[76]

The request fell on deaf ears, and indeed, the hostile attitude of the U.S. government in 1926 is plainly revealed by the fact that the Soviet ambassadress-designate to Mexico, the remarkable Aleksandra Kollontai, was denied permission even to travel through the United States en route to Mexico because "she has been actively associated with the International Communist subversive movement."[77] The official U.S. attitude was still the same when President Franklin D. Roosevelt was inaugurated in 1933.[78]

Litvinov's instructions to Rakovskii are significant, however, despite the lack of success with the U.S. government, because they reveal Litvinov's desire to reorder the Soviet Union's foreign policy. In 1926, the Soviet Union was again quite isolated in Europe, despite the Berlin Treaty. The German connection was no longer the shield Chicherin had envisioned, relations with Britain and France remained perfunctory at best, and Soviet policy in East Asia stood on the verge of disaster.[79] At the same time, Chicherin's health was rapidly deteriorating, and he was in constant pain from diabetes and polyneuritis.[80] Both the policies and the man who was their architect were failing. It was time for a change, and Litvinov stood waiting in the wings.

There were other reasons for a change, too. Stalin and his policy of "socialism in one country" were rapidly gaining absolute sway over the last elements of opposition, a process that Litvinov accepted as

preferable to the "violent internationalism" of Trotskii.[81] Forced industrialization and collectivization were on the horizon. It is perhaps
ironic that while turning inward, the Soviet Union should also elevate
to the top post in foreign affairs a man identified with the Soviet
Union's reintegration into European affairs. But the vast domestic
reorganization could not be carried out unless the Soviets had a
breathing spell with regard to international relations, and it was to be
Litvinov's formidable task to provide this respite. The first step was
taken at Geneva in 1927, despite Chicherin's protests,[82] and under
Litvinov's guidance, Soviet foreign relations entered something of a
new phase. To be sure, good relations with Europe's other pariah,
Germany, remained of utmost importance, and Moscow continued a
policy of avoiding "groups and combinations, hostile to each other
. . . and leading unavoidably to war."[83] Nonetheless, the mere appearance of Soviet representatives at the League constituted a significant
policy shift. If Litvinov, however, thought the USSR could reap
substantial benefit from this change, he was soon disillusioned.

Seven

PROPAGANDA AND DISARMAMENT

1927-1928

THE YEARS FROM 1928 TO 1934 are often viewed as something of an isolationist period in Soviet foreign relations.[1] This interpretation has some merit, because during those years there was an intense focus on massive internal change. The New Economic Policy was completely scrapped, and the Soviet Union, under Stalin's leadership, plunged into an unprecedented experiment of forced industrialization and collectivization under the First Five-Year Plan adopted at the Fifteenth Party Congress in December 1927.[2] More than ever in its brief history, the Soviet Union needed to abstain from foreign adventures and, on a more positive note, seek to project itself as a staunch supporter of disarmament and peaceful coexistence. Such a policy would favorably influence foreign public opinion.

In an address to the party Central Committee on 23 October 1927, Stalin spoke of the approaching internal upheaval:

> History shows that not a single young state in the world has developed its industry, particularly its heavy industry, without foreign help and foreign loans, or without plundering foreign countries, colonies, etc. England developed her industry in the past by plundering other countries and colonies. . . . We, however, can not follow either of these two ways. Our whole policy excludes colonial robbery. We do not get any loans. There remains to us only one way, that indicated by Lenin: developing our industry and reequipping it by domestic means.[3]

A few weeks later, at the Fifteenth Party Congress, Stalin declared that there was "a struggle between two tendencies of the capitalist

87

world." The "aggressive military tendency" was led by Britain, and Germany and Turkey were the main capitalists prepared "to continue peaceful relations."[4] Stalin concluded that this analysis was not new but harked back to the earlier period of the *peredyshka* (breathing space) under Lenin: "We can not forget Lenin's words that in building [socialism] much depends on how we will succeed in delaying war with the capitalist world. Such a war is inevitable, but it can be delayed. The preservation of peaceful relations with the capitalist countries is, therefore, a necessary task for us."[5] Thus Stalin formulated the party's "line": in domestic affairs, an emphasis on industrial development and in foreign affairs, the maintenance of peace.

With Chicherin's passing from the scene, the task of translating Stalin's general instructions into action largely fell to Litvinov. And there was no better place to gain the attention of the world and to present the Soviet Union as a leader in the struggle for peace than at the Preparatory Commission for the Disarmament Conference in Geneva (henceforth referred to as the Preparatory Commission), for it was upon these talks that much of the world's attention was focused.[6] However, the tactics that Litvinov pursued in Geneva were contradictory and therefore failed. He called initially for complete and universal disarmament and ignored France's well-known demand that some type of security arrangement must precede any disarmament. Litvinov, however, was not concerned so much with France's reaction as with putting forth the Soviet Union as the leading force for disarmament. Having made his admittedly propagandistic proposal, Litvinov then put forth a quite realistic, graduated program for arms reductions. But the original maximum plan had aroused so much ire in Geneva that Litvinov's more sensible program was simply dismissed out of hand. He therefore returned to Moscow empty-handed.

Litvinov, however, could not just inform the League of Nations that the Soviets were ready to come to Geneva; there were serious obstacles to overcome. Broadly speaking, Soviet rhetoric toward the League had been mostly hostile for almost ten years. Probably more important, however, was the 1923 murder of the Soviet diplomat V. V. Vorovskii in Switzerland, where the headquarters of the League were located.

The hostility of the Soviet government toward the League clearly emerged in 1926 when Germany joined that organization, but the Soviet attitude was not wholly antagonistic. For example, before taking office as British prime minister for the first time, J. Ramsay MacDonald had said in 1923 that both Germany and the Soviet Union should enter the League. This remark was prominently published in *Pravda* without any thundering editorial denunciations.[7] More significant, the Soviets had participated since 1922 on various technical committees of the League concerned with sanitation and health problems, although after 1923 they refused to return to Switzerland.[8] And it is often forgotten that the Soviet government sent representatives to the League's Naval Conference in Rome in 1924. In accepting the invitation to that conference, Chicherin emphasized that no change had occurred in the Soviet Union's attitude toward the "so-called League of Nations" but said that his government "desired to participate in the business of naval disarmament . . . and to assist the establishment of a general peace and reduction of armaments." Since the Swiss government had given "no satisfaction" in the matter of the Vorovskii murder, however, Chicherin flatly refused to accept a conference on Swiss soil.[9] Because the Soviets refused to budge on this issue of the conference's location, originally slated to be held in Geneva, it was transferred to Rome. It was, however, a conference of experts, not plenipotentiaries, and its results were so meager that plans for an "international naval conference with full powers were tacitly abandoned."[10]

Although Soviet hostility toward the League was not unqualified, and even clear precedents existed for participation in the Preparatory Commission, the Soviets' anger toward Switzerland because of Vorovskii's murder was virtually boundless and probably quite sincere. The matter can be summarized briefly. Vorovskii had been in Switzerland as part of the Soviet delegation to the 1923 Lausanne Conference. On the evening of 10 May, he was dining with two other Soviet diplomats at the Hotel Cecil when Maurice Conradi, a Russian émigré whose family had been ruined by the revolution, walked up to him and fired once, killing the diplomat instantly. At his trial, Conradi was successful in politicizing this murder of an unarmed man without warning. As Alfred Erich Senn has noted that all of Europe's boiling tensions came to the surface during the trial, all but obscuring the actual assassination. Despite the testimony of eyewitnesses and Conradi's defiant confession, he and an accomplice were acquitted.[11]

After the acquittal, the Soviet Union and Switzerland "stood in a virtual state of war,"[12] a situation that continued until 1927 despite mediating efforts by the French government and clear signals from the League of Nations that the Swiss must settle the affair or face the possibility of seeing the League leave Switzerland.[13] For his part, Litvinov tried to cut through such problems as monetary compensation for Vorovskii's orphaned daughter and a demand that the Swiss government admit complicity in the murder. He wrote to Nikolai Krestinskii, the Soviet *polpred* in Berlin who handled most of the negotiations with the Swiss and various intermediaries, that the actual compensation was not important but it could serve as a "special expression of regret." Litvinov, added, however, that his remarks were not official, and the Soviet government later rejected so lenient a settlement.[14]

In the end, the matter came down to a Swiss proposal that used the word *durchaus* ("thoroughly") to characterize how regretful and critical the Swiss government felt about the murder. After Moscow rejected this proposal, Krestinskii and his Swiss counterpart added *sehr* ("very") to *durchaus* and a provision for compensation, thereby ending the affair.[15] The road to Geneva was finally open.

As in the past, the League invited the Soviet Union to send representatives to the Preparatory Commission, which was scheduled to resume sessions in Geneva in late November 1927.[16] This time the Russians accepted and announced that Litvinov would head their delegation.[17] Two days later, on 22 November, Litvinov issued a press statement concerning the Soviet decision to go to Geneva, and his remarks constituted the first official public statement on the shift in Soviet policy.[18]

Litvinov immediately asserted the need to correct recent "rumors and unfounded assertions" regarding the Soviet government's attitude toward both disarmament and the League. "The government of the Soviet Union has never concealed its disbelief in the willingness and ability of capitalist countries to abolish the system of wars among nations, and consequently to achieve disarmament,"[19] he said. This skepticism was based on the "steady and systematic growth of the armed forces of the capitalist states" and on "seven years' fruitless activity concerning disarmament at the League." A sure symptom of the reluctance to disarm was the fact that "even the date for convening [the actual Disarmament Conference] cannot yet be determined."[20]

By attending the Preparatory Commission, however, the USSR was "depriving its enemies of the possibility of attributing to it, even in the smallest degree, the possible failure of the conference, and its neighbors of an excuse for their refusal to disarm on the ground that the USSR was absent from the conference."[21] Litvinov thus emphasized that the Soviet Union had precious little hope for positive results but could, by its simple attendance, avoid the charge of blocking disarmament itself. It is clear that the Soviet government intended to derive as much propaganda value from the sessions in Geneva as possible.

Litvinov then gave the essentials of the proposals to be placed before the commission. The Soviet Union would do no less than "insist on the necessity of complete and universal disarmament" either at "one stroke" or "by stages." He would "fight against any attempt to divert attention to third-rate questions," clearly a warning to those people who wished to emphasize security first, then disarmament.[22] Whatever charges can be leveled at Litvinov, it cannot be said that his proposals at Geneva were a bolt from the blue. One can only wonder why almost all the other delegates were so stunned when Litvinov did precisely what he had said he intended to do.[23]

Having thus warned Europe of his proposals, Litvinov and the Soviet delegation (which included his wife, Ivy)[24] left for Geneva where they put up in a small "family hotel," the Pension d'Angleterre. In Geneva, Litvinov and the other Soviets went out of their way to be unobtrusive, forsaking the distinctive red ties worn at Genoa. Litvinov's only eccentricity, as far as dress was concerned, was his broad-brimmed black hat.[25] Litvinov's uncharacteristic desire for anonymity outside the conference hall was perfectly understandable. In the period just before his arrival in Geneva, Britain had severed diplomatic relationships with the Soviet Union, and the Soviet diplomat P. L. Voikov had been murdered in Warsaw.[26] High visibility in Switzerland would have been asking for more trouble, and Litvinov probably feared for the safety of the Soviet delegation.

In any case, the fourth session of the Preparatory Commission began its deliberations on 30 November, and Litvinov gave his opening speech that same day. His blatantly propagandistic remarks were directed, not at the Geneva delegates, but to world public opinion, which he managed to reach. But perhaps Litvinov was playing the role of gadfly; he might have thought that by exposing the inactivity of the Preparatory Commission, he could goad it into action. Such an idea, however, puts the best possible interpretation on the motivations of

Litvinov and the Soviet leadership. He labeled capitalism the fundamental cause of armed conflict, calling World War I the principal
"imperialist" war, yet as a result of that war, "people in all countries"
had become "imbued with the determination to struggle against imperialist wars and for guarantees of peace." This change in public
opinion had made possible Soviet participation in the Preparatory
Commission and the League's work on disarmament.[27]

Litvinov then openly acknowledged the propaganda factor in
Soviet policy: "The Soviet Government demonstrates in the face of
the whole world its will to peace between the nations and wishes to
make clear to all the real inspirations and true desires of the other
states with regard to disarmament."[28] Continuing his theme of the
difference between Soviet and League disarmament efforts, Litvinov
blasted the failure of the League to advance "even a single step" toward
disarmament or even a limitation of military budgets. This record, he
claimed, contrasted sharply with Soviet proposals to limit arms at the
Genoa and Moscow conferences. Now, with the settlement of the
Vorovskii affair, the Soviet efforts toward disarmament could be
transferred to Geneva, and, presumably, the Soviets could get the
League moving toward concrete action.[29]

Litvinov then presented the Soviet proposal, which Louis Fischer
impishly called Litvinov's Fourteen Points.[30] This plan called for "the
complete abolition of all land, naval and air forces." To accomplish this
goal, Litvinov specifically proposed:

1. The dissolution of all land, sea, and air forces and the inad-
   missibility of their existence in any concealed form whatsoever;
2. The scrapping of all warships and military airplanes;
3. The destruction of all weapons and military supplies;
4. The discontinuance of calling up citizens for military training
   either in armies or public bodies.

Litvinov concluded that the scheme could be accomplished "in one
year's time" and that it was "the simplest and the most conducive"
means to achieve peace.[31] However, Litvinov recognized that such a
far-fetched plan was doomed, so he asserted that "in case" the capitalist
states rejected his first proposal, he would suggest that complete
disarmament be achieved "by gradual stages, during a period of four

years." Moreover, according to Litvinov, the Soviet government was ready "to participate in any and every discussion of the question of the limitation of armaments whenever practical measures really leading to disarmament are proposed."[32]

At this point, the other delegates must have thought Litvinov was ready to behave more like a conventional statesman, but the revolutionary aspect of Soviet diplomacy reemerged. Speaking of the need to prohibit "chemical and bacteriological substances," Litvinov proposed "the establishment of workers' control" over those chemical industries that could be most easily used to produce such materials.[33]

Litvinov conceded that many people would regard his proposals as "complex and difficult," if not "Utopian," but Litvinov claimed that it was more "Utopian" to think that the Preparatory Commission could ever settle the problem of European security. He felt it was simply impossible to achieve any common approval on "what constitutes security for each country and, individually, the extent and importance of its international obligations, its geographical peculiarities and other special features, before the level of its effective, technical armaments, military and air vessels, etc., can be established."[34]

Essentially, Litvinov was proposing that diplomacy should be repudiated and that peace and security be obtained through total disarmament. This approach was Bolshevik propaganda at its most transparent. Undaunted, though, Litvinov presented a formal resolution that the Preparatory Commission forthwith adopt the Soviet proposals and prepare to convene the actual Disarmament Conference, not later than March 1928, for the "discussion and confirmation" of the Soviet plan.[35] Litvinov concluded by anticipating the most likely and most serious criticism his plan was to encounter:

> We are fully aware that certain circles will endeavor to stigmatize our program and resolution as propaganda. We are quite ready to accept this challenge and declare that we are making propaganda for peace and shall continue to do so. If [the commission] is not a suitable place in which to make peace propaganda, then apparently we are here under a misunderstanding. We shall not let slip a single opportunity for making the most intensive propaganda for peace and disarmament.[36]

Having returned to the arena of European diplomacy after a hiatus of over five years, Litvinov took his seat. In the ensuing brief discussion, the French delegate charged that disarmament would be useless "if there was no international organization taking charge of security, if you had no international force to ensure the maintenance of this security, if you had no international law such as we are endeavoring to lay down here." In short, disarmament and security were indivisible, and such was the position of the majority in Geneva. The commission, therefore, voted to shelve the Soviet proposal "for the time being."[37] The Soviet response was simply to reintroduce the proposal for general and immediate disarmament at the fifth session of the Preparatory Commission.[38]

The fifth session met from 15 to 24 March 1928, and Litvinov spoke on 19 March. Indefatigably, he reiterated that general and total disarmament could solve the problems of "general security and peace." With no armaments, technical security issues, like freedom of the seas, would become moot. And Litvinov denied that enforcement or verification would present a problem, because "it is absolutely obvious that control over the achievement of general disarmament would be significantly easier than control over partial disarmament."[39]

Litvinov then asked for a "clear and definite, and not a theoretical, answer to the question of whether the Preparatory Commission accepts in principle a general disarmament" over the course of four years. To underscore the popularity of the Soviet position, Litvinov produced a declaration signed by the presidents of 124 peace organizations from thirteen countries in support of his proposals. Litvinov closed by turning to the U.S. observer, Hugh Wilson, and declaring that in light of the recent proposal of the U.S. government to outlaw war as an instrument of national policy,[40] he felt justified in expecting U.S. support for proposals that he deemed were entirely consonant with the U.S. plan.[41]

Wilson was under instructions not to respond to the Soviet plan, but Secretary of State Frank Kellogg considered it "so impractical that no detailed discussion appears called for."[42] The German and Turkish delegates, however, took the floor to declare their support for at least a discussion of the Soviet proposals.[43] After these two statements, "there was a long and embarrassing silence, following which the chairman said as no one appeared anxious to speak," he would adjourn the session until the following day.[44]

The opponents of the Soviet plan were in a state of disarray. As Wilson told Secretary Kellogg, "All the delegations, as far as I know, are anxious that there should be a prompt disposal of the Russian proposals . . . but it appears that no-one has the courage to stand up against the attacks [?] of the Russians."[45] The *New York Times* correspondent agreed with Wilson and wondered if "anyone on the commission was able to compete with M. Litvinov."[46] The British delegate, Lord Cushenden, met the challenge.

Speaking the next day for a full hour and a half with only a few notes,[47] Cushenden began by asking Litvinov not to take personally the remarks he was about to make. He then castigated the Soviets for their prior negative position on the disarmament work of the League. Not only had they made no contribution during the first seven years of this labor, but they had "lost no opportunity for reviling the League and overwhelming it with scorn and derision." Now, he continued, the Soviets appear, apparently intending "to unmask the capitalist states—which evidently means the whole civilized world outside their own borders—and to disclose the sabotage of the Soviet proposals."[48] But if there was sabotage afoot, Cushenden said, it came from the Soviet side and was directed at the League and the establishment of world peace.

> For years past the Soviet policy expressed by its leaders has been to produce armed insurrections in every nation where they can exercise influence. We must have assurance given by M. Litvinov that there is a complete change of policy. Has the Soviet government decided to no longer interfere in the affairs of other nations? Unless they [sic] are prepared to make such an assertion we are faced with the unpleasant fact that they [sic] are the largest obstacle toward the carrying out of their own proposals.[49]

In such an atmosphere of distrust and outright hostility from both sides, it was hardly surprising that nothing concrete ever came from the work of either the Preparatory Commission or the subsequent Disarmament Conference.

Following this withering attack, Litvinov informed Moscow that at least a staunch opponent of even discussing the Soviet proposal had been forced to do just that. Litvinov, however, feared that the plan would be sent to a "subcommission" at Britain's insistence, thereby killing it. He added that only the Germans had responded favorably.[50] Litvinov failed to note that almost everyone had greeted Cushenden's speech with prolonged applause.[51]

On 23 March, the Preparatory Commission resolved that the Soviet draft, "while in harmony with the ideals of mankind is, under the existing world conditions, incapable of being carried into execution" and therefore "cannot be accepted by the Commission as a basis for its work."[52] Litvinov had expected this rejection, and the same day he introduced a proposal for partial disarmament, which he hoped would meet a better reception.[53] This extensive new plan consisted of forty-nine articles covering land forces and their material supplies, naval forces, air armaments, chemical warfare, a timetable, and provisions for control and ratification.[54] The articles detailed precise provisions for reducing the levels of the various forces and their equipment. For example, states "maintaining armed land forces numbering over 200,000 men . . . or having in the cadres of the armed land forces more than 10,000 regular officers or more than sixty regiments of infantry" must reduce these levels by one-half. States with armed land forces of over 40,000 men, more than 2,000 regular officers, or more than twenty regiments of infantry would reduce those levels by one-third, and so on.[55]

Concerning arms themselves, Litvinov proposed that they be reduced similarly. The exceptions were "tanks and heavy artillery with very long range" and "all implements of war directed primarily against the civilian population" (military aircraft and chemical weapons). These weapons "must be destroyed."[56]

Naval powers with a fleet in excess of 200,000 tons would be obliged to reduce their naval forces by one-half. Those nations with smaller fleets would reduce by smaller percentages. Aircraft carriers were to be dismantled entirely. The proposal also provided specific tonnage limits and "age-limits" for specific types of warships, along with exact limits on the permissible caliber of guns mounted on the ships.[57] Similar percentage reductions would be made in the numbers of military aircraft, and chemical and bacteriological warfare was to be banned entirely.[58]

The Soviet Union had thus presented a quite specific and sensible program for arms reduction, but it damaged its own case with a gesture toward proletariat internationalism. Litvinov added that the reduction process would be supervised by "an equal number of representatives

of the legislative bodies and of the trade unions and other workers'
organizations of all states participating in the present Convention."
On the other hand, the proposal provided for on-site inspections,
something necessary for any arms control agreement to be effective.[59]

As remarkable as it may seem, there was no general discussion of
the new proposal. The French objected that to examine Litvinov's
proposal would necessitate the Preparatory Commission's starting
work anew, a strange objection since the commission had achieved
nothing upon which all parties could agree.[60] Instead, the new Soviet
plan was to be referred to the various governments. Litvinov immediately responded to this new rejection. He seemed genuinely stunned.

> I find myself in a very difficult situation. The President has told
> me that the proposal, which the Soviet delegation just made and
> with which the other delegations are still not familiar, will not
> be submitted for discussion in the course of the present session.
> He gave no reason for this and did not explain why there will be
> no discussion. Why will there not be any discussion at this
> session? For what reason have we gathered here? Only to decide
> that nothing will be decided; that we will return home, having
> done nothing? Did we not come here to discuss disarmament? I
> introduced a disarmament proposal and nothing else. Why will
> the Preparatory Commission of the Disarmament Conference
> not concern itself with the proposal? I would like an answer to
> this question.[61]

Litvinov concluded with apparent sadness that the Soviet delegation
could not expect to be treated on an equal basis with the delegates of
other states, but that French and British proposals at earlier sessions
had at least received a hearing when they were first put forward.

Litvinov was not the only person distressed by the proceedings.
The German representative, Count Bernsdorff, declared: "I have been
a member of this Commission for more than two years, and on no less
than twenty occasions I have heard it asserted here that all our work
would be futile because Russia was not represented; but now Russia is
here and the Commission decides to do nothing."[62] The German then
attacked not so much the Treaty of Versailles itself as the failure of
the victorious powers to abide by it and begin their own disarmament.

Thereupon, the French delegate, Count Clauzel, went into action and charged that it was Germany that had not lived up to its obligations.[63]

As a U.S. reporter quipped, "For some time the debate got far away from the subject on the agenda."[64] Finally, the Canadian representative observed that the hour was late and everyone was exhausted. He therefore moved for an adjournment, and "the Chairman grasped the idea eagerly."[65] Thus ended the fifth session of the Preparatory Commission.

Litvinov tried via telegram to put the best possible interpretation on the futile session, telling the Politburo that "Soviet prestige" had been greatly increased. He observed with satisfaction that the French press was disappointed that Soviet-German relations had survived intact despite "the arrest of the engineers. From Germany I received as always, a good press."[66]

On 21 April, Litvinov reported to the party Central Committee about the recent sessions of the Preparatory Commission. He bluntly repeated that the purpose of the proposal for "complete, thorough, and immediate disarmament" was to remove even a "hint" that the Soviet Union was an obstacle to disarmament. As expected, that proposal had been rejected, but "to our astonishment, most of the delegations were almost more bitterly opposed to our proposal for partial disarmament." In retrospect, Litvinov acknowledged that the Soviet delegation had been "simple" in expecting anything else.[67] Previously he had had little hope for achieving disarmament; now he felt it was "useless to expect reasonable, logical, and well-grounded discussion" in Geneva.

Litvinov added that if the Soviet intention had actually been "simply to discredit the League of Nations, to expose the capitalist states represented in it, and, as Lord Cushenden expressed it, to tear from it the mask of pacifism, we might be highly satisfied with the results of the Fifth Session." Even the "bourgeois press" had written openly of the breakdown and failure at the League. Despite this dismal experience, Litvinov proclaimed that, while maintaining its military defenses, the "primary aim of Soviet policy and Soviet diplomacy is to secure peaceful conditions for our internal creative work, without infringing on the national interests of any other." He added that there were abundant rumors that the Soviet Union planned an attack "on its nearest neighbors—Latvia, Estonia, Romania, and, of course, 'inoffensive' Poland."[68] Later, as an answer, Litvinov would come forth with a plan to draw the fangs from such accusations—the Litvinov, or Moscow, Protocol.

For the moment, Litvinov left for his favorite vacation spot, Carlsbad, Czechoslovakia. He told his wife that he was "happier in Carlsbad than anywhere else in the world;" he especially liked the "comfortable, relaxed atmosphere," so much more congenial than Moscow.[69] Ivy, for her part, spent her 1928 vacation in Berlin.[70]

After Litvinov's experience at Geneva, the Soviet leaders should have realized that Soviet propaganda only ruined their more serious proposals. This lesson, however, was lost on Moscow, and the advocacy of general and total disarmament continued. It seems, therefore, that the primary Soviet goal was to stand before the court of public opinion as the world's staunchest champion of disarmament, while at the same time doing nothing to address the much more complex problem of disarmament and security. This Soviet policy would remain in place until the German connection completely collapsed.

Eight

BECOMING THE
NEW FOREIGN COMMISSAR

IN THE LATE 1920s, Litvinov was already de facto commissar for foreign affairs, and in 1930 he formally assumed the position. Precisely why he received the appointment is unknown, but his long experience in foreign affairs certainly helped. His main rival for the position was probably Lev Karakhan, another deputy commissar whose specialty was Asian affairs, and the fact that Karakhan was passed over in favor of Litvinov suggests that the Politburo's main concerns were in Europe. If that was the case, Litvinov clearly had the best qualifications, and his appointment was quite predictable. Something that also helped Litvinov's candidacy for Chicherin's post was the signing of the Litvinov, or Moscow, Protocol in 1929. As will be shown, the protocol was largely symbolic, but after almost twelve years of ostracism, even symbols were better than nothing.

Immediately after Litvinov's first experience at the Preparatory Commission in Geneva, he told German Foreign Minister Gustav Stresemann that he was especially pleased by the German-Soviet cooperation there.[1] He certainly was sincere, because only Germany, for its own reasons, had strongly supported Litvinov's proposals. Almost immediately after the Geneva talks, however, relations with Weimar Germany experienced a mild and brief strain; the cause was the Litvinov Protocol. It is ironic that Stresemann should have been alarmed by Litvinov's actions with regard to the protocol, because the latter, it can be argued, was merely following Stresemann's own example of expanding his country's international ties and reducing European tensions. Indeed, the Litvinov Protocol can be viewed as a Soviet response to Locarno. Litvinov, no more than Stresemann, wanted a policy oriented exclusively toward one state. In the late 1920s and early 1930s, Litvinov wanted to reintegrate the Soviet Union into Europe and, above all, avoid conflicts. In this desire, he was merely doing what any realistic statesman would have tried to do as Europe's years of stability were entering their twilight.

The idea for the Litvinov Protocol grew out of events in France, the United States, and, strangely enough, Lithuania. On 6 April 1927, the tenth anniversary of the U.S. entry into World War I, the French Foreign Minister, Aristide Briand, proposed that the United States and France sign a pact outlawing war as an instrument of their national policies. The U.S. government, however, preferred a "much more spectacular contribution to world peace" by including "all the main world powers" in a declaration renouncing war.[2] More important, in such an arrangement, the United States "would not commit [itself] any more than any other nation to the security of France, and both powers would appear to have taken a forthright stand in favor of peace." On 27 August 1928, Secretary of State Frank Kellogg signed the agreement, the Kellogg-Briand Pact, in Paris.[3]

The Soviet government at first reacted unfavorably to the new proposal. In an address to the Central Committee on 21 April 1928, Litvinov charged that if the French and Americans really wanted peace, they should support a general disarmament more firmly: "It would seem easier to have confidence in a neighboring state which showed its devotion to peace by destroying all offensive weapons, than if it stood before us fully armed and increasing its armaments, confining itself merely to a promise not to attack us."[4]

Nonetheless, it would have been difficult and counterproductive for the Soviets to remain aloof from the pact. Although the Soviet Union was not one of the original signatories, the State Department made it plain that the treaty was open "to all the countries of the world,"[5] and finally, on 29 August 1929, the Soviet Union received through the French ambassador in Moscow an invitation to adhere to the agreement. In addition to his own misgivings, Litvinov knew there was some distrust within the Soviet government concerning even such an innocuous pact. Therefore, he asked Ambassador Jean Herbette for all documents and materials relative to the pact and a list of all signatories.[6] Having examined the materials, Litvinov recommended to *Sovnarkom* that the Soviet Union adhere to the pact.[7]

There ensued what was probably the last round in the Litvinov-Chicherin feud. According to Louis Fischer, Litvinov and Politburo member Nikolai Bukharin argued that the Soviet Union should sign the pact because it was advisable "to participate in any instrument which even remotely" was conducive to peace. Chicherin charged that the pact would allow the great powers "to interfere in Russia's relations with other countries," but he added that the pact really lacked any means of enforcement, an admission that would seem to have negated his first objection.[8] Litvinov and Bukharin, however, won the debate, and on 6 September, *Izvestiia* announced Soviet adherence to the pact.[9]

The Kellogg-Briand Pact would not become valid, however, until all the signatories had ratified it, a process that would take until July 1929.[10] In the fall of 1928, Litvinov was mulling over this point when the Soviet *polpred* to Lithuania, S. I. Rabinovich, told him that the Lithuanian government was contemplating proposing a pact similar to Kellogg-Briand that would include the Soviet Union, Poland, Germany, Lithuania, and Latvia. This pact would come into force regardless of the fate of the Kellogg-Briand agreement.[11] Litvinov seized on this idea as a way of drawing Poland and the Baltic states into a general agreement through Russian initiative.[12] Thus, the idea for the Litvinov, or Moscow, Protocol actually originated in Kaunas with the Lithuanian prime minister, Augustine Voldemaras.

Litvinov explained his plan before *Sovnarkom*, arguing that his proposal would constitute a large step toward a Soviet-Polish non-aggression treaty, something the Soviet government had first proposed in September 1925.[13] Litvinov added that if Poland refused to sign the protocol, Warsaw's aggressiveness would be exposed "to all the world."[14]

Poland had rejected earlier Soviet proposals for a bilateral neutrality and nonaggression pact modeled on the agreement signed between Russia and Turkey in 1925 because Warsaw saw such moves as both an effort to isolate Poland and a "bluff and expression of Russian two-facedness."[15] Also in the past, the Poles had responded to Soviet inquiries with their own proposal for a general nonaggression agreement among the Soviet Union, Poland, the Baltic states, and Romania. Litvinov had, in turn, objected that such a scheme was an attempt to create a regional bloc headed by Poland and hostile to the Soviet Union because it implied Soviet acceptance of Romania's seizure of Bessarabia.[16] Obviously, neither the Soviet Union nor Poland had had much desire for a nonaggression pact.

In an effort to ease this stalemate, Litvinov presented his plan to the Polish ambassador, Stanislaw Patek, on 29 December 1928. Surprised by the offer, the Pole said he could make no official statement, but he agreed with Litvinov that Soviet-Polish relations could certainly be improved.[17] However, Patek felt that the Soviet proposal would meet a fate similar to previous efforts.[18] Litvinov replied that the new proposal was simply a nonaggression pact; it had no additional provisions for neutrality or nonadherence to blocs deemed hostile to one of the signatories. Patek promised to forward the proposal to his government,[19] and on 1 January 1929, Litvinov made his proposal public.[20]

Despite the fact that the Litvinov Protocol was only a specific application of a rather innocuous general agreement and could hardly be interpreted as a threat to anyone,[21] it aroused alarm in Berlin. Stresemann feared that the pact could be regarded as an attempt to create a bloc of border states under Polish leadership, and he thought that the Soviet Union would not agree.[22] For his part, the new German ambassador to Moscow, Herbert von Dirksen,[23] stated bluntly that the Litvinov proposal was an expression of the deputy commissar's "disapproval of the Locarno policy."[24]

Litvinov tried as best he could to calm these exaggerated fears. He told the Germans that the pact was designed merely to ease tensions in eastern Europe, especially with regard to the chronic hostility between Lithuania and Poland, and if Germany wished to sign the protocol, it was welcome to do so.[25] The Germans soon realized their fears had been unfounded and accepted the signing of the protocol.[26]

The ceremony itself took place in Moscow on 9 February 1929. The main Polish reservation had been that all the Baltic states and Romania should participate in the agreement,[27] and Litvinov had agreed to this proviso even though there were no formal relations between Bucharest and Moscow. He noted that both the Soviet Union and Romania were already signatories of the Kellogg-Briand Pact; his proposal, Litvinov said, was merely an extension of that treaty.[28] In his public address, however, Litvinov took care to emphasize that although he welcomed Romanian adherence, it was a country with which the Soviet Union "had serious old difficulties—difficulties not settled by this protocol."[29] Still, the mere signing of a pact of any sort with Romania was a significant departure from past Soviet policy.

The immediate results of the Litvinov Protocol were meager, and Soviet-Polish relations remained strained until the beginning of a Franco-Soviet rapprochement in April 1931.[30] Nonetheless, a change for the better had taken place. Historian Josef Korbel has summarized well the broader significance of the protocol, noting that everyone gained something. Owing to Litvinov's initiative, Poland and the Soviet Union had at last worked out an agreement that both were willing to sign. It is true that the protocol was largely symbolic, but it was also a step in the direction of easing eastern European tension.[31]

Litvinov could indeed be pleased with his work, despite its limited value. He could not, however, rest for long on this achievement, because on 15 April 1929, the Preparatory Commission reconvened for its sixth and final session. Little can be gained by recounting in any detail the commission's final deliberations, because they largely duplicated those of the earlier sessions, but as far as Litvinov is concerned, it must be noted that during those spring days, on the eve of the Great Depression, the commission voted overwhelmingly to reject the principle of proportional arms reduction, thereby killing Litvinov's proposal submitted to the fifth session.[32] Historian Francis Walters noted that the Preparatory Commission had made "no progress."[33] Count Bernsdorff of Germany, who had frequently supported Litvinov, observed that the fundamental problem was that virtually no one was really determined to achieve disarmament. Bernsdorff's only hope for the Disarmament Conference was that the various governments might "furnish their representatives with quite different instructions than had been the case" for the Preparatory Commission.[34]

Of much greater importance for Soviet foreign policy in 1929 was the Sino-Soviet dispute over control of the Russian-built Chinese Eastern Railroad and the resumption of diplomatic relations with Britain. With regard to the former, Litvinov played virtually no role; the entire episode was handled by the deputy commissar for Far Eastern affairs, Lev Karakhan.[35] Litvinov did enter the picture on 3 December to respond to a declaration made by the new U.S. secretary of state, Henry Stimson. The secretary reminded the Chinese and the Russians that they had ratified a treaty renouncing the use of force and expressed the "earnest hope" that the two powers would settle their dispute without further hostilities.[36]

Litvinov's reply, dated 5 December, could hardly have been encouraging for Stimson. The former briefly reviewed the origins of the conflict and concluded that the Red Army had acted defensively and had not violated any of "the obligations, whatever they may be, resulting from the Treaty of Paris." In concluding, Litvinov stated that "the Government [of the Soviet Union] cannot fail to express its astonishment that the [United States], which by its own will, does not entertain any official relations with . . . the Soviet Union, should find it possible to address to [the] latter advice and recommendations."[37] From these remarks, it seems quite clear that the Soviet Union ultimately took a decidedly skeptical view regarding the value of the Kellogg-Briand Pact and that the Soviet desire for normalized relations with the United States had its limitations.

Litvinov did supervise the negotiations for the resumption of Soviet-British relations, and again, it was a change in British policy, occasioned by the formation of a second Labour government under Ramsay MacDonald in 1929, that brought about the resumption of relations. The Soviet position remained essentially the same as it had been in 1924. Moreover, despite the renewal of diplomatic relations, the Soviet Union and Britain remained on very poor terms.[38]

The Norwegian chargé in Moscow told the Soviet government on 17 July that Britain was ready to open talks preliminary to a resumption of diplomatic relations. Karakhan accepted the proposal[39]— Litvinov was probably vacationing in Carlsbad, as was his summer habit[40]—but on 6 September, Litvinov announced that the talks were off unless Britain accepted the standard Soviet formula: first, full recognition; then negotiations of outstanding issues. On 12 September, the British accepted Litvinov's terms.[41]

The talks in London resulted in a compromise embodied in a protocol signed in London on 3 October, which provided for the negotiation of outstanding issues "immediately on the resumption of full diplomatic relations."[42] The issues in question included a commercial treaty; claims, counterclaims, and other financial questions; fisheries; and an application of previous treaties and conventions. A special paragraph reaffirmed that both nations would refrain from propaganda aimed at the other, as had been provided in the abortive 1924 treaty.[43]

With the formalities settled, Sir Esmond Ovey arrived in Moscow to assume his duties as the new ambassador, and his reports throw light on Litvinov in the period just before he became commissar for foreign affairs and on the problems of Anglo-Soviet relations. Writing from the Soviet capital on 23 December 1929, Ovey described Moscow as being in a "state of siege." Stalin had just initiated his violent program to eliminate the wealthiest peasants, the kulaks, "as a class," and the tension in the air was palpable. Ovey found Litvinov gloomy but, as usual, outwardly concerned only with foreign affairs. He was especially exasperated with the British, who, he claimed, had put "special conditions" on diplomatic relations with the Soviet Union that they did not apply to "capitalist states." Litvinov singled out British objections to the Soviet state monopoly on foreign trade, clearly feeling that the policy should be accepted by London. Nonetheless, Ovey found Litvinov personally agreeable and noted that even in criticizing Britain, he is "not without a sense of humor."[44]

The issue of propaganda had long been a bone of contention between the Soviet Union and Britain, despite the 1924 and 1929 pledges. The dispute, of course, centered on the activities of the Comintern. Litvinov never had any direct connections with that organization, but it was his unfortunate job to claim from time to time that the Comintern was an independent organization. He clearly despised this charade and wished the problem would go away. Discussing the British Communist Party with Ovey in December 1929, Litvinov grimly suggested that London deal with its Communists as the Soviet authorities handled its domestic troublemakers, stating, "You can hang them or burn them alive if you catch them."[45] During a discussion with Ovey in February 1930, Litvinov lost his composure. He called the Comintern "hopeless" and added: "Why don't you take the thing? You are a free country. We don't want it here. Do arrange for it to hold its sessions in London." Ovey told his superiors that Litvinov's remarks must be kept absolutely confidential, any leaks might prove "his undoing."[46]

Meanwhile, in London, talks were continuing on the outstanding issues enumerated in the October protocol, and as usual, the most serious stumbling block was the debt/loan impasse. In a forty-five-minute conversation with Ovey on the evening of 4 April, Litvinov became quite animated and, according to Ovey, "jumped all over the place." Litvinov could not understand why the two countries could not just reactivate the 1924 treaty, which had provided in a roundabout way for a government-backed loan. Regaining some self-control, Litvinov admitted that such a financial arrangement was impossible, but he still kept talking of the "necessity" of some type of "guaranteed loan." Finally nailing him down, Ovey learned that Litvinov meant "a loan by the Bank of England or a group of banks," which Ovey accurately called "an ordinary commercial loan." But Litvinov warned that the Soviet government would not spend all the loan in the country that granted it, only a "certain portion." On the other hand, Litvinov wanted to ease the way for the British to grant the loan. He said that a loan clause did not have to be in the formal settlement as long as there was an informal agreement that a loan would be extended—a "happy coincidence," in Litvinov's words. Ovey favored such a solution, calling it "perfectly sound common sense."[47]

Turning to the issue of claims and counterclaims, Litvinov fervently hoped that the negotiators would limit themselves to setting the monetary amounts owed to both sides. Those numbers could then be used as the basis for further negotiations after a loan had been settled. Litvinov possibly wanted to get a British loan, and afterward the Soviet government would simply refuse to discuss the specifics of mutual claims, but he pointed out quite correctly that the whole issue was enormously complex. For Britain, it involved confiscated foreign properties as well as municipal and private bondholders; for the Soviet Union, it meant claims for damages arising from the intervention. But regarding British loans to Russia during World War I, Litvinov brought out his knowledge of English slang and exclaimed "Nothing doing!" Echoing Chicherin at Genoa, he added that Russia had already lost enough from the war, especially in terms of territory. Ovey then asked Litvinov if the Soviets "really wanted a loan very much or not." Litvinov replied evasively to the effect that they could get along without it, but a loan might be "useful." Ovey, however, concluded that a loan was "important for them." It could help in the completion of the First Five-Year Plan and would thereby help stabilize the regime, but he offered no personal recommendations to the Foreign Office.[48]

Ovey may have felt Litvinov's proposal was "perfectly sound common sense," but London did not share his opinion. There were further desultory discussions, but no agreement was ever reached. The British refused to budge from a position of "no payment—no loans or credits," and the Soviets were equally obstinate in the reverse.[49]

Litvinov's priority was to obtain a loan, which the Soviet Union sorely needed, but he clearly could not promise that the entire sum would be spent in Britain. On the other hand, he seemed almost desperate to prevent the issues of the Comintern and prerevolutionary debts from blocking some type of settlement. Neither government would compromise, but once again, it is clear that Litvinov was making an effort to bridge somehow the chasm between imperial Britain and the Soviet Union.

Despite the dispute with Britain, international relations in general were mostly quiescent in 1930 and most of 1931.[50] As the Great Depression deepened, the USSR and the capitalist countries turned increasingly inward, trends that were clearly revealed in Britain's adoption in 1932 of the Imperial Preference System[51] and the United States' retreat into economic nationalism as announced at the London Economic Conference of 1933.[52] Germany and Japan were to employ different means to solve their economic hardships.

For Litvinov, however, 1930 was an important year because on 21 July 1930, his appointment to the office of People's Commissar for Foreign Affairs was announced in Moscow. The internal politics behind his appointment are heavily shrouded in mystery, but it must be emphasized that by the summer of 1930, Stalin's political ascendancy was secure and Litvinov and Stalin could usually get along with one another. This is not to say that Litvinov always agreed with Stalin, but on some very important issues, for example, Stalin's power struggle with Trotskii, Litvinov backed the Georgian, privately telling his own family that although Stalin was bad, Trotskii would be worse.[53] Litvinov also was certain that Stalin's greatest fear in the 1930s was a war, which led the general secretary to support Litvinov's policies of nonaggression pacts and efforts to build a collective security system.[54] Finally, it was probably important to Stalin that Litvinov was recognized more as a foreign affairs expert than as a party man.[55] He had no following within the party and therefore could not pose a threat to Stalin's personal power.

Nonetheless, Litvinov's relationship with Stalin was not close or without disputes. Once Mikhail Litvinov overheard his father on the phone talking with Stalin. After the conversation, Mikhail asked him why he used "vy" in addressing Stalin instead of the familiar "ty" used between friends. Litvinov eyed him and said, "Because I don't wear high boots," a reference to Stalin's affectation of a worker's costume.[56] Years later, Ivy recalled that her husband never had a close personal relationship with Stalin or any of his cronies. She felt that her bourgeois background was a factor, but more important was the fact that Maxim was "a Jew, a Westernizer, a civilized body. And [he was] one who did not drink or hunt or join into the Byzantine hierarchy." His position was "more like that of a 'specialist' called from 'abroad,' his specialty happening to be foreign affairs." Maxim was, in short, "grave and high-minded."[57]

Litvinov's feelings toward Stalin were mixed but in the end negative. Speaking with the writer Ilya Ehrenburg after World War II, Litvinov said that he considered Stalin "the greatest living statesman," a statement probably explained by Litvinov's low opinion of then President Harry Truman. Litvinov then laughed softly and quickly "changed" the subject. Speaking of ancient Rome, he said:

> Titus was notorious for his cruelty. When he seized power, he seemed magnanimous to the Romans, and flatterers called him an "ornament to the human race." In the same year Vesuvius destroyed Pompeii and Herculaneum. Quite possibly the volcano was carrying out the new Emperor's instructions: there were many influential personalities in Pompeii, and Herculaneum was famed for its philosophers and artists.[58]

Ehrenburg also says that the Soviet diplomat Iakov Surits told him that in 1936, after Litvinov had presented his views to Stalin on foreign policy, the dictator put his hand on Litvinov's shoulder and said, "You see, we can reach agreement." Litvinov pushed Stalin's hand away and replied, "Not for long."[59]

Another issue that requires consideration is Litvinov's role in foreign policy formulation while he was commissar. Historians have been perplexed and divided on this issue, owing largely to the paucity of solid evidence, and even Adam Ulam and Max Beloff, two leading specialists on Soviet foreign policy, have been ambiguous. In a reconsideration of his two-volume study on Soviet foreign policy in the 1930s,[60] Beloff concluded that he probably did not stress sufficiently Litvinov's subordinate role.[61] Ulam largely dismisses Litvinov as a mere tool of Stalin, yet credits the foreign commissar with educating the Soviet leadership on the changing realities of international relations.[62] In a more recent study, Jonathan Haslam asserts that "Litvinov was largely free to pursue an outgoing foreign policy," Stalin being absorbed in the massive tasks of industrialization and collectivization.[63]

Litvinov did not do much to clarify the situation. In September 1938, at the height of the Munich crisis, Litvinov told his friend Louis Fischer, "I am merely a messenger boy; I hand up papers."[64] But during the same month, the German diplomat Gustav Hilger claimed that he learned from a "very reliable source" that Litvinov, when asked if France could expect Russian assistance if war came over Czechoslovakia, replied, "If I remain Foreign Commissar, yes; otherwise, no."[65]

While in Moscow and Britain as a research fellow, I attempted to resolve this problem. Litvinov's daughter, Tatiana, quoted her father as saying, "We do only what Stalin wants."[66] However, Soviet historian Vladimir Trukhanovskii asserted that the Politburo regularly sought the advice of the foreign commissar on policy matters. A specific instance of this interaction was in late 1933 when the Politburo summoned Litvinov and informed him that the international situation had changed dramatically with the rise of Hitler. How did he think Soviet policy should react to this new situation? Litvinov reported back with his recommendation that the Soviet Union should enter the League and work for a defensive alliance with France and its ally, Czechoslovakia.[67]

Trukhanovskii's account received independent confirmation in an interview with the late Evgenii Gnedin, an acquaintance of Litvinov who worked as a journalist and as the chief of the Press Department of *Narkomindel* in the 1930s. Gnedin was somewhat surprised that there was any controversy on this point. He said that the Politburo had its own Commission for Foreign Policy, the staff of which changed periodically. As a correspondent for *Izvestiia*, Gnedin attended one evening session of the commission sometime between 1930 and 1935, when the commission consisted of Viacheslav Molotov, chairman of *Sovnarkom*, and Lazar Kaganovich, a crony of Stalin's. Two deputy foreign commissars, Nikolai Krestinskii and Boris Stomoniakov, made their reports and offered suggestions for Soviet policy. Their requests were either granted or rejected; no further discussion was allowed.

Gnedin added that Litvinov, as foreign commissar, had frequent contact with the Politburo and because of his foreign affairs expertise, he was able to influence that body's decisions. But, as the "cult of personality" around Stalin grew and the "total regime" was fully accomplished, foreign experts were consulted less frequently. What Gnedin clearly had in mind was that after about 1936, Litvinov's influence declined while that of Molotov increased.[68] Thus, it seems safe to conclude that during the early to mid-1930s, foreign policy discussions were made at first on some type of collective basis but that gradually this arrangement gave way to total and direct control by Stalin and Molotov.

In any case, Stalin had selected his man, and on 25 July 1930, Litvinov met with members of the press for the first time as foreign commissar. His remarks were uncharacteristically staid and flat. He began by belittling his own promotion, asserting that because Soviet foreign policy "is wholly determined by the will of the working and peasant masses," there would not be "any change whatever" in that policy. It would continue to be based on the principles of the October Revolution and "the defense of conquests of the revolution from external action and intervention." Alluding to the Five-Year Plan, Litvinov said that the "greater our plans of development, the more rapid their pace, the greater is our interest in the preservation of peace." This peace could be maintained by "the discovery and implementation of peaceful coexistence" between the Soviet Union and the rest of the world.

Looking more closely at the other "five-sixths of the earth's surface," Litvinov affirmed the standard line that it was still divided between the "so-called victors and vanquished" of the world war. Although the Soviet Union "maintained with some of these states, wholly correct, normal, and even in some cases friendly relations," his government had no intention "to take part in the grouping of some states against others."[69]

Turning to foreign trade matters, Litvinov claimed that the Soviet Union desired to expand its economic intercourse, but

> certain hostile capitalist groups . . . are conducting a campaign
> for a severance of economic relations with our Union. Their
> efforts appear to be directed chiefly at our exports, but in fact
> they are against our entire foreign trade, for a reduction in our
> exports would inevitably mean a corresponding reduction in our
> imports. These anti-Soviet campaigns are doomed to failure.[70]

In that statement, Litvinov was referring to the recent accusation of Soviet "dumping," or the sale abroad of goods at prices below the cost of production, and as the world depression deepened, the desperate search for causes, or scapegoats, included an increasingly broad movement against the Soviet Union that focused on the charge of dump-ing.[71] By the fall of 1930, the United States and France had developed special licensing procedures for Soviet goods, which had the effect of sharply reducing Soviet exports to those countries, and soon other countries joined in discriminatory practices against Russia.[72]

The importance of this trend, however, should not be overstated. Reviewing Soviet foreign policy and the international situation in January 1931, Molotov asserted that "by and large our relations with the majority of foreign states have developed along normal channels."[73] Nonetheless, it was not in Moscow's interest to have its foreign trade severely curtailed by governmental decrees, because the Soviet Union was already suffering enough as a result of the general economic crisis.[74] Litvinov was called upon to answer the charges of dumping, which he did in an address to the Commission of Enquiry of European Unions on 18 May 1931.[75]

Repeating his proposals made to the Soviet government on the eve of the 1922 Genoa Conference, Litvinov declared that the entire postwar economic order was in need of reorganization. The basic problems of reparations and indebtedness and continued heavy military spending were serious obstacles to economic stability and prosperity and had yet to be solved, and now this unfavorable situation was aggravated by increased economic nationalism.[76]

Litvinov then argued that there was something very strange about singling out the Soviet Union for censure. He noted that the amount of Canadian grain on the international market had increased almost five times since 1913, yet no one had protested. He concluded that the whole attack was politically inspired,[77] and added that "the special conditions of our agricultural system and our foreign trading system" made it possible for the USSR to sell grain at prices below those of other states. If those other states suffered as a result of the Soviet Union's new "special" methods of procuring agricultural products for sale abroad, that was their hard luck. "I must point out that the prices on the world market are determined by supply and demand."[78] Soviet policies clearly were not about to be changed, because the need for foreign currency was simply too great.

Taking a more conciliatory line, Litvinov proposed what he called "a sort of economic nonaggression pact,"[79] which provided for an "abstention from hostile measures in the economic sphere against any country or group of countries from political or other motives—in other words to declare economic war illegal."[80] Like so many other Litvinov proposals, this one died quietly and largely unmourned. This time, the death blow came from the already mentioned growing economic nationalism.[81]

By late 1931, the world of the 1920s had changed greatly. The preparations for the Disarmament Conference continued in Geneva, but no progress was made, and Litvinov introduced no new proposals. Germany was increasingly chaotic, with unemployment reaching staggering proportions and political extremism, both from the right and left, in the ascendant, and the steadying presence of Stresemann had been lost because of his untimely death in 1929. Then in September 1931, the Japanese moved into Manchuria, opening the long road to the disaster of 1939-1945. On the horizon were significant foreign policy changes, and not just for the Soviet Union.

Nine

LITVINOV AND
SOVIET FOREIGN POLICY ON THE
EVE OF HITLER'S ASCENDANCY

FROM THE MIDDLE OF 1931 until the end of 1932, Soviet foreign policy saw some changes that were more superficial than substantial. Specifically, nonaggression pacts were negotiated with France and Poland, two countries that had long been distinguished by their openly anti-Soviet positions. Although the initiatives came from Paris and Warsaw, the French believed that Litvinov attempted to meet them halfway on this specific issue.[1] Nonetheless, relations with France remained quite poor. Economic talks collapsed, and Franco-Soviet hostility at Geneva remained a byword, as Litvinov campaigned against any efforts to establish a security arrangement as a precondition to disarmament. At the same time, Weimar Germany's death rattles were reverberating throughout Europe. No one could say what German policy would be even in the most immediate future, and in East Asia, Japan stopped talking and openly attacked.

Still, Soviet policy underwent no drastic outward change. Moscow vigorously rejected collective security in Europe and Asia, and talk of "total and general disarmament" remained the main Soviet slogan. What was happening behind the scenes in the Kremlin is unknown, but there is no evidence that a serious policy reevaluation was occurring. Soon, however, Soviet policy would be forced to change. Like it or not, the Soviets would be transformed into defenders of the Versailles system and collective security. That, however, is a topic for subsequent chapters.

Weimar Germany in the early 1930s was quickly crumbling before onslaughts from both the right and the left. This deterioration para-

115

lyzed German foreign policy because any diplomatic initiative was subject to thundering criticism from one, or both, of the extremes.[2] Thus, when the Berlin Treaty came up for renewal in the spring of 1931, the Germans refused to extend it for five years, as *Narkomindel* wished; instead, the treaty was to run only until 30 June 1933, after which either party could cancel it with just one year's notice.[3] This limited renewal marked the beginning of the end of the special relationship that had begun in 1922. Now Litvinov, forced mainly by circumstances, was to guide Soviet policy further away from Berlin and toward rapprochement with France.[4]

Litvinov never was a man to seek bad relations with another country, having a preference always for normal and peaceful relations with all states that were willing to reciprocate.[5] Thus, he was able to accept and eventually to embrace the Rapallo connection, despite his initial inclination toward working out an arrangement with Britain. It is not surprising, therefore, that when the French began to show signs of a readiness to end the pointless tension in relations over economic differences, Litvinov was ready to accommodate them. Indeed, at the height of Franco-Soviet hostility, Litvinov made it clear to Ambassador Herbette that he was ready at any time to reopen negotiations.[6] As the German connection became even more tenuous, Litvinov told the French even more bluntly that he was ready to ameliorate tensions.[7]

French hostility, however, remained firm until shortly after the shock of the announcement of a proposed Austro-German customs union on 21 March 1931. France, supported by Britain, immediately protested to the International Court of Justice in the Hague. Austria and Germany dropped the idea before the court handed down a decision against the proposed customs union, but French complacency had been badly shaken.[8] Since French hostility toward the Soviet Union was producing no benefits, common sense dictated that France change its policy.

The French initiative began on 20 April in an extraordinary manner. The French secretary general, Philippe Berthelot, asked the Soviet *polpred*, V. S. Dovgalevskii, to come to the Quai d'Orsay, but because the *polpred* was ill, he declined. Berthelot then asked if Dovgalevskii would receive him that same day, and the Russian agreed.[9]

After Dovgalevskii reviewed briefly the "unfriendly" conduct of the French, he reported that Berthelot had said "the French government was prepared to give us proof of its peacefulness, and with this goal in mind, asked me how we would receive an invitation from the French government for the conclusion of a nonaggression pact." The arrangement would also provide for a "trade agreement based on the principle of equality."[10] Dovgalevskii's official report of the talk was accompanied by a letter to Deputy Foreign Commissar Krestinskii, in which the polpred was somewhat perplexed, writing that "if my memory serves me well," the Soviet Union had already proposed a nonaggression pact to France but had been turned down. He was therefore suspicious about French motives regarding this sudden change.[11]

The next day, Litvinov took over the correspondence between Moscow and Paris. He apparently shared none of Dovgalevskii's misgivings, for he sent the following terse message to the polpred:

> Tell Berthelot that the Soviet government accepts the French
> government's proposal concerning the immediate initiation of
> negotiations for the conclusion of a pact on nonaggression . . .
> and that in the immediate future we will be prepared to deliver
> both a draft treaty on nonaggression and a trade agreement.[12]

Litvinov added that the draft treaty would arrive that same day by telegraph and a proposed commercial agreement would arrive soon in a diplomatic pouch. He also wanted to know immediately if Dovgalevskii's health had improved sufficiently for him to begin the negotiations.[13]

It is true that the Soviet Union had made a standing offer in 1925 to sign nonaggression pacts with all countries with which it maintained normal relations,[14] but Litvinov's unhesitating alacrity in 1931 was most likely stimulated primarily by the rapidly deteriorating situation in Germany. In a meeting with the British ambassador on 26 July, Litvinov was in despair over events in Germany. With remarkable prescience, the commissar, who had recently been to Berlin, told Ambassador Ovey that he feared the "possibility of some form of fascist government emerging in Germany." Ovey felt that Litvinov and the Soviet government "in their heart of hearts would deprecate serious upheaval in Germany at this moment." Above all, the Russians wanted "peace and credits,"[15] and one way to bolster peace was through nonaggression pacts. In such an atmosphere, it is hardly surprising that the Franco-Soviet Nonaggression Pact was initialed in the summer of 1931. By the terms of the agreement, both states accepted essentially negative obligations. Specifically, they pledged not to attack each other, either directly or indirectly, and not to aid or assist by any means a third party should it attack one of the signatories.[16]

The French, worried about public reaction to the new pact, asked Dovgalevskii to keep the agreement secret. The *polpred* expressed understandable doubt that absolute secrecy could be maintained because leaks about the early negotiations had already appeared in the French press. Nonetheless, he promised to inform Moscow of the request.[17] News of the initial agreement, however, appeared in the press almost immediately, despite Litvinov's efforts to prevent it,[18] and in an effort to placate the French press and public, Berthelot insisted that the Russians conclude a similar pact with the Poles, France's eastern ally.[19]

As has been observed, the Soviets were perfectly willing to conclude a bilateral nonaggression pact with Poland, but Warsaw insisted on a regional agreement including Romania, which Moscow would not accept, notwithstanding the very vague Litvinov Protocol. As far as Litvinov was concerned, this policy was firm, and the matter lay "with Warsaw and not with us."[20]

The French stood by their refusal to formally sign the pact with the Soviet Union until a similar arrangement could be reached between Poland and Romania. Recent events in Germany also worried Poland, and Marshal Josef Pilsudski, Poland's dictator, had ordered Josef Beck, his foreign minister, to "give his attention" to a nonaggression pact with Moscow.[21] In October 1931, Litvinov met with the Polish chargé in Moscow, and they agreed that the two countries would soon open formal negotiations for a nonaggression pact.[22] The actual talks began in December, and a nonaggression pact was signed in the summer of 1932, but the negotiations did not greatly concern Litvinov.[23] Indeed, after September 1931, he was obliged more and more to give his attention to East Asia, where he lacked any expertise, because the Japanese invaded Manchuria in that month, which posed a serious threat not only to China but also to Soviet territory.

Despite his lack of familiarity with the region, Litvinov recognized the seriousness of that threat, and on 22 September, he voiced Soviet concerns to the Japanese ambassador, Hirota. He told the Japanese that the Soviet Union was especially concerned about the advance into Manchuria because it threatened the Soviet-owned Chinese Eastern Railroad. Hirota told Litvinov that the Russians would be kept abreast of events in Manchuria and assured him that talks had begun between Japanese officers and the Chinese authorities in Nanking.[24]

Two days later, in a meeting with the British chargé, William Strang, Litvinov reiterated Soviet concerns about the Japanese aggression but added that Moscow would not "complicate the situation." He also said that the Soviet Union lacked formal relations with the Nanking authorities and had no intention of attempting to invoke the Kellogg-Briand Pact.[25] Clearly, aggression so near the Soviet Union's border required the foreign commissar's attention, but it is equally clear that Litvinov was not excessively worried about the incident. Indeed, if the situation had been viewed as genuinely dangerous, it is highly unlikely that Litvinov would have traveled to Turkey in October for ceremonies renewing the 1925 nonaggression treaty.[26]

Nonetheless, the situation did not augur well for Soviet-Japanese relations. Litvinov characteristically sought to clarify Japanese intentions by offering a nonaggression pact, telling the Japanese foreign minister in a 31 December meeting in Moscow that the Soviet Union would soon have nonaggression treaties "with all our neighbors, with the exception of Japan. We think that this gap should be filled." The signing of such a pact would also help to end speculation in Europe and America regarding Soviet-Japanese relations. Litvinov recorded that the foreign minister was "clearly caught off guard by this proposal" but promised to deliver the suggestion to the Japanese cabinet.[27]

Nothing ever came of Litvinov's offer. Speaking with Ambassador Ovey in mid-January 1932, Litvinov was pessimistic about long-run events in the east. Ovey said Litvinov "very definitely gave me the impression that it was his own considered view that one of these days Russia and Japan must come to an armed conflict," but Ovey emphasized that "there was nothing immediate in this fear."[28]

Without doubt, the Soviet government wanted to avoid a military conflict with Japan in the midst of the dislocations of the First Five-Year Plan, a worsening and politically inspired famine, and the steady disintegration of the special relationship with Berlin. Moreover, by early 1933, much more serious problems confronted the Soviet Union in Europe, and therefore the Russians offered to sell to Japan their country's interest in the Chinese Eastern Railroad, thus eliminating a constant source of trouble and freeing them to concentrate on Europe.[29]

After this brief incursion into Asian affairs, Litvinov packed his bags again and departed for Geneva and the long-awaited Disarmament Conference. He had absolutely no hope of achieving anything positive,[30] but he returned to Geneva to propagandize again that disarmament was Europe's only hope of peace.

On 2 February 1932, the conference formally convened, with representatives from "all the sixty-four recognized countries of the world" in attendance.[31] It is important to note that this opening session had to be delayed for an hour so that the League Council could consider the latest news from Asia, the Japanese aerial bombing of Shanghai. "It was an ill-omened beginning."[32] No disarmament was achieved at the Disarmament Conference, but it is of significance for a study of Litvinov's career, if only to reveal his views on collective security just before the ascendancy of the Nazis.

When Litvinov addressed the conference on 11 February, Franco-Soviet differences again came to the fore despite the recently initialed nonaggression agreement. Litvinov made his obligatory references to the international capitalist system as the true source of all wars and also denigrated the League as impotent to do anything about the de facto, if not de jure, war in China. Attacking the position of France, Litvinov said that disarmament must be addressed "without digression for the study of continually arising preliminary conditions."[33] What Litvinov had in mind was the French proposal for "the formation of an international force, under the aegis of the League of Nations, to which all states would submit their offensive weapons," an idea that necessitated a clear definition of aggression and aggressor plus a system of compulsory arbitration.[34] With words that should have haunted him later, Litvinov derided this plan for collective security. These proposals, he said, would be "fruitlessly debated" and would "put the clock back years if not decades." The "only infallible way" to secure peace was "by way of general and total disarmament."[35]

The Soviet Union's wholly negative attitude toward some type of security agreement, as opposed to simple disarmament, was given concrete expression when the issue arose of Soviet participation in the League's Lytton Commission. This body, created to investigate the Sino-Japanese conflict, eventually condemned Japan as an aggressor and recommended that Manchuria be placed under Chinese sovereignty and that Japan receive economic concessions there. The Japanese response was to withdraw from the League.[36] The Soviet Union refused invitations to cooperate with the Lytton Commission on the grounds that the USSR was not a member of the League,[37] but obviously, the real reason was Moscow's desire not to "complicate" the situation, as Litvinov had told Strang. Collective security was still in the future.

Having attacked the French proposals and indulged in a flight into the fantasy of total disarmament, Litvinov came back to reality to assert that the Soviet delegation "is ready to discuss . . . any proposal tending to reduce armaments, and the further such reduction goes, the more readily will the Soviet delegation take part in the work of the conference." He then listed certain aggressive types of armaments, "for example tanks and heavy long-range artillery," which he thought should be completely banned, and repeated the earlier Soviet proposals for proportional reductions of other arms and armed forces,[38] an idea that the Preparatory Commission had already rejected. The day after his address to the conference, Litvinov telegraphed Moscow that the best that could be hoped for was a stabilization of the present level of armaments, but he considered even this unlikely. There was a better chance of a ban on bacteriological weapons, although Litvinov's general pessimism was undiminished.[39]

In April 1932, the Disarmament Conference faced a crucial decision. The German chancellor, Heinrich Brüning, confronting catastrophic conditions at home, hoped to achieve a success at Geneva that might stabilize his government, so with British, U.S., and Italian support, Brüning proposed that Germany be allowed to reduce the period of military service from twelve to six years and to increase the number of men under arms from 100,000 to 200,000. The French premier, André Tardieu, refused to give his support, and Brüning returned to Berlin empty-handed. On 30 May 1932, President Paul von Hindenburg dismissed him and named Franz von Papen the new chancellor. "German democracy had received its death blow."[40]

The Bolsheviks were not ones to mourn the death of German democracy, but they were horrified when the French press announced in late June that Papen had met with Prime Minister Herriot and proposed a Franco-German alliance. The French were extremely skeptical, at best, and the British were totally against such an alliance. Therefore, the idea vanished as quickly as it had appeared.[41] An indication of the Soviet apprehension is found in a meeting between the Soviet *polpred* in Germany, L. Khinchuk, and General Kurt von

Schleicher on the very day the French press broke the story. Schleicher assured the Russians that they "had nothing to be disturbed about,"[42] but that statement failed to allay Russian fears. Indeed almost three years later, Litvinov still recalled vividly the anxiety felt in Moscow at the prospect of a Franco-German rapprochement.[43]

Meanwhile, the conference in Geneva lumbered on, but by mid-June, it was "totally bogged down in a morass of technical obstacles and complications . . . which were [actually] put forward to block the concrete suggestions for reduction of existing armaments."[44] On 22 June, President Herbert Hoover proposed the abolition of obviously offensive weapons and a reduction of other weapons by one-third. This proposal seemed to revive the conference, and Italy and the Soviet Union announced their support for the proposal,[45] even though Litvinov had little, if any, hope for its adoption.[46] When the French addressed the issue, they effectively killed it, pointing out the lack of security arrangements.[47]

In late July, the Papen government in Germany announced that it would no longer participate in the conference "until the principle of equality of rights had been definitely recognized,"[48] meaning Germany's right to equality of arms. By December, Germany, Britain, France, and Italy, with U.S. support, had accepted in principle that Germany should have "equality of rights in a system which would provide security for all nations." With this resolution, which left all substantial matters up in the air, the conference adjourned.[49] "The first year of work had ended where it should have begun."[50]

At the end of 1932, the general foreign policy situation of the Soviet Union was uncertain at best. Relations were somewhat better with France and Poland, but Moscow's improved dealings with Paris were mainly owing to French initiative and Soviet receptivity, both of which were prompted by fears of a destablized Germany. Litvinov was in the forefront of the fight for better relations with France, and in late 1932, the French ambassador in Moscow wrote gushingly that "Litvinov has imposed his policy and this policy is one of mutual interests between the USSR and France." But he added that Litvinov's Soviet opponents were still active and that they were "the defenders of an exclusive German orientation," against which the commissar fought "with tenacity and not without success."[51] East Asia's future was still problematic, but for the present, the Japanese threat had largely been countered by a Soviet military buildup in the area and a firm refusal to get involved so long as Soviet borders were not crossed.[52] The situation in Germany worried Litvinov, but about all he could do was wait for things in Berlin to sort themselves out.

On 30 January 1933, Europe saw an ominous sign of the path Germany would take when Adolf Hitler became the new chancellor. Far from being a pragmatic politician without clear goals,[53] Hitler had some very definite ideas about Germany, its goals, and the tactics needed to achieve them. Hitler had preached repeatedly that the Germans were the master race destined to supremacy at least in Europe, if not the world. As such, the Germans were naturally entitled to all the land they needed to flourish—the famous doctrine of *lebensraum*. "Racial vitality and spatial expansion were directly related."[54] Moreover, Hitler openly proclaimed that German expansion would come by military conquest—other peoples "would be expelled or exterminated, not assimilated"[55]—and war was the point at which German racial superiority and the need for expansion met.

Hitler made no effort to conceal the fact that German expansion would take place primarily at the expense of the Soviet Union.[56] (Poland was dismissed as "incidental," in keeping with the Nazis' notorious contempt for that nation.)[57] France, the chief beneficiary of the hated Versailles system, would be smashed first, a chore in which Italy could be expected to help.[58] As far as Britain was concerned, Hitler felt that that island nation could probably be bought off by giving it a free hand in the colonial world. Also, Britain's differences with France and the Soviet Union were to be exploited fully.[59] The road to the east would thus be open.

Besides buying off Britain through a colonial deal, Hitler sought to implement his policy through the method of divide and conquer. Hitler in power, therefore, showed a consistent aversion to all multilateral treaty commitments.[60] Instead, he sought specific bilateral agreements that could be more easily torn up once their usefulness was over. The only way to contain a policy that rejected outright any collective agreements was to confront it with a strong mutual-assistance alliance system that would guarantee the aggressor a general war if it attacked an individual state. The natural, if not only, Continental states to lead such a system were the Soviet Union and France, because they were Hitler's main targets and because they possessed the combined strength to defeat Nazi aggression. As will be seen, for a brief moment it appeared that such a system might come into existence, but for many reasons, collective security failed, and Hitler was able to launch World War II.

Ten

REORIENTING
SOVIET FOREIGN POLICY

HITLER CAME TO POWER on 30 January 1933, and at the Disarmament Conference on 6 February, Litvinov announced a startling change in Soviet policy. Previously, the Soviet Union, through Litvinov, had consistently rejected the French demand that some type of security arrangement must precede disarmament. Litvinov, moreover, had refused to cooperate with some early efforts to bind the disarmament conferees through a definition of aggression. He now accepted both ideas. In a speech that "awakened many a bored delegate,"[1] Litvinov said that although the Soviet delegation still favored total disarmament as the best way to achieve real security, it recognized that the French would not relent in their insistence on some type of security arrangement. Therefore, the Soviet Union would henceforth be willing to discuss such a security system as a precondition to subsequent disarmament. Litvinov admitted that such a task, in the face of Europe's complex international rivalries, would be extraordinarily difficult and that "to grapple with this problem means an end to all work on disarmament for a very long time." But with Soviet support, the problem could be dealt with more rapidly, and then the delegates could get to the business of disarmament.[2]

Litvinov noted that a security system would, "obviously," require some provision for determining who was the aggressor, a point on which there must be "complete candor and mutual understanding."[3] He therefore offered for discussion a Soviet "Draft Declaration Regarding a Definition of Aggression," which would brand as an aggressor any state that declared war on another state, sent its armies across the borders of another state, fired across its borders into another state, or established a naval blockade.[4] He then listed circumstances that could not be accepted as justification for crossing another state's borders. First and foremost, Litvinov insisted that "no considerations of the political, strategic, or economic order [of the state attacked] can serve as a justification for aggression."[5]

Thus, only one week after the advent to power of Hitler, Soviet policy had undergone a dramatic change. The rise of Hitler doubtless spurred the Soviets to change their policy, but it must be repeated that for a long time, Litvinov had been quite unsure about the future of Soviet-German relations—the revelations of the Papen proposal to France particularly causing grave concern. Exactly when the Politburo changed its policy is unknown, but it is highly unlikely Litvinov would have acted without its approval.

The same day, Litvinov telegraphed the Soviet government that the French foreign minister, Joseph Paul-Boncour, had come to see him in obvious elation. He had thanked Litvinov for his remarks and had announced the French cabinet's decision to submit the nonaggression treaty to the Chamber of Deputies for ratification immediately.[6] Perhaps the Soviet motivation was simply to facilitate just such a step, but it is also possible that Litvinov hoped to build a Franco-Soviet rapprochement as a hindrance to the so-called four-power pact then being discussed by Britain, France, Germany, and Italy. Speaking with the French ambassador in April, Litvinov made no effort to conceal his concern: "Anything that is done without us, could be something done against us."[7] In any case, it must be emphasized that after the early months of 1933, "Franco-Soviet cooperation became a prominent feature" of what was left of the Disarmament Conference.[8] This change was a significant step on the path to the Mutual Assistance Pact of 1935 and one the Soviets had initiated.

Further evidence of the Franco-Soviet rapprochement came during Litvinov's visit to Paris on 6–7 July 1933. At a government reception, Litvinov spoke glowingly about relations with France and the Soviet Union's "nearest neighbors," and he publicly recognized that improvements with these neighbors had been facilitated by "the French government and French political circles." He concluded on an upbeat note: "Neither politically nor economically do our interests conflict with those of France in any part of the world and therefore in our view there is no obstacle to further political and economic rapprochement."[9] In private talks with Paul-Boncour, Litvinov was more direct, urging the French to sign a protocol with the Soviet

Union that defined aggression in the terms of Litvinov's Geneva proposal of 6 February.[10] The French declined, claiming that they needed to discuss the matter with the British.[11] France's reluctance to sign an agreement as innocuous as the one defining aggression was clear evidence that the rapprochement with Moscow was still a topic of serious controversy in Paris. As an authority on Franco-Soviet relations in the early 1930s, William Scott, has observed, the July discussions were "only exploratory in nature, but they contained the germ of future negotiations."[12]

While in Paris Litvinov sent an extraordinary telegram directly to Stalin (which indicates that the two men were working closely in the development of Soviet policy) saying that both Paul-Boncour and Premier Edouard Daladier had alluded to "Polish-German negotiations" in a way that "merited serious attention." He felt their remarks were "in the capacity of a warning to us."[13] Clearly, Litvinov wanted the general secretary to know that something potentially unfavorable for Moscow was in the works between Berlin and Warsaw and that a German-Polish rapprochement only made an understanding with Paris more urgent. The alternative, as even Stalin must have understood, was a wholly isolated Soviet Union, a prospect unappealing to even a world revolutionist.

The next important event in the improvement of Franco-Soviet relations followed soon after Litvinov's visit to Paris when the French air minister, Pierre Cot, paid an official visit to the Soviet Union, the first French ministerial visit to that country. At almost the same time, Edouard Herriot went there as well, although his visit was unofficial.[14]

On 19 September, Litvinov met with Herriot. Despite the "unofficial" nature of his visit, Litvinov understood well that Herriot's prestige was significant in French politics, and Litvinov therefore sought to convince the Frenchman of the change in Soviet policy. "I told him of our firm decision and desire to enter into the closest rapprochement with France," and specifically, Litvinov proposed that France and the Soviet Union "conclude a gentlemen's agreement for an exchange of information," an idea that "especially interested" Herriot and one that he promised to support.[15]

The next day, Litvinov met with Cot, who had arrived in Moscow after touring Soviet aeronautical factories and observing Soviet air maneuvers. Cot opened the conversation with praise for Soviet power, "both actual and potential" and added that the members of the French delegation were "convinced of the necessity and desirability of a rapprochement between our two countries." Litvinov agreed, but expressed concern that "the right" might come to power in France and not share this desire for closer relations.[16] (If Litvinov had Pierre Laval in mind, his fears were well-founded.)

It is true that the visit with Cot was quite cordial, but there is no evidence from Soviet sources that Litvinov proposed a Franco-Soviet security pact, much less an "unconditional" alliance that would provide for automatic mutual assistance in the event one of the parties was attacked. But such a proposal was made according to both the foreign minister, Paul-Boncour, and the secretary general of the French Foreign Ministry, Alexis Saint-Leger Leger.[17]

Regardless of who first suggested an alliance, it is quite clear that both countries felt increasingly uneasy with the new German state by late 1933. Speaking with the French ambassador, Litvinov "repeated . . . that he was persuaded that Germany will make war within two years," although he added that Nazi interests were directed more toward the east, including the Ukraine, than toward Alsace-Lorraine.[18] Although these remarks hardly constitute the offer of an alliance, they could hardly have been clearer in stating Soviet fears of Hitler.

In any case, it is obvious that the decisive impetus toward a mutual assistance pact occurred when Germany announced its withdrawal from the League of Nations on 14 October 1933. Now the French seemed almost panicky. Paul-Boncour rushed to Dovgalevskii and proposed that "if the situation in Germany does not change, then with time the issue would arise of supplementing the Franco-Soviet Pact . . . with a pact of mutual assistance."[19]

On 31 October, Litvinov met with Paul-Boncour in Paris for further talks, and the commissar described the discussions as even "more friendly than anytime in the past." Paul-Boncour first broached the issue of whether the Soviets wished to continue with the disarmament talks, and Litvinov pointed out that further discussion seemed pointless in the face of Japanese aggression in Asia and Germany's withdrawal from the League. Next Paul-Boncour raised the issue of a mutual assistance pact and the USSR's entry into the League "in case of German rearmament and preparation for war" and Litvinov responded that the Soviet Union had "to think not only about the West, but also about the East and that France should take some interest in our complications in the East." The French, however, rejected obligations in that region. They also insisted that the Soviets must join the League because a mutual assistance pact would have to operate through the machinery of the League in order to have any hope of receiving Polish support.[20] The French thought that Litvinov was clearly pleased by these proposals, but he said they were much too important to be settled without consultation with Moscow. Nonetheless, he and Paul-Boncour agreed that while Moscow was considering the proposal, they "would think about possible means of cooperation."[21]

While the men in the Kremlin were evaluating the possibilities of a Franco-Soviet rapprochement, they had to consider it within the broader context of European diplomacy. In particular, Soviet-German relations had worsened considerably over the course of 1933. After Litvinov had announced the change in Soviet policy on security and disarmament in February, the commissar reported that the German representative in Geneva, Rudolf Nadolny, had "expressed satisfaction, but it was hardly sincere."[22] On 1 March, Litvinov discussed the general state of Soviet-German relations with Germany's new foreign minister, Konstantin von Neurath, who assured the commissar that Germany had no desire to abandon the Rapallo policy, but he reported to Berlin that Litvinov was unconvinced. "Litvinov," the German asserted, "is thinking of developing relations with France further"[23] and added that Litvinov was unusually hostile during their meeting. Unlike his usual practice, Litvinov objected heatedly to the recent repression of the German Communists in the wake of the Reichstag fire. Neurath pointed out that Litvinov previously had assured him "that German-Russian relations had in no way been influenced by the attitude of the German government toward German communism."[24]

Another bitter and perhaps more revealing meeting occurred on 11 March when in speaking with Ambassador Dirksen, Litvinov was almost incoherent. He astonished Dirksen by saying that the USSR intended to check Germany's anti-Soviet plans by means of "closer relations with France," a policy that would have the added advantage of depriving Germany of French support for any *Drang nach Osten*. Litvinov bluntly stated that a "chief goal" of Moscow's policy was to prevent a German-French alliance.[25]

As Litvinov's talks with the French and Germans indicate, he was an early advocate of better relations with Paris while Rapallo was collapsing, but there is good reason to believe that Litvinov was somewhat taken aback with how quickly the special relationship with

Berlin disintegrated. In a more tranquil conversation with Neurath in Berlin in June 1934, Litvinov revealed that "before the Nazis came to power, we assumed that in due course they would disavow their anti-Soviet programs and would continue the policies of the previous German regimes regarding the USSR. We ourselves assumed cooperation [with the Nazis] on the same basis as before." Unfortunately, Litvinov added, such had not been the case, and Hitler's program as outlined in *Mein Kampf* still held true. Litvinov emphasized that the "differences" between the nature of the two regimes was not an issue; the problem was the Nazi plans for eastward expansion.[26]

Thus, it seems impossible to assert that Litvinov and the Soviet leadership had become proponents of collective security and opponents of Nazism on the basis of principle, as Soviet historians have so often asserted. The ultimate issue for Moscow and Litvinov was the security of the state and how best to achieve it.

While Litvinov was moving Soviet policy toward France, the Soviet press also began to change its tone on foreign policy issues. Beginning in May 1933, *Pravda* and *Izvestiia* published a remarkable series of articles by Karl Radek, a prominent Soviet politician and publicist, in which he asserted that while Versailles was bad, the new proponents of revision were worse. They were after "the peace of the prison" and were openly preparing for war, so the new task of the international proletariat was to prevent the destruction of Versailles by "the fascists who seek to redistribute the world by a new war."[27] So that there could be no confusion about who the "fascists" were, Radek later wrote that Versailles was "better than revision by the Nazis, which would mean world war."[28] In two final articles, Radek warned that the Soviet Union would have to look to "pacts of defense"[29] in order to stop the Nazis, and that treaty revision according to Berlin meant a change for the Soviet Union "along the lines of Brest-Litovsk."[30] If Radek meant that some sort of Nazi-Soviet rapprochement involving Soviet territorial concessions was possible, it is certain that Litvinov was not an advocate of such a deal.[31]

In the midst of the reevaluation of Soviet policy in Europe, a new opportunity arose elsewhere. In the United States, Franklin D. Roosevelt had been elected president and had decided to end the fifteen-year break in diplomatic relations between the United States and Russia. At almost the same time, the Soviet-Japanese talks for the sale of the Chinese Eastern Railroad broke down.[32] Because the Soviet leadership viewed the United States as a Pacific power that should be concerned with Japanese aggression, it decided to send no less than the foreign commissar to negotiate the establishment of relations. As early as 1918, Litvinov had recognized the new and important role the United States played in international relations, and throughout the intervening years he had tried to keep the lines of communication open between Moscow and Washington. Now he was at last going to the United States.

Litvinov landed in New York on 7 November 1933, and he arrived at the White House to open negotiations the next day.[33] It immediately became clear that the Russians were extraordinarily desirous of reaching a quick settlement with the U.S. government because Litvinov laid aside the standard Soviet policy of formal recognition before discussing particular issues. For its part, the U.S. government insisted upon a settlement of the following points before formal recognition: the repudiated debts of the imperial and Provisional governments and confiscated property of American nationals; propaganda activities of the Comintern; and the rights of Americans who might reside in Russia subsequent to recognition, especially the right to freedom of worship. Litvinov grudgingly accepted these conditions.[34]

Now it was time to get down to business. Litvinov, uncomfortable in what he later admitted was a "very nervous situation,"[35] replied immediately to the debt issue. He insisted that the Russians could not be expected to pay for guns used to shoot other Russians by the troops of Aleksandr Kerenskii,[36] but William C. Bullitt, Roosevelt's chief Soviet adviser, charged that at least two-thirds of the money sent to Kerenskii had been used to fight the Germans and therefore the Soviets must pay.[37] Bristling, Litvinov shot back that in that case, the Russians had counterclaims arising from the U.S. military intervention in Russia in 1919–1920.[38] Sensing an impasse, Bullitt startled Litvinov by changing course to note that soon the Congress would pass the Johnson Act, which would forbid loans to nations in default to the U.S. government, and if the Soviets continued to bicker, they would be unable to obtain any credit in the United States.[39] Litvinov felt obliged to retreat.

A financial settlement was reached on 15 November and embodied in a "gentlemen's agreement" between Litvinov and Roosevelt. Foremost, the Soviet government agreed to pay the United States "a sum not less than $75,000,000 in the form of a percentage above the ordinary rate of interest on a loan to be granted to it" by the U.S. government or its citizens. (The use of the word "loan" turned out to be quite unfortunate for the United States, as we shall see.) The Soviets also agreed to waive claims against U.S. activity during the intervention in Siberia after World War I,[40] and Litvinov further pledged that the Russians would not allow any organization on Soviet territory that aimed at the overthrow of the U.S. government.[41] He also assured Roosevelt that the rights of Americans in the USSR would be carefully protected under the Soviet Constitution.[42]

Litvinov then revealed the reasons for the Soviets' conciliatory policy: They wanted a Soviet-U.S. nonaggression pact in the Pacific. The president, however, quickly passed over the matter, promising only to give it further consideration.[43] In short, the Soviets were so anxious for U.S. cooperation that they agreed to conditions that Beatrice Farnsworth has succinctly referred to as "the most sweeping the Soviets ever signed."[44] But if they thought doing so would buy active U.S. involvement against Japan, they were rapidly disillusioned.

Before that, however, each government appointed its ambassador. The Soviets pointedly selected their foremost Japanese specialist, career diplomat Aleksandr Troianovskii—and Tokyo clearly understood the implications of Troianovskii's appointment;[45] not surprisingly, Roosevelt sent Bullitt to the Soviet Union.

When the U.S. ambassador arrived in Moscow in December 1933, the Soviet leadership set out to flatter him, though Litvinov had already developed a distaste for the affluent American,[46] a feeling that would intensify and be reciprocated. The Russians held a grand reception at the home of Soviet Marshal K. E. Voroshilov, where Stalin met with a foreign ambassador for the first time. Numerous toasts of vodka and red wine were consumed, and Bullitt began to sense an atmosphere of sincere congeniality. On a more serious side, Stalin introduced Bullitt to another marshal, Aleksandr Egorov, adding that Egorov would victoriously lead the Red Army against Japan "when Japan attacks."[47] Stalin continued his anti-Japanese theme by asking Bullitt to help the Russians immediately obtain 250,000 tons of U.S. steel rails to complete a second rail line to Vladivostok, explaining that the Russians would defeat Japan without the rails but that the task would be easier with them.

On December 21, Bullitt met with Litvinov, and the latter revealed his government's most important ambition: The Soviets wanted the Americans to propose nonaggression pacts among the United States, the Soviet Union, China, and Japan.[48] Bullitt remarked without elaboration that such an arrangement was highly improbable. Litvinov then asked if the Americans would send a warship or squadron to Vladivostok or Leningrad; Bullitt's reply was again discouraging.[49] The American would later conclude in a report to Washington that the Russians would "do anything" for U.S. "moral support" against Japan,[50] an odd statement in the face of Soviet requests for concrete U.S. action.

After this unmistakably firm rebuff, talks opened on the implementation of the debt agreement discussed earlier in Washington. They got nowhere. The Soviets insisted upon an outright loan, to be spent by them wherever they pleased.[51] Aghast, the Americans refused to consider such an arrangement, insisting that they had actually meant a "credit" to be spent in the United States under government supervision.[52] As a result, "no loan was ever granted, no debt was ever paid"[53]—meaning the $75 million the Soviets had agreed to pay the United States was never received.

Why would the Soviets, who wanted to purchase U.S. goods, not back down and adhere to the American interpretation of the debt agreement? Primarily, they did not do so because the Russians no longer felt a need for U.S. help in East Asia. Relations with Japan began to improve, a development communicated by Ambassador Troianovskii to President Roosevelt in February 1934[54] and confirmed by Ambassador Bullitt in April.[55] Indeed, in the summer of 1935, the Russians sold the Chinese Eastern Railroad to the Japanese-controlled state of Manchukuo, and thus the threat of war in the east receded.[56] No longer needing U.S. aid, the Soviet Union lacked a compelling reason to pay the old debt, and subsequent talks got nowhere. The brief Soviet-U.S. rapprochement thus bore no fruit, and Soviet attention once again turned toward Europe.

There is genuine irony in the story of Litvinov's role in U.S. recognition. According to his daughter, he felt that his talks with Roosevelt were the "high point" of his diplomatic career,[57] yet it seems that he was not entirely aboveboard in his dealings with the Americans and perhaps not even with his own government. The debt issue continued to plague relations,[58] and the main problem revolved around the terms "loan" and "credit." This difficulty was in fact a deception, because the night before signing the recognition agreement, Litvinov had told the U.S. journalist, Walter Duranty, that he "clearly understood that no 'loan' would be available in the United States but that the most that could be expected would be credits along the line of those available in Great Britain."[59] Litvinov never made any similar acknowledgment to U.S. officials and, as mentioned, insisted on a "loan" for Moscow. This was hardly Litvinov's finest hour. If Litvinov did understand the U.S. meaning as early as November 1933, the lack of agreement hardly redounds to his credit—despite his thereby "saving" the Soviet Union $75 million.

The year 1933 saw some of the most dramatic changes ever in the history of Soviet foreign policy. The country's previous positions on disarmament and European security were scrapped, as was the policy that full recognition must precede any negotiations on debts or propaganda. It is, of course, impossible to give precise reasons for these policy changes, but the Soviet moves were understandable reactions of a state that found itself threatened on two fronts. The change in policy was directed at France and the United States, two logical partners for the USSR in the event of conflict with Nazi Germany and/or militarist Japan. The next year was to bring even more significant Soviet policy reversals.

Eleven

THE FRANCO-SOVIET
MUTUAL ASSISTANCE PACT

LITVINOV FAILED to achieve U.S. support against Japanese aggression, and on the European front, he achieved only an illusion of success—the Mutual Assistance Pact signed between the Soviet Union and France in May 1935. This accomplishment, which at the time appeared substantial, turned out to be virtually meaningless. Almost immediately after its conclusion, the whole system of collective security, of which the pact was a cornerstone, unraveled, and events demonstrated that appeasement and accommodation were the western powers' true policies toward Hitler and Mussolini.

In December 1933, Litvinov stopped in Rome on his way back to Moscow from Washington. In a meeting with Mussolini, Litvinov tried to convince him that "the militarist tendency in German policy" was also a threat to Italian interests. More significant, he explained the new direction of Soviet policy. He said that German rearmament and that country's aggressive policy were Russia's real concerns and that, because of them, the Soviet Union had decided to take "a resolute path toward a rapprochement with France."[1]

Also while in Rome, Litvinov took time to promote the improving relationship with Paris. Speaking with Charles Pineton de Chambrun, the French ambassador to Italy, the commissar decried Germany's rearmament and expressed his desire "to draw the bonds even closer" between France and the Soviet Union. He hoped the two countries would consult on "all European issues" and that "ultimately he would witness the establishment between France and Russia of the intimate affinity of former times."[2]

Back in Moscow, Litvinov continued to sound the tocsin against the Nazis, and he urged France to at least maintain its present level of armaments. He believed that Hitler needed "two or three" years to prepare his aggression, and in the meantime, the Nazis would sign "any pacts or treaties"—to which they would attach "no importance." The essence of Hitler's thought remained "revenge and expansion toward the east and the reconquest of Alsace-Lorraine." Litvinov emphasized that *Mein Kampf* had just come out in an edition of 1 million copies and not one point had been modified from previous editions.[3]

As the direction of Soviet foreign policy was clearly undergoing a serious change, Litvinov met with the German ambassador in Moscow, Rudolf Nadolny, on 13 December. Perhaps Litvinov wanted more ammunition for his argument in favor of collective security agreements; if so, he certainly got it. After a bitter review by both men of the poor relations between Moscow and Berlin, Litvinov brought matters up-to-date, asserting that "some people in Germany" liked Japan's aggressive course, which concerned the Russians so much. In Litvinov's words, "Nadolny then unleashed absolute blackmail—that is, a rapprochement of Germany with Japan was possible and depended on Soviet conduct."[4]

If Stalin and the Soviet leadership's main concern really was in Asia, and if they wanted at all costs to maintain the Rapallo connection, this would perhaps have been a good opportunity, as Nadolny seemed to be hinting at a Soviet-German rapprochement as a way of restraining Japan, although the offer was contained within a threat. Litvinov declined, saying that past disagreements, for example, Locarno, paled before the person of Adolf Hitler and his Nazis, and he recounted some especially virulent anti-Soviet remarks made recently by Nazi leaders. If Nadolny still felt that Moscow was the cause of the deterioration in Soviet-German relations, he was not confronting "facts that were clear and obvious to all." Litvinov repeated to the ambassador that *Mein Kampf* continued to circulate in Germany and that Hitler had not disavowed one word of it. With such a man making foreign policy, a Soviet-German rapprochement was out of the question.[5]

The Politburo had come to realize as much. Although the details of its debates remain unknown, Soviet sources assert that on 19 December 1933, the Politburo accepted the collective security policy that had been the subject of discussion since at least the previous February. The party leadership approved a resolution calling for the conclusion of a regional treaty system that would provide for mutual assistance in the event of German aggression and for the entrance of the Soviet Union into the League of Nations. Vladimir Trukhanovskii, a leading Soviet authority on foreign policy who enjoyed access to party and state archives, told me that the resolution was drawn up by Commissar Litvinov.[6]

On 28 December, Dovgalevskii formally communicated the Soviet decision to Paul-Boncour, and Moscow also announced its agreement to the French precondition for a mutual assistance pact: The Soviet Union was willing to join the League of Nations. Soviet membership, however, was qualified by Moscow's refusal to recognize the League's right to arbitrate in disputes with a third country that had existed before the Soviet Union joined the League. The Russians also rejected any role in the League's mandate system.[7] Once these conditions were satisfied, the Soviet Union was prepared "to conclude within the framework of the League of Nations a regional agreement for mutual defense against aggression from the side of Germany." The nations eligible for this regional pact were Belgium, France, Czechoslovakia, Poland, Lithuania, Latvia, Estonia, and Finland, "or several of these lands, but with the obligatory participation of France and Poland."[8]

Litvinov had succeeded in changing completely the direction of Soviet foreign policy.[9] Long the League's harshest critic, the Soviet government now intended to join that organization. For years, Soviet-French hostility had been a byword in European diplomacy; now the two nations had agreed in principle to an alliance. Litvinov, however, should not be overly praised for these achievements. Forever the realist, he simply saw a drastic change taking place in Germany and responded accordingly. Ultimate "credit" for the change in Soviet policy, therefore, should go to Hitler. On the other hand, it is undeniable that Litvinov can in no way be put into that ignominious group of statesmen, led by Neville Chamberlain and Pierre Laval, who made the fatal mistake of seeing Hitler as just another German statesman with whom one could reason.

On 29 December 1933, before the Central Committee, Litvinov made the most important public speech of his career. He began by announcing that the Soviet Union stood at "the junction of two eras" and said that the past fifteen years had taught the Soviet leadership much about the capitalist world and its "imperialist nature." Litvinov asserted, however, that "not all the capitalist states always want war" and that at some times "any of the capitalist states may become profoundly pacifist." Such an event could occur after defeat in a war, when a state needs peace to recover and marshal its forces for revenge, and such had been the general situation in Europe after World War I, because in that terrible ordeal, there had been no real winners. But "that era of bourgeois pacifism is over." The talk heard now was about, not disarmament, but "armaments or rearmament." There is "a new militarist spirit" and "new parties, new cliques, and new people with new ideologies, which have not been bound or compromised in any way by the pacifism of the past." To these people, "war alone is able to ennoble, to renew, to rejuvenate mankind." And their proclaimed targets in this "civilizing mission" are "Marxism, communism, and radicalism."[10]

This struggle, however, also had a more narrow and immediate purpose—"the revision of treaties and the seizure of lands both mentioned and unmentioned in the treaties they propose to revise." Just a cursory reading of the literature of this "new ideology" reveals that its immediate territorial aims are areas "under control of the hated Marxists, but it does not reject additional pieces of bourgeois lands." So that there could be no confusion as to whether Litvinov had in mind Germany or Japan, he specifically stated that "so things stand . . . with one of the European countries."[11]

Despite the unmistakably clear meaning of his remarks, Litvinov said: "You will have received, however, an incorrect representation of the international situation if, on the basis of what I have said, you think that all the capitalist states are now striving for war and making direct preparations for it. Far from it." True, antagonisms existed among all the capitalist states, but "these rivalries have still not reached such an acute point that war is being actually considered." These powers, however, "may have nothing against a small fight among other states in which they are not involved and from which they might be able to derive some benefit," in particular, "if this fight causes our Union to suffer."[12]

In spite of Litvinov's cautious tone, an indisputable change had publicly taken place in Soviet foreign policy. The oft-heard assertion that Litvinov was attempting to explain to the Soviet leadership that not all the capitalist states were equally dangerous,[13] however, is not entirely true. No doubt Litvinov emphasized a growing division within the capitalist world, but acknowledgment of the existence of such divisions had always been a cardinal point in Soviet policy. What was unique in Litvinov's speech was his placing Germany in the more hostile capitalist grouping. In the 1920s, Soviet leaders never tired of pointing out that Germany was, in general, the best friend Soviet Russia had and that France was the most hostile of the capitalist states. Now that configuration was reversed.

Turning to a description of relations with individual states, Litvinov for the most part merely elaborated his introductory remarks. He noted that relations with France were marked by "an absence of any political antagonism" and a mutual desire to preserve the peace. Relations with fascist Italy received unqualified praise, and although Anglo-Soviet relations remained poor, Litvinov denied that there were any "objective causes" for this situation.[14]

With respect to Germany, Litvinov publicly admitted that there had been hope that once in power, the Nazis would drop their more extreme ideas. Unfortunately, that had not been the case, and the idea of "conquest in the east" continued to be expressed. He repeated the assertion that he had put to Nadolny: The cause for the collapse in Soviet-German relations lay with Berlin and Germany's new aggressive policy. The Soviet Union derived no joy in this deterioration of a relationship that for years had been mutually beneficial, but there was nothing to be done while the Nazis held power.[15]

Turning to Japan, Litvinov described that country as the "darkest cloud on the international political horizon."[16] Litvinov could indeed say this, not because Japanese policy had changed much since 1931, but because it was becoming increasingly clear that any proposals to restrain Japan through collective action with either France or the United States were bound to fail. (As it turned out, isolated in East Asia and facing a threat there that was clearly less powerful than a resurgent Germany, the Soviet leadership elected to cut its losses. In 1935, therefore, after lengthy negotiations, Moscow completed the sale of the Chinese Eastern Railroad).[17]

Litvinov's speech provoked a storm of speculation within the Moscow diplomatic corps. The British ambassador reported that there was "a growing impression" that France and the Soviet Union were moving toward a mutual assistance pact. He refused to credit such rumors, because they contradicted the "most basic principles of Soviet policy," but if such a pact actually was being planned, he concluded, there could be no doubt that the Soviets were "really afraid of German aggression."[18]

At the Seventeenth Congress of the Communist Party in February 1934, Stalin gave definitive notice that the spirit of Rapallo was dead. "The point is that Germany's policy has changed," he said. At present in Germany, the "upper hand" belongs to a group espousing a policy "which, in the main, recalls the policy of the former German Kaiser, who at one time occupied the Ukraine, marched against Leningrad, and converted the Baltic countries into a *place d'armes* for this march." He concluded with the ominous observation that the Soviet Union stood ready to renew the friendship but only after Hitler showed a readiness to reciprocate.[19]

This speech was typical of the well-known caution and reserve that Stalin displayed in uncertain situations until he felt that the time was ripe for action. But, as emphasized earlier, Litvinov, always carrying a memory of Brest-Litovsk, had long harbored a deep distrust of the Germans. It is probably more than a coincidence that when Stalin came forth publicly to criticize Germany, his words should echo the thoughts of his foreign commissar.

In any case, the focus of diplomatic activity now shifted to France where the new foreign minister, Louis Barthou, had to fight a battle to get a pact with the Soviets accepted.[20] First, however, the new French government was so preoccupied with domestic affairs that consideration of the Franco-Soviet mutual assistance pact "simply lay dormant for two months."[21] In the meantime, Litvinov attempted to clarify the situation with Poland.

On 26 January 1934, that country announced its conclusion of a nonaggression pact with Germany, with both states pledging to consult directly on all issues affecting their mutual relations and to refrain from the use of force in settling any dispute.[22] Litvinov certainly disliked the Polish government in general and Foreign Minister Josef Beck in particular;[23] the new Polish move only increased this feeling. The fact that Soviet-Polish relations had reached a new low was apparent from discussions held in Moscow between Litvinov and Beck in the middle of February. Litvinov asked Beck why he supposed Hitler had concluded a pact with Poland of the sort that Brüning and Stresemann had rejected, and how did Beck reconcile it with the Nazis' ideology. Beck replied that the Nazis, in power, now understood that Poland was "not a weak, young state." Litvinov derided the idea that the Nazis had changed their ultimate goals since coming to power, saying that "we judge the aspirations of the Nazis on the basis of their past publications and not on some political speeches, which Hitler is now making and in which he has switched over to some pacifist phraseology." Beck objected that Germany presented no immediate threat and that if he "was able to make Poland secure for the present that was sufficient." Beck even scolded Litvinov for "looking too far into the future."[24]

And so the conversation continued. Obviously, Beck felt that he had achieved a real measure of security through his arrangement with Hitler. As a result, however, Poland could not be expected to participate in any defensive mutual assistance pact to check German expansion because such a policy would have angered Hitler. The policy of collective security, still very much embryonic in form, had received a serious blow.

Litvinov clearly recognized this fact. In a memorandum for the Politburo, Litvinov outlined Poland's hostility to collective security and wrote that it was even possible that the Poles had some type of secret agreement with Germany. Litvinov argued the following:

> Poland considers it useful for its new orientation . . . to disguise
> its contents by outwardly good relations with us. This disguise
> can be useful to us and therefore we ought to meet the Poles
> half way. This masking [of the poor nature of relations] will
> demobilize Polish public opinion regarding us and in the future
> will somewhat complicate Polish efforts to switch over to open
> hostility to us. We should therefore encourage this
> demobilization by means of a further cultural rapprochement
> with Polish social circles. For us to mobilize our public opinion
> in the desired direction in the event it should become necessary
> will be an easier matter.[25]

The Soviets never got much of a chance to implement Litvinov's suggestion, because Soviet-Polish relations went into a deep freeze. The Poles were a leading force opposing Soviet entry into the League of Nations,[26] and they played a similar role in blocking the proposed regional guarantee system known as Eastern Locarno.

With Poland adamantly refusing to cooperate with the Soviet Union, Litvinov turned to Germany with his policy of influencing public opinion by outwardly friendly acts. However, the public opinion he actually wished to influence was French, and his goal was to stir the French into action on the mutual assistance pact. Thus, Litvinov proposed on 28 March that the Soviet Union and Germany pledge "to take into account in their foreign policies an obligation to preserve the independence of the Baltic states."[27] When Hitler adamantly rejected such a commitment,[28] his decision received wide publicity in the Soviet press.[29] On the heels of Germany's refusal, Litvinov told the Soviet chargé in France:

> The Germans are attempting to depict our proposal chiefly as an attempt to secure a new rapprochement with them. Through the press and personal explanations it is necessary to fight such efforts. We wanted either to force the Germans to bind themselves with regard to the Baltic (which we did not seriously consider possible) or to expose the false and hypocritical Nazi pacifistic statements. In this we have succeeded. In talks with Barthou, you must, even in the event of the Boncour offer being withdrawn as a result of Poland's position, convince him of our desire for a rapprochement and cooperation with France in the securing of peace.[30]

Litvinov's attempts to prod the French into action were success-ful, and in late April, Barthou decided "to grasp the Russian alliance."[31] It was not an easy decision for the Frenchman. He realized that a close relationship with Moscow could facilitate Communist infiltration in France, and he had no doubts that the Poles and the British would not like the pact. But Barthou had also read *Mein Kampf* and also had no illusions about Hitler. He knew, too, that the Franco-Russian alliance before World War I had been important in saving France when the war broke out. If Germany wanted to start trouble in Europe again, France must have allies, not just moral support. Moscow and Litvinov were offering what France needed.[32]

Litvinov "was unable to conceal his satisfaction" that Barthou had made up his mind. The French ambassador to the Soviet Union also pointedly noted that "in the years since I have been following Soviet policy I have been unable to detect a deviation in the general line conducted since the signing of the [1932] nonaggression pact. [This policy] tends to a rapprochement with France and its allies and

Litvinov (at right) with unidentified persons, probably Soviet diplomats, ca. 1930s. Location unknown. (Photo courtesy of the Hoover Institution Archives, Joseph Freeman Collection)

an indifference, every day greater, toward Hitlerite Germany." He concluded that the "principal champion of this policy is obviously Litvinov."[33]

Low-level negotiations were resumed in Paris late in April,[34] and on 18 May, Litvinov and Barthou met in Switzerland. Litvinov attempted to make the security arrangement as broad as possible, but Barthou reluctantly asserted that such proposals were not feasible. The Baltic states were one stumbling block. Litvinov wanted that area included, but Barthou, who had recently been in Prague, said that the Czechs, claiming they had no vital interests in the Baltic, would not agree to this. Barthou felt that Czech participation in the security arrangement was more important than Baltic adherence. Moreover, it was unstated, but obvious, that Poland would in no way consent to a Soviet guarantee of Baltic independence. Barthou added that he would work for an inclusion of the Baltic states, but he did not seem hopeful.

Another problem was Litvinov's "preoccupation" regarding the "precision and rapidity" of the assistance France could give the USSR, and the commissar also argued "that our political accord should be accompanied by a technical convention."[35] Both men agreed that Germany should be invited to participate, but when Litvinov asked Barthou if France would accept a pact without Germany, assuming that the latter would not return to the League, Barthou said that could be the subject of "separate negotiations."[36] As William Scott has observed, the talk of including Germany in a pact everyone knew Hitler would reject was done "for the sake of appearances."[37] Now Litvinov had a commitment from both Barthou and the Politburo for a Franco-Soviet mutual assistance pact.

On 29 May, speaking before the Disarmament Conference, Litvinov admitted that the disarmament efforts had failed and hinted at the developing alliance. He observed that the conference had accepted the principle of equality of armaments for Germany in early 1933 and that Hitler's response has been to withdraw from the conference and the League. It was time to recognize that disarmament was a hopeless cause and that "new measures" had to be devised to protect the peace.

> The Conference of course must do everything in its power to induce every state to accede to such measures. I hope that that would be so and that consideration of their own interests would induce even states which did not sympathize with these measures not to stand aloof from the general system that would be set up. But even if there should be dissident states, that should by no means prevent the remainder from coming still closer together to take steps which would strengthen their own security.[38]

In other words, Germany was perfectly welcome to take part in collective security, but such an arrangement should not be sacrificed because of German obstruction.

The speech making continued at Geneva, but in the background Litvinov and Barthou were moving ever closer to a firm agreement. On 4 June, Litvinov telegraphed Moscow that he and Barthou had met "for the final elucidation of the details of the pact. I insisted on an immediate answer to the principle of the agreement from the French cabinet," and Barthou promised to act as quickly as possible.[39]

Finally, on 6 June 1934, an agreement was reached.[40] The essence of the arrangement was an eastern pact of mutual assistance including the Soviet Union, Germany, Poland, Czechoslovakia, Finland, and the

Baltic states. A separate Franco-Soviet treaty would guarantee the general pact and would provide for direct mutual assistance between the two nations in the event of war. Litvinov also confirmed his government's readiness to join the League of Nations.[41] He knew, however, that the battle was still far from over and told the Politburo that

> the French increasingly express doubt concerning the position of
> Poland. [Litvinov knew already that Beck was lost as far as
> collective security was concerned.] From all sides the French are
> being subjected to pressure to tear themselves away from us and
> to return to the path of a Franco-English and Franco-German
> agreement. In essence, the struggle here at the Conference is a
> struggle between us and the Germans.[42]

Litvinov could not have been more correct, and the battle was already all but lost in favor of Germany. During the discussions in the French cabinet about the pact, Pierre Laval declared himself categorically in favor of "an accord with Germany and hostile to a rapprochement with Russia which would bring [France] the International and the red flag."[43] In October 1934, Pierre Laval was to become France's foreign minister.

However, before that event occurred, Barthou scurried about Europe seeking support for Eastern Locarno and the supplementary Franco-Soviet pact. His most important stop was in London, where he arrived on 9 July. The shock of Hitler's "night of the long knives" (30 June) had still not worn off in Britain, but the British, nonetheless, had grave reservations about the French rapprochement with Russia. The German Ambassador Leopold von Hoesch told his government that British Foreign Secretary John Simon had made it clear to him that "the inclusion of Russia in the European security combination" was "on the whole not very congenial to him."[44]

However, Barthou was firm. He told the British that if Eastern Locarno fell through, he might well substitute a simple Franco-Soviet alliance for it. Simon objected strenuously to that idea, so Barthou suggested an arrangement whereby France would give Germany a guarantee in the event of a Soviet attack (which Barthou knew was a ridiculous idea) and the Soviet Union would give Germany a guarantee in the event of a French attack (an idea so preposterous as to be laughable). Simon said he liked this proposal and would "recommend" it to Germany,[45] thinking he had gained an important concession from Barthou and had forestalled a Franco-Soviet alliance that would "divide Europe into hostile camps" (as if that were not already the case).[46] Knowing that a proposal that expected Hitler to accept aid from the Red Army was doomed and therefore meaningless, Barthou accepted Simon's offer.[47]

Barthou, however, was less willing to accept Simon's proposal for German rearmament. In language tortuous even for diplomats, Simon wanted to tell Hitler that this new treaty system "would afford the best ground for the resumption of negotiations for the conclusion of a convention as would provide, in the matter of armaments, for a reasonable application of the principle of German equality of rights."[48] Upon reflection, Barthou accepted Simon's formula, but as Scott observed, if "Germany refused to join Eastern Locarno, then the revival of arms talks negotiations fell to the ground,"[49] so, again, Barthou had made a meaningless concession to the British. Moreover, the British had hoped to prevent a Franco-Soviet alliance by supporting Barthou and Litvinov's plan for an Eastern Locarno, but that plan, owing to the policies of Hitler and Beck, "had no chance of success."[50] Soon Barthou and Litvinov would be able to proceed with a defensive alliance, having first offered Hitler a place in a general pact.

Litvinov, however, was getting a bit fed up with all this diplomatic haggling, and he basically refused even to discuss Eastern Locarno with the German ambassador in Moscow, despite the fact that Germany was to be invited to join. For example, on 9 August 1934, the German chargé in Moscow, Fritz von Twardowski, informed Berlin that he had learned from the Italian ambassador in Moscow that Litvinov was ready for German participation in Eastern Locarno but that if the general pact failed to materialize, "Litvinov flatly replied that there would be a Franco-Soviet Pact." The Italian ambassador, whom Litvinov was obviously using as a conduit, was excited, urging the Germans to sign a pact with Paris and Moscow because such an arrangement would facilitate an arms settlement and remove the danger of German isolation.[51]

Hitler was unmoved by these suggestions, and in a meeting with the Polish envoy on 27 August, he flattered and almost pleaded. He opened with the announcement that the German legation in Warsaw would be raised to embassy status and then made an astounding analogy: He claimed that both Germany and Poland were victims of the "unreasonable stipulations" of Versailles but that this unfortunate circumstance was "nothing in the face of the threatened development on the Russian side." He predicted an eventual Russian military defeat at the hands of the Japanese, which would only make the Soviets assert "political and military pressure" on the west. "There was no reason for either Poland or Germany to serve as a shield for Russia"![52]

Having made these observations, Hitler got to the point—"what was Poland's attitude toward the Eastern Pact proposals?" He suggested that "if they were negative, then we should cooperate as closely as possible in the matter." The ambassador immediately replied that "the Polish government's attitude had been negative from the start and still was so."[53] Eastern Locarno was dead; the road, however, was open for the Franco-Soviet alliance.

Still, as noted earlier, the French insisted from the outset that any mutual assistance pact must operate through the League of Nations, and in August 1934, the Soviet Union was not yet a member. That problem finally disappeared when a formal invitation was sent to Moscow on 15 September, but arranging for League membership had been no easy battle for Litvinov. As late as 30 July, he had told the Estonian Foreign Minister that opinions within the Soviet government on the issue of League membership "were about evenly divided" and that it was vital that the League issue an appropriate invitation immediately.[54] Litvinov was apparently able to carry the day by arguing that without League membership, the pact with France was impossible,[55] so fourteen years of hostile Soviet policy toward the League finally ended.

But the League had to approve Soviet membership, and Litvinov and the Soviet delegation (including Ivy) awaited the final decision in a "delightful farmhouse" outside Geneva. The mood was hardly delightful; indeed, Ivy recalled that everyone had "haunted expressions on our faces." However, Maxim "kept his cool better than the rest. To the astonishment of everyone he took me to the cinema after lunch" while awaiting word from Beneš. Alone, he confided to his wife, "I don't think Beneš would let me down," but he spoke "doubtfully." Soon, however, they learned the good news; the USSR was accepted.[56]

On 18 September, the day the League approved Soviet membership, Litvinov addressed the Assembly. Apologizing, he said that he felt he must first review briefly the early unhappy history of Soviet-League relations,[57] but that done, he said:

> The Soviet government, following attentively all developments
> of international life, could not but observe the increasing
> activity in the League of Nations of states interested in the
> preservation of peace and their struggle against aggressive
> militarist elements. Moreover, it noted that these aggressive
> elements themselves were finding the restrictions of the League
> embarrassing and trying to shake them off. All this could not be
> without its influence on the attitude toward the League of
> Nations of the Soviet government.[58]

He continued with the usual observations that the Disarmament Conference had failed and that now was the time to devise "more effective means" of securing the peace against those people who wish to "refashion the map of Europe and Asia by the sword."[59] He called bluntly for unity among the peaceful states, warning that "in the present complicated state of political and economic interests, no war of any serious dimensions can be localized and any war, whatever its issue, will turn out to have been but the first of a series."[60]

Litvinov added that he did not "consider it the moment to speak in detail about effective means for the prevention of impending and openly promulgated war,"[61] and indeed, he could not. That task had to be taken up in Moscow in the final push for the signing of the pact with France. Still, an agreement in principle was secure, and the prospects for a Moscow-Paris alliance were good.

Shortly after Litvinov's return to Moscow, Louis Barthou, his staunchest ally in the cause of collective security, was assassinated in Marseilles on 9 October 1934,[62] and Pierre Laval took his place. Immediately after Barthou's murder, the French ambassador to the Soviet Union, Charles Alphand, reported that Litvinov felt "genuine anxiety concerning its consequences" and specifically that Litvinov feared a French policy "less favorable to the USSR."[63] From Paris, M. I. Rozenberg, the acting Soviet chargé, quickly informed Moscow that Laval had said he intended to continue Barthou's policy, but in direct contradiction to that policy, Laval had also said he "would strive for an agreement with Germany, for the peace of Europe was impossible without a Franco-German agreement." Moreover, "if an agreement with Germany was possible only by means of a French agreement with Moscow, then he was prepared to take such a path."[64] As far as Laval was concerned, the road to Berlin ran through Moscow.

Litvinov was certainly disheartened. On the same day he received Rozenberg's telegram, he replied that although Laval's remarks could be construed as indicating that the French were ready to work toward a Franco-German-Soviet arrangement, Litvinov felt that it was "much more probable" that Laval intended to use the rapprochement with the Soviet Union, "only for the goal of intimidating Germany in order to get from it more concessions; in other words, France is only playing a trick on us."[65] Litvinov had lost confidence that the French would ally firmly with the Soviet Union against Germany; the game was all but over before it had begun.

Litvinov suddenly was faced with a very possible Franco-German rapprochement. In desperation, and despite Laval's misgivings, Litvinov succeeded in getting France's signature on a protocol that pledged that neither party would enter into an agreement with another state that might wreck the plans for a "regional Pact of the East or of the agreements connected thereto, or which would be contrary to the spirit by which they were inspired."[66] Even this mild declaration was unpopular with the new French government headed by Pierre-Etienne Flandin, and when French diplomats informed other governments of the protocol, they characterized it "as an interim affair, designed to placate Litvinov."[67] Before the French Senate, Laval announced that "the French government will never do anything which justifies Germany in thinking that we intend to practice a policy of isolation towards her. The Franco-German rapprochement in an international framework is an effective guarantee of peace."[68]

That was not all. Laval also wanted, more than anything, an agreement with Mussolini, and from 4 to 8 January 1935, Laval held talks in Rome during which the two men swapped some territory in Africa and made a mutual commitment to uphold Austria's independence.[69] Litvinov had no objections to a Franco-Italian rapprochement, but he added that no arrangements of any sort should allow German rearmament.[70]

It is hardly surprising that in these new circumstances, Soviet policy should begin to waver. On 28 January 1935, Molotov indirectly told the Seventh Congress of Soviets that the French connection was not something on which the Russians could depend.

If our foreign policy is clear and stable, it is impossible to say the
same for those countries where, because of various influences,
changes take place from this or that government, where power
changes from one bourgeois party to another. Everyone knows ·
well, for example, the important changes and zigzags which have
taken place in the course of the current period in the policy of
certain countries which we have been discussing in our foreign
policy.[71]

Those remarks completely negated Molotov's subsequent bland assertion that Soviet-French relations had recently "significantly improved."
In speaking of Germany, Molotov was plaintive:

It is impossible to close one's eyes to the changes that have taken
place in Soviet-German relations since the National Socialists
have come to power. For ourselves, we can say that we always
have and still do want to have good relations with Germany.
Everyone knows that the Soviet Union is filled with a deep
desire to develop its relations with all countries, including states
with fascist regimes.[72]

Molotov then mentioned Nazi racial theories and the notion of
innate German superiority over all other peoples. Although such ideas
were an obstacle to good relations, he observed that "we do not conceal
our profound respect for the German people as one of the great people
of the contemporary epoch."[73] To make such a statement while the
Nazis held to their expansionist goals does not reflect particularly well
on Molotov, but here, however, was a man who would have no qualms
in signing a pact with the "great people" of Germany and their new
leader.

In the meantime, Laval went to London, and the British renewed
their efforts to reverse the Franco-Russian rapprochement.[74] Litvinov's
despair increased.[75] However, just as it seemed that an agreement with
France was impossible, none other than Hitler came to the rescue
when on 16 March, he announced the renewal of universal military
service and fixed the number of divisions for the new army at thirty-
six.[76] The French ambassador rushed to Litvinov and asked him what
he thought of the news. Showing his disgust with France and Laval,
Litvinov said that "on this issue I should turn to him, as [German

rearmament] broke the provision of Versailles, which we had not signed," adding that recent British and French policy had only served to encourage German aggressiveness.[77] Litvinov obviously felt that France had gotten pretty much what it deserved.

Nonetheless, the French were faced with isolation before an openly resurgent Germany.[78] On 2 April, Litvinov bluntly warned Laval that his "wavering is well known . . . and is creating an unfavorable impression" in the Soviet Union.[79] On 9 April, Laval ended his delaying tactics and informed the Soviet government that he was ready to sign a mutual assistance pact no later than 1 May.[80] Litvinov replied on the following day. He wanted the pact strengthened beyond the original proposals, and specifically, he wanted a mutual obligation for "immediate military assistance in the event of clear aggression" without waiting for a judgment from the League's Council. This aggression could be determined on the basis of the criteria he had proposed in February 1933 at the League.[81]

The French responded with a proposal that France would be obliged to aid the Soviet Union "only if [France] is satisfied that such aid is compatible with the application of the Locarno general treaty."[82] The Russians rejected this proviso, and the French remained equally firm.

On 18 April, Litvinov and Laval met in Geneva to discuss the treaty for the last time. Laval resisted the commissar's efforts to include any guarantees for the Baltic, insisting that the treaty be restricted to mutual assistance regarding Germany. Laval also repeatedly raised a most thorny issue: the USSR's lack of a common border with Germany. The foreign minister insisted that this geographic fact meant that France's obligations were greater than Russia's. How Litvinov responded to Laval's remarks is unknown, but to the Soviet government he acknowledged that Laval had a valid point. He insisted, however, that "the pact will have great political significance as a factor reducing the temptation of an attack on the part of Germany, Poland, and Japan" and added pointedly that the agreement would help "prevent the establishment of close relations between France and Germany." He concluded his dispatch a bit abruptly, telling the leadership that "you must now decide in principle the question of signing the pact and communicate on this to me by telephone in Geneva."[83]

In the final treaty, signed by Laval and the Soviet *polpred*, Vladimir Potemkin, no mention was made of Locarno, but paragraph

two of the protocol attached to the treaty stated that the mutual
assistance pact "in no way invalidates existing treaty obligations,
accepted earlier by the USSR and France with third governments."[84]
The "heart" of the treaty was Article 2. In admittedly awkward
language it stated:

> In the event of the USSR or France, in circumstances specified
> in article 15, paragraph 7, of the League of Nations Covenant,
> being the object, in spite of the genuinely peaceful intentions of
> both countries, of an unprovoked attack on the part of a
> European state, France and reciprocally, the USSR, shall
> immediately give aid and support to each other.[85]

This treaty must be viewed in a larger context. Just before its
signing and after four days of negotiations, Britain, France, and Italy
announced their support of Austrian independence and "complete
agreement in opposing, by all practical means, any unilateral repudiation of treaties which may endanger the peace of Europe." Also, lest
Hitler not get the point, Britain and Italy specifically "reaffirmed their
obligations as guarantors of the Treaty of Locarno."[86] Finally, as a
result of the successful completion of the Franco-Soviet pact, the
Soviet Union signed a similar pact with Czechoslovakia, France's ally
and a state with much to fear from Germany and Poland.[87]

It would therefore seem that in the late spring of 1935, Hitler's
stated territorial ambitions had been checked by an alliance system of
most of Europe's main powers. The ink, however, was hardly dry on
these agreements when they started to collapse.

Twelve

THE DECLINE AND FALL
OF LITVINOV

WITH THE SIGNING of the Franco-Soviet pact, the most important task of Litvinov's career was completed. Now it was up to the respective governments to ratify the treaty and put some teeth into it by means of military talks. The latter endeavor was a complete failure from the outset.

> The [French] military did not want a Military convention, which
> would set up intimate collaboration between the two armies.
> They feared Communist infiltration among French troops and
> they were influenced by purely military considerations. They
> were skeptical that the Red Army could take the offensive, and,
> in any case, they did not think that the French Army needed a
> Russian offensive.[1]

French military thinking was dominated by a defensive strategy. In the event of war with Germany, the French intended to hold their positions at the Maginot Line and in Belgium and hoped that the Russians would open a second front to divide Germany's forces.[2] Also, the alliance had the purely negative effect of depriving Germany of access to Russia's enormous amounts of raw materials. Flandin told British Foreign Secretary Anthony Eden that France's motivation in agreeing to the pact had been to block the possibility of "a treaty between Germany and the Russian Soviet," and the British were relieved that Paris did not take the alliance more seriously.[3]

The Soviet leadership, including even Litvinov, also harbored few illusions about the true value of the French alliance. Writing in *Pravda* on 29 March 1935, the Soviet marshal, Mikhail Tukhachevskii,

observed that "the French army, with its twenty divisions, its hastily
assembled units, and slow rate of expansion by stages under mobiliza-
tion is already incapable of active opposition to Germany."[4] Litvinov
also realized that the alliance had lost much of the significance he had
wanted it to have. At about the same time that Tukhachevskii was
disparaging French military power, Litvinov was doing the opposite
regarding Germany.

> The rearmament of Germany in every sphere has surpassed all
> expectations. There is no doubt whatsoever that Germany will
> now or in the immediate future have numerical superiority over
> France as regards ground forces. She will very soon overtake
> and surpass France in military aviation. France is thus losing her
> position as the most powerful state in Europe. Germany has a
> much greater military potential as regards manpower and war
> production than France.[5]

It should hardly be surprising in these circumstances that on 8
May, Litvinov offered Nadolny a nonaggression pact between Germany
and the Soviet Union as a way to "lessen the significance of the Franco-
Soviet Pact."[6] Nadolny promised to report back, but, as is well known,
the Nazi-Soviet nonaggression pact was not achieved until August
1939.

This last incident can be interpreted in many ways. First, despite
almost two years of building Franco-Soviet rapprochement, Litvinov
and the Soviet government had virtually abandoned this effort owing
to the policies of Laval—or perhaps Litvinov was looking for more
ammunition for his anti-Nazi policies through Hitler's rejection of a
nonaggression pact. In any case, Soviet feelers and requests for improved Soviet-German relations continued throughout the 1930s,
although Litvinov played no further role.[7]

Or perhaps Litvinov's offer of 8 May to Germany represented his
ultimate strategy for Soviet policy in Europe. By that time, Litvinov
realized that the French alliance had only a "psychological" importance
in that it might cause Hitler to "think ten times" before resorting to
aggression.[8] If a nonaggression pact with Germany were added to this
"psychological" alliance, Soviet security would unquestionably have
been strengthened in Europe. And the more secure the western flank,
the better Moscow could deal with threats from the east. The main

problem with creating such a system was that Hitler wanted nothing to do with it.

In this atmosphere it is understandable that the French legislature did not ratify the pact until February 1936 and that no effort was made to achieve military collaboration until the summer of 1939.[9] By then, Litvinov had "retired," and Stalin was rapidly moving toward his pact with Hitler. Moreover, the Franco-Soviet alliance was to function through the League of Nations. If the League proved a broken reed on which to build collective security, then an already mortally wounded alliance would be even further vitiated. The League had been unable to do anything about Japanese aggression, and when a European power attacked another nation without provocation, it was similarly helpless.

Given these circumstances, it seems reasonable to conclude that, in fact, there never was any real collective security in the years before World War II. Among the USSR, France, Germany, and Britain there existed so much distrust, hatred, and contradictory goals that it is difficult, if not impossible, to envision how any collective security system was possible. Nonetheless, Litvinov deserves credit, along with Barthou, for understanding most clearly the nature of the Nazi regime, and acting accordingly.

The tragic story of European aggression began in early October 1935 when Italy attacked Ethiopia. Military operations, however, were the result of a crisis that had been building for some time. Anticipating Italian aggression, Litvinov met with the British foreign secretary, Samuel Hoare, and told him "again and again . . . that he regards the present controversy as the test case for the League." Litvinov added that he had already "warned" Moscow of the possibility of economic sanctions. Such measures might harm Russia, but "he was prepared to risk it, provided that the League was ready collectively to take effective action."[10]

As the Italian troops advanced, Litvinov, who was then in Moscow, instructed the Soviet representative in Geneva to vote in favor of sanctions against Italy "on condition of their application by the other members of the League."[11] On 7 October, the League's Committee of Thirteen, which had been formed to study the Italian-Ethiopian conflict, reported that "After an examination of the facts . . . the Committee has come to the conclusion that the Italian government has resorted to war in disregard of its covenants under Article Twelve of the Covenant of the League of Nations."[12] A few days later, the League's Assembly voted overwhelmingly to apply economic sanctions against Italy under Article 16 of the Covenant.[13] For a moment, it seemed that Mussolini had seriously misread Europe's resolve to resist aggression, but in fact, he had not.

Litvinov returned to Geneva on 13 October. Two days later, Krestinskii sent him word that the Politburo had accepted the League's decision on sanctions but reiterated that it must be coordinated with the other members of the League. To help with this coordination, the Politburo ordered the Soviet military attaché in Berlin, General Orlov, to proceed to Geneva.[14]

Britain and France, however, had no intention of following a policy that was hostile to Italy. They wanted a peaceful settlement of the war, but their dominant desire was to prevent a German-Italian rapprochement. According to Anthony Eden:

> Laval said that we must not threaten Mussolini with sanctions, which might be regarded as an act of war. If Mussolini, thinking himself blockaded, were to bombard Malta or attack the British fleet, the principles of the Covenant might be preserved, but Germany would come in and disturb Europe. So the argument continued, Laval failing to perceive the truth that, if Mussolini could be shown that lawlessness did not pay, Hitler would take note.[15]

Laval's policy reached fruition in the famous Hoare-Laval pact of December 1935. This "solution" to Italian aggression gave Italy large parts of Ethiopian territory and designated much of the remainder as Italy's sphere of influence. What was left of independent Ethiopia received a corridor to the sea as its only compensation.[16]

The revelation of this arrangement had a profound effect. In London, the public received the news with "stunned disbelief, then indignation too strong to be resisted. On December 19 Hoare resigned." Laval had also been mortally wounded politically. Socialist Léon Blum led the call for Laval's ouster, and in January 1936, Laval lost his majority and resigned.[17] With the collapse of the Hoare-Laval plan, the League went ahead with limited sanctions. Italian exports fell by 40 percent and imports by 50 percent. However, oil, a vital war material, was excluded from banned imports, and this fact significantly lessened the impact of the sanctions on Italy's ability to make war.[18]

Upon hearing the news of the Hoare-Laval pact, Litvinov confidentially told a Soviet official:

[It] means a partition of Abyssinia and a violation of its
territorial integrity. This violates the Covenant of the League,
which guarantees each member's inviolability and the integrity
of their territory, in the name of which the League has both
intervened in the conflict and begun to apply sanctions. The
League of Nations can not therefore approve such a proposal.[19]

He added later that if Abyssinia accepted such conditions, there was nothing the Soviet Union could do about it. But he was adamant that such plunder could not be condoned under the aegis of the League.[20]

Soon Litvinov's attitude hardened, and, like Eden, he came to see Italian aggression within a broader context. On 22 January 1936, he told Eden that the Soviet Union would participate in oil sanctions against Italy if all the other powers in the League would do likewise. He added that Germany "must be made to understand that a close understanding exists among the peaceful nations." Those states "must be strong; Germany only understands force."[21]

The League did nothing, and while the other European leaders were distracted with other matters, Mussolini completed his conquest of Ethiopia. Faced with Italy's fait accompli, the League Assembly voted to end sanctions. As an instrument of collective security, the League had failed dismally, and henceforth, it was "ignored in the crisis of European and world politics."[22] The most significant result of the war was an Italian-German rapprochement, which meant that western policy had neither preserved Ethiopia nor kept Mussolini from Hitler's embrace. In the midst of the Ethiopian fiasco, however, a much more serious crisis occurred, this time in the heart of Europe.

On 7 March 1936, Hitler reoccupied the Rhineland, an event that Litvinov had foreseen.[23] The French foreign minister, Pierre-Etienne Flandin, turned to Britain, arguing truthfully that Hitler's action violated both the Versailles and Locarno treaties. He said that Britain and France must take a "firm stand" and be prepared to accept military action if Hitler refused to back down.[24] The British cabinet would have none of this, telling Flandin that British public opinion would not support "sanctions of any kind."[25] Instead, the cabinet suggested that the French, Belgians, and Germans should take their argument to the International Court in the Hague.[26]

The Soviet Union was scarcely consulted at all. Flandin merely asked the Soviet ambassador, Vladimir Potemkin, what the Russians' "attitude" concerning Hitler's bold move would be. Litvinov instructed Potemkin to tell the French that if they took the matter to the League, they could count on "my full support." Litvinov then tried to prod the French into action, asserting that he would "feel freer in Geneva" if Franco-Soviet relations had been clarified by a "final ratification of the pact." He added that ratification "without debate would be a fitting reply to the aggression of Germany and a timely demonstration of the unity of the French nation in the face of such aggression."[27] Litvinov also attempted to create some resolve among the British. Through Ambassador Ivan Maisky, he stated that

> negotiations with Hitler on the second day after the violation of the Locarno treaty would have more serious consequences than the Laval-Hoare plan. It would be the final blasting of confidence in England. We . . . are ready to support any action collectively taken against Germany. Right now there is the full possibility to halt German aggression and diminish its dangers. Negotiations with Germany now would mean a strengthening of this danger and encouragement not only of Germany but Italy and Japan.[28]

In the end, the French, lacking support from Britain, simply did nothing.[29]

Litvinov's evaluation of the Rhineland crisis was right on the mark. Had France acted militarily with Soviet diplomatic support, it is virtually certain that London would have been forced to stand with Paris. Hitler's three battalions that had crossed the Rhine were under orders to withdraw if they met military resistance,[30] and such a humiliating withdrawal may well have had a sobering effect on Hitler and strengthened the contempt with which many German officers viewed the fuehrer in 1936. Certainly, the tragic couse of history would have been different. Litvinov was again right about Hitler, but that was his only consolation.

During the March crisis, Litvinov sent a telegram directly to Stalin from London that France had capitulated and that he had failed to obtain even a discussion of security in eastern Europe. The commissar suggested a renewal of the proposal for a Soviet-German guarantee of the Baltic states, although he thought Britain and France would prefer some type of Soviet-German pact of nonaggression. He concluded with uncharacteristic deference: "I request instructions."[31]

The next day, Stalin responded through Deputy Commissar Nikolai Krestinskii, saying the Soviet Union desired the "restoration of the east European pact, i.e., adherence of Germany to the Soviet-French pact . . . which is open to all countries." However, Stalin told Litvinov that "if the problem of eastern Europe is not now decided finally, then the authority of the League and the problems of limiting arms in the future will be placed under a serious threat and that the USSR . . . will consider that it is left on its own."[32] On 28 March, Litvinov told Moscow that he had failed. In discussions with Flandin and Leger, the Frenchmen had said that an eastern pact was "impractical."[33] It requires only a little imagination to realize how the Politburo must have "greeted" such news.

There can be no doubt that the Ethiopian and Rhineland crises finished off what there was of Litvinov's policy of collective security with France and the League. The Ethiopian war was the second time the League had condemned an aggressor and then done nothing. More serious, the French had refused to fight when the Germans had brazenly marched right up to their border, thereby greatly increasing the chances for a successful surprise attack against France. In Moscow, Litvinov must have been asked how the Russians could possibly put any hope in an ally that would not fight on its own doorstep. There was only one possible answer: One could not rely on such an ally.[34]

Litvinov, nonetheless, continued to speak publicly in favor of collective security, but his speeches had a hollow, depressed tone. On 17 March, in addressing the League Council, he reviewed the League's failure to do anything about German rearmament, the Ethiopian war, or the recent occupation of the Rhineland: "Such a League of Nations will never be taken seriously by anyone. The resolutions of such a League will only become a laughing-stock. Such a League is not required . . . because it will lull the vigilance of the nations."[35] He added, however, that

> we are not less, but on the contrary, more interested than others
> in the maintenance of peace, both today and for decades to
> come. We stand for an international agreement which would not

only consolidate the existing foundations of peace, but, if possible, would likewise create new foundations. We stand for the participation in such an agreement of all countries which so desire.[36]

Unfortunately for Litvinov, no one desired. He had again put the Soviet Union on record as advocating collective security, but that policy had failed, and Molotov publicly acknowledged that fact two days after Litvinov's speech at the League. Talking with a correspondent of the French newspaper Le Temps, Molotov, a man much closer to Stalin than was Litvinov, asserted that there were two "tendencies" within the "Soviet public." One group had an "attitude of thoroughgoing irreconcilability to the present rulers of Germany," but the "chief tendency, and the one determining the Soviet government's policy, thinks an improvement in Soviet-German relations possible."[37]

Litvinov knew the game was almost over. Talking with Eden in Geneva in October 1936, he said that he "did not see what use it was coming to Geneva just to make speeches. Nothing ever seemed to result from the speeches. After each failure the League said that it would make efforts to strengthen itself against the next trial, but in fact nothing was done, and we merely sat and waited for the next aggression."[38] Because the French had abdicated as a great power in March 1936, Litvinov added that "the only real chance of peace in Europe was for this country [Britain] to make it clear that she would stand by the victims of aggression in Europe. If we [the British] did that there would be no war."[39] At Munich in 1938, the British were to reveal most vividly their feelings toward the victims of aggression.

While the Rhineland crisis was still rocking Europe, the Spanish military revolted against its constitutionally elected government. "Hitler and Mussolini intervened at once, and possibly decisively."[40] France was inclined to aid the Spanish republic but was restrained from doing so by Britain. The result was a "nonintervention pact" by which most countries stayed aloof while the republic was slowly crushed with blatantly obvious Italian and German assistance.[41]

Perhaps Litvinov felt he could win support in the west by adhering to the nonintervention agreement. He told Eden that he personally favored nonintervention but that the way it was working out "had resulted in favoring the rebels."[42] In a separate conversation on the same day, Eden reported that when he asked Litvinov for the

Soviet position on "indirect intervention," the commissar said he did not know what Eden was talking about. Litvinov declared that such matters "were being dealt with directly from Moscow."[43]

At about the same time, Litvinov sent a dispatch to Aleksandrov-skii, the Soviet ambassador in Prague, insisting that there had been no changes in the Soviet policy toward Germany. He emphasized that Kandelaki, the Soviet emissary who handled economic negotiations with Germany, had received no "new instructions" and that any rumors about "changes" being sought regarding Germany were groundless.[44] In fact, it seems that Kandelaki was then untiring in his efforts to improve economic and political relations with Berlin.[45] The two incidents suggest that Litvinov had not only lost his influence over Soviet foreign policy but was even in the dark about what that policy was.

Then in April 1937, Potemkin, the Soviet ambassador to France returned to Moscow to lead the Western Section of the Foreign Commissariat,[46] which had been Litvinov's preserve. Moreover, according to Tatiana Litvinov, Potemkin was a "Molotov man."[47] Litvinov would linger on as commissar for two more years, but that period was reminiscent in some ways of Chicherin's last years, in office but with little to do.

These were especially trying times for Litvinov. In Europe, his policies were constantly rebuffed, and at home, the great terror of 1936–1938 threatened to devour the country. Afraid to sleep at night, he usually stayed up playing cards with Ivy. He did not want to be taken away half-asleep in his pajamas.[48] But Litvinov was never a patient man, and he drew the line one day when a young officer of the People's Commissariat for Internal Affairs strutted unannounced into Litvinov's office in the Foreign Commissariat. The officer demanded that Litvinov "tell all the details about the wrecking going on in *Narkomindel.*" According to an eyewitness, Litvinov feigned surprise and asked, "Don't you get enough names from the newspapers?"[49] Soviet history is not replete with similar examples of defiance before the police.

On the other hand, it is true that Litvinov felt compelled to defend Stalin's terror to foreigners. He told the U.S. ambassador, Joseph Davies, in 1938 that the Soviet government "had to protect itself against traitors within their gates, who . . . were conspiring with Germany and Japan." He could not believe that the defendants would "confess to crimes which they knew were punishable by the death penalty, unless they were guilty."[50] But surely Litvinov knew that death could be preferable to the torture and degradation so freely used by the NKVD, and in a private moment, he surmised that Nikolai Bukharin, a leading Bolshevik, had confessed to outrageous crimes in order to save his family.[51]

In June 1937, domestic terror and foreign policy came together and destroyed the last remnants of hope that Litvinov could possibly have held for collective security with the west. In that month, Stalin ordered the execution of most of the leadership of the Soviet officer corps, and of all the events of the terror, this one had the most serious repercussions for foreign policy. When Litvinov heard the news, he realized that no nation would ally itself with a government whose top military leaders had been accused of being spies out to overthrow their own government.[52] Litvinov had said that Hitler understood only force; now the Soviet Union had suffered a "catastrophic weakening" of its military power.[53] Talk of collective security had become a joke.

In the west, this disaster for the Red Army produced complete unity in the British cabinet against the Soviet Union. According to Eden, there had been two "strongly held" viewpoints among Britain's leading politicians.

> Some, religious in their views, regarded communism as anti-Christ. Others were brave enough to consider supping with the devil, but doubted whether he had much to offer. When Stalin executed the leadership of the Soviet armed forces . . . [these] critics combined to see in this the ruin of any military efficiency the Russians might have possessed.[54]

This view remained dominant until 1941.[55] In France, the historian Jeane-Baptiste Duroselle notes simply that the assault on the army and the executions "put an end to all serious negotiations" with Moscow.[56]

Litvinov continued his public policy of denouncing aggression; there was little else to do. Speaking before the League Assembly on 21 September 1937, he again called on the members to follow a "resolute policy" in the event of further aggression. Such a stand would convince every state "that aggression does not pay; that aggression should not be undertaken."[57]

Litvinov was no fool. Judging from his conversations with the French, he was disgusted with the west's appeasement. He intimated to the French ambassador, Robert Coulondre, that the USSR was moving away from an attachment to western affairs, and Coulondre warned Paris that these remarks were not some diplomatic tactic, but "policy."[58] Litvinov realized that collective security against Nazi Germany was a dead letter, and in December 1937, he publicly dropped a genuine bombshell in an interview with the Moscow correspondent of *Le Monde*. He said that the way things stood, "no one wants anything to do with us" but that the Soviet Union would wait and see what might arise. The correspondent then initiated the most significant part of the conversation:

> "What do you mean by that, Commissar?"
> "There are other possible combinations," Litvinov replied.
> "With Germany?"
> "Why not?"
> "But is a German-Soviet rapprochement possible?"
> "Perfectly possible."[59]

It was now largely a matter of waiting for Hitler to grasp the Soviets' offer.

In the meantime, Litvinov's personal life worsened. Ivy had been sent to Sverdlovsk to teach English—and for her own safety during those murderous years—and Ivy's copy of a letter from Maxim dated 11 June 1938 appears in her papers. It reads in part: "I cannot even think of a holiday. This year, so far, no one is even speaking of holidays. Anyhow, I shall certainly no more go abroad." The letter closed, "Love kisses Maxim."[60]

Litvinov was right when he observed that 1938 was no year for holidays. Although Stalin's terror was winding down, the USSR's international position had reached its all-time nadir during the crisis over Czechoslovakia. In the midst of this situation, Litvinov gave one of his most outstanding speeches when in Leningrad, he finally let loose in public all his feelings against Germany. The Germans, even before the Nazis, he asserted, had been racists with their talk of "pan-Germanism," and Germany had been aggressively expansionist before Hitler with the Kaiser's vision of "*Mitteleuropa*." Now these virtually innate German tendencies had reached a hideous fruition with the

Nazis and their talk of "the historic right of existence only for the German race." Austria had been swallowed up, "which, in many respects, more than compensates for the provinces lost in the war." Now Czechoslovakia was threatened.

And most surprising to Litvinov was that "without firing a single shot," Germany had completely emasculated the victors of World War I. "The entire diplomacy of the western Powers in the last five years resolves itself into an avoidance of any resistance to Germany's aggressive actions, to compliance with its demands and even its caprices, fearing to arouse its dissatisfaction and disapproval even in the slightest degree." This policy had only encouraged Hitler and weakened the west so that when war came, Germany would be in a better position than it had been in 1914. And it would be a terrible war. Although Brest-Litovsk had been bad, still "less can one expect a just peace from Hitlerite Germany, with its medieval racial theories, its antihumanism, its belief in crude material force as the supreme law." In short, it would be a massive slaughter until complete victory by one side.[61] This speech, however, received marginal coverage in the Soviet press—perhaps Stalin and Molotov feared it might offend Hitler.

As the crisis over Czechoslovakia developed, Litvinov tried two tactics. First, he assured the Czechs on 13 March that the USSR would provide an "absolute minimum" of 1,000 airplanes for which airfields were being prepared. Czech President Edvard Beneš also expected to receive an unspecified amount of Soviet equipment.[62] Second, turning to the French, Litvinov tried to encourage them to take a resolute stand, with Soviet support, and to warn Paris of the consequences of further appeasement. Speaking in late April with Coulondre, Litvinov offered his "opinion" that Britain was treating France poorly and urged that Paris "must follow its own path in order to repulse German maneuvers."[63] A little later, Litvinov said there was no doubt that if Germany attacked Czechoslovakia and France "will exert itself," the USSR would keep its treaty obligations. "But if, after Manchuria, Abyssinia, China and Austria, the western powers still allow the strangulation of Czechoslovakia, the Soviet government will, in that case, break with this policy and reconcile itself with Germany."[64]

In late August, Litvinov reiterated that if Germany attacked Czechoslovakia and France came to that country's aid, the Soviet Union "will carry out its obligations." Jean Payart, counselor of the French Embassy in Moscow, added that this was the position Litvinov had already stated "many a time."[65] Even the German ambassador warned his government that if France stood by Czechoslovakia, the Soviet Union would come in against Germany.[66]

On 2 September, when Payart and Litvinov met once again, the commissar repeated that the USSR would fulfill its obligations "by all possible means" on condition that France did the same. But Litvinov also brought up the concrete problem of transit for Soviet troops and suggested that the matter be put before the League. He also advocated both a conference among Britain, France, and the Soviet Union and Franco-Soviet-Czech staff talks.[67] However, when the French foreign minister, Georges Bonnet, met with the British, he suppressed Litvinov's suggestion for staff talks, and the Political Directorate of the French Foreign Ministry on 6 September declared that Litvinov's response was "evasive."[68] Thus, the USSR was shut out of the September crisis, but the western leaders hardly considered this exclusion an unfortunate event. Neville Henderson, the British ambassador to Germany, neatly summed up British thinking about the Soviet Union when he observed that the "great advantage" of direct talks among Britain, France, Germany, and Italy on the Czechoslovakian crisis was "the exclusion of the Soviet Union."[69]

In the wake of Munich, the British ambassador to the Soviet Union, Areta Akers-Douglas Chilston, reported that Litvinov "has scarcely been visible and speculation is rampant" regarding his future. It was clear to Chilston that the commissar's efforts to "realize his policy of collective security against Germany appear (for now) to have fallen into the water."[70] Regarding Berlin, Litvinov negotiated an agreement with the Germans to cease the mutual "mudslinging" that had been a prominent feature of the Soviet and German press.[71] Meeting with Coulondre, Litvinov characterized French behavior during the Czech crisis as a "cruel deception" and added, ominously, that the USSR "safe behind its borders would look on henceforth at the establishment of German hegemony in central and southern Europe." He predicted that Hitler would then establish German control over "Europe" and then turn on the British. But not, however, before he has "come to an arrangement with the USSR."[72]

In fact, Litvinov made one last effort at a collective rebuff to Hitler. During the crisis over Poland in 1939, he proposed a tripartite mutual assistance pact among Britain, France, and the USSR. The treaty he envisioned, however, also granted the powers the right to render military assistance to the states bordering the USSR from the Baltic to the Black seas. Moreover, Britain was to "announce that the assistance promised by it to Poland concerns exclusively aggression on the part of Germany."[73] Even so strong an anti-Nazi as Winston Churchill conceded that the prospect of the Red Army marching into eastern Europe for any reason was an "obstacle" to an alliance, although he also felt it was worth the risk.[74] On 3 May, the British told Litvinov they were still undecided regarding the Soviet proposal.[75] The game was finished.

That same day, Litvinov was summoned to the Kremlin where he received a thorough critique of the collective security policy. Understandably, he made no defense and accepted his dismissal in silence. The lack of reaction apparently infuriated Molotov, and, as Litvinov was leaving the room, Molotov stood up and screamed, "You think we are all fools!" Litvinov did not answer.[76] The next day, *Pravda* announced simply that the Soviet government "had relieved comrade M. M. Litvinov at his request from his duties as People's Commissar for Foreign Affairs."[77]

In fact, although Litvinov was down, he was not quite out. After his dismissal, he sat on a government commission whose task was to retain or purge members of *Narkomindel*'s staff as the commissariat entered the Molotov era. Beside Litvinov sat Molotov; Lavrenty Beria, head of the NKVD; and a few others. Aleksei Roshchin had worked at *Narkomindel* in Moscow since 1937 when he nervously entered the interrogation room in May 1939. Beria immediately attacked Roshchin on the grounds that the latter had worked with one Gershelman who had been exposed as an "enemy of the people." According to Roshchin, Litvinov immediately came to his defense, telling Beria that Roshchin's relations with Gershelman had been purely "formal." Roshchin added that "the intervention of Litvinov saved me from enormous unpleasantness. Any connection with an 'enemy of the people' in those times could lead to the most tragic consequences for the fellow involved. I greatly appreciated Maxim Maximovich's action."[78]

It is hard to reject the idea that Litvinov perhaps welcomed his retirement. He told his family that they were "turning over a new leaf," but the actual changes in their life were slight. The Litvinovs lost their Moscow apartment for about a year in 1939 and 1940 but were allowed to retain the use of a comfortable dacha just outside the city. Litvinov arose each morning at the same time and was driven by his chauffeur to the Lenin Library. There he worked all day on a dictionary of Russian synonyms, a project he undertook because of a lifelong love of word games. He quickly completed his work and submitted it to a publisher, but the editor wanted to avoid dealing with a former high official and placed various conditions upon publication. After some arguments, Litvinov eventually gave up.[79]

Thirteen

THE LAST YEARS

ON 22 JUNE 1941, Nazi Germany invaded the USSR, thus tearing up the Nazi-Soviet nonaggression pact of 1939 and starting the Great Patriotic War. Litvinov immediately asked for "any kind of work," but other than being allowed a brief radio address, his request was ignored. However, when W. Averell Harriman and Lord Beaverbrook, representing the United States and Britain, arrived in Moscow in late September to receive Stalin's formal requests for military aid, they asked that their mutual acquaintance, Litvinov, serve as their interpreter. The Soviets produced him in a matter of hours. The talks started out somewhat stormily, but in a final meeting a cordial atmosphere was established as the western representatives strove to meet Stalin's requests. It seemed that Litvinov's long-awaited rapprochement with the west was about to come true, and beside himself with joy, Litvinov jumped to his feet in the middle of a session and shouted, "Now we shall win the war!"[1] That prediction was to come true, but wartime hopes that there might be a lasting relaxation of tensions between the Soviet Union and the west were soon dashed.

In late 1941, however, Stalin needed foreign help desperately, and to underscore his willingness to improve relations with the United States, he sent Litvinov to serve as the new Soviet ambassador in Washington. That did not work well at all. Litvinov conducted a vigorous public campaign for the opening of a second front, an effort that only annoyed President Roosevelt,[2] and on the other hand, Stalin apparently informed Litvinov of the Kremlin's own annoyance with the absence of a western offensive against Germany, because in the spring of 1943, Litvinov "insisted" that Stalin allow him to return to Moscow to explain the situation in the United States.

From left: Flora Litvinov, the late Evgenii Gnedin, the author, and
Mikhail Litvinov. November 1982, Moscow.

Behind the diplomatic scene, Maxim and Ivy underwent a
wrenching personal crisis: the decision whether to defect or not.
Writing on 20 January 1943, Ivy records that "for months" Maxim
"has been hinting" that his position "is so intolerable that if it weren't
for [the] children," he would "simply write and break off" with the
Kremlin. The main reason Litvinov wanted to stay was "to write his
memoir," which he had already started.[3] (Litvinov did write a memoir
of sorts, but unfortunately, Ivy had the work destroyed.)[4] Ultimately,
the Litvinovs decided to return although Ivy remained in New York
for a few months after Maxim left. Mikhail Litvinov believes his
parents probably never were entirely serious about remaining in the
United States, knowing the swift retribution he and Tatiana would
have suffered.[5]

Before he left Washington, however, Litvinov had an off-the-record conversation with Under Secretary of State Sumner Welles that went beyond the usual issue of a second front and revealed the extent of Litvinov's pessimism regarding Soviet-U.S. postwar cooperation. According to Welles:

> Mr. Litvinov . . . went on to say that in his judgment the future peace of the world depended very largely upon understanding and cooperation between the Soviet Union and the United States. He said that the way things were now going, he did not see any prospect of the achievement of that kind of understanding and cooperation. [In Moscow] . . . he would do his utmost to persuade Stalin that the policy [he] had in mind should be followed in the interests of the Soviet Union itself. He said he was far from optimistic as to the outcome of his impending mission.[6]

Litvinov also emphasized the reasons for his profound pessimism. He said that his influence with Stalin was "nonexistent today" and that he did not even believe "that his messages were received by Stalin: in any event none of his recommendations had been adopted." The source of the trouble, according to Litvinov, was Molotov, who had "removed from the Foreign Commissariat every important official who had any experience with the outside world."[7] Litvinov's hopelessness was surely genuine, but placing the blame on Molotov was disingenuous at best. Litvinov knew better than most people that Molotov did nothing without Stalin's direct approval. *Narkomindel* had been purged thoroughly[8] but hardly at Molotov's initiative.

Nothing occurred in the last years of World War II or the first years of peace to change Litvinov's gloomy outlook about Soviet-U.S. cooperation. In August 1943, he was relieved as ambassador to the United States and again made a deputy commissar, this time a powerless sinecure he was to hold until August 1946.[9]

For a time, Litvinov threw himself into his work but to little advantage. In what appears to have been October 1943, he wrote to Ivy that he was busy "in connection with the coming conferences" but "my mood is sometimes very gloomy and hopeless. Perhaps your coming will cheer me up."[10] On another occasion, he wrote that he feared that any real diplomatic work "may be very interesting but also a source of new frictions."[11]

Indeed, Litvinov saw frictions coming between the USSR and the United States and tried to justify and explain the Soviet position. By 1944, the two allies were already parting ways over the issue of Poland, and in speaking with Harriman and Eden, Litvinov "expounded the concept that it was unreasonable to consider that the interests of thirty million Poles should be given equal weight with those of one hundred eighty million Russians. Where the interests of the Russians conflicted with those of the Poles, the Poles would have to give way."[12] Litvinov certainly believed in this concept, especially in view of Poland's policy before the war, but surely he was also trying to warn Roosevelt that resistance on the Polish issue was futile.

And back in Moscow new frictions did arise, as Litvinov revealed shortly after the war. Two months before his final dismissal in 1946, he gave a lengthy interview to Richard C. Hottelet of the Columbia Broadcasting System. It was Litvinov's last detailed conversation with a Westerner, and he clearly intended it as his political testament.

Hottelet had only recently arrived in Moscow and had sent formal requests for interviews to all commissars and deputy commissars. Only Litvinov had responded, telling Hottelet to visit him at his office on 18 June 1946.[13] When the American entered Litvinov's office, he found the aged diplomat bending over his desk sifting through his papers. Despite the hot summer day, a large fire was blazing in the fireplace. It was clear that Litvinov was putting his files in order—destroying what he did not want or did not want known. At Litvinov's invitation, they sat opposite one another at the office's long conference table.

Hottelet asked Litvinov what he thought of the international situation and sat back, prepared to hear the "usual polite evasions." Instead, Litvinov said: "The outlook is bad. It seems as though the differences between East and West have gone too far to be reconciled."[14] Hottelet gulped with amazement but quickly recovered and asked Litvinov why East and West could not live together in peace. Was it not possible, for example, that the United Nations could be instrumental in creating postwar harmony? Litvinov replied that he did not think so, and he was unequivocal in explaining why: "As far as I am concerned the root cause [of the Cold War] is the ideological conception prevailing here that conflict between the Communist and capitalist worlds is inevitable."[15]

Hottelet almost desperately tried to determine if a full capitulation to Soviet demands might ease tensions. Litvinov replied, "slowly and deliberately," that such blanket concessions "would lead to the West being faced, after a more or less short time, with the next series of demands."[16] The American continued his attempt to find a way out of the dilemma that Litvinov felt was insoluble. "I asked him whether it might not be true that much of the mutual suspicion between East and West might lie in the difficulty of drawing a line between genuine security and imperialist aggression. Litvinov . . . regarded me sadly. He spoke almost gently as though to lessen the impact of his words." Well might Litvinov soften his tone because the words were a genuine bombshell. "Hitler . . . Hitler probably felt sincerely that his demands were justified, that he was entitled to *lebensraum*. Hitler was probably genuinely convinced that his actions were preventive and forced on him by external circumstances."[17] Neither man had previously mentioned Hitler. The topic of conversation was Stalin's foreign policy, but Litvinov's meaning was clear. It is quite understandable that several times during the course of the interview Hottelet wondered "if the man had gone crazy or whether this was some fantastic frame-up."[18]

It is, of course, impossible to say precisely why Litvinov should have been so incredibly reckless during the interview. One thing is clear, however: His disgust with Soviet politics and foreign policy was simply boundless. No other explanation makes much sense. All he wanted to do was to disassociate himself from Stalin's regime, and he told Hottelet that he no longer had influence within the government and that "I'm glad to be out of it."[19]

After August 1946, Litvinov was indeed finally "out of it," and other matters occupied his time. Ivy recalled that Maxim was "pathetically happy spoiling" his grandchildren, especially taking them to the zoo.[20] Nevertheless, his health began to deteriorate, and life grew difficult in other ways as well. Ivy records that the family became accustomed to "seeing that plump finely molded hand upon the printed booklet beside the Kremlin Telephone . . . strike out a name and number that would never be required again. Gradually whole pages showed neither names nor numbers, only long black lines from margin to margin."[21] Still, he kept up a fairly active correspondence, some of which has been published. In a letter to Aleksandra Kollontai dated 2 July 1951, Litvinov wrote that he had just read an unpublished memoir about Lenin written in the 1930s by his widow, Nadezhda Krupskaia.

He was particularly pleased that the work had brought out vividly Lenin's "humanity." Litvinov added, however, that it was "a pity that [the book] is inaccessible to our youth. They know so little about Ilich as a man."[22] Litvinov probably did regret that the Soviet youth knew only Stalin and Stalinism, but he also was very close to burning his bridges with even Lenin, despite his sincere admiration of the man who had opened up new revolutionary horizons so many years ago. Shortly before his death, Litvinov was resting on a couch at home reading Leo Tolstoi, one of his favorite writers and one of history's greatest pacifists. He sighed loudly, let the book drop from his hands, and turning to his wife, said, "After all, perhaps Tolstoi was right— you don't accomplish anything by force."[23] At about the same time, Litvinov's daughter-in-law asked him how he felt about his life of service to the party, and his ambivalent answer might well serve as his epitaph. He said it was like meeting a beautiful young woman and falling hopelessly in love. So you get married. But with time she "has grown into an ugly witch. Still you're married to her."[24]

The end came on the night of 31 December 1951, when Litvinov was stricken with a heart attack and died almost immediately. The body lay in state for a few hours in the ceremonial conference hall of the Foreign Commissariat, now called the Foreign Ministry, and on 3 January 1952, the remains were interred in a corner of the lovely cemetery beside the Novodevichey Monastery in Moscow. The failures were over at last.

Litvinov's grave, Moscow.

CONCLUSION

BY THE END OF Litvinov's life, his belief in revolution had been seriously undermined. He had made the long ideological journey from a gunrunning revolutionary to a man who doubted the utility of violence in any situation. Because he lived through the terrible excesses of Stalinism, it was quite natural that he should reexamine his early years in the light of what followed them. He watched as Stalin's grim gulag mocked his own youthful desire for a Russia "without prisons" and drew his conclusions.

But the ultimate irony of Litvinov's career is that he, perhaps more than anyone, gave at least a veneer of respectability to Stalin's murderous regime. It is easy to imagine how much worse the Kremlin's international position might have been in the 1930s if Litvinov had not been around as the personification of a businesslike diplomat. Litvinov was genuinely, if grudgingly, respected in the west (and detested by the Nazis), and this respect surely served to lessen hostility toward the Soviet Union in Paris, London, and Washington. As the U.S. diplomat John Wiley put it, Litvinov's "courage, effrontery, articulate and irrepressible energy have been invaluable [to the Kremlin] at a time when Soviet representatives are usually regarded as nuisances." Under Litvinov, he added, the Soviets' role in international affairs had "evolved from intrusion to participation."[1] In a sense, Litvinov was the diplomatic shield of the Stalinist 1930s.

But viewed from another perspective, Litvinov's professional legacy could be useful to Gorbachev today. Litvinov, the diplomat, sought to reintegrate the Soviet Union in its new socialist, or Stalinist, form into the world community as a nation-state, downplaying the global revolutionary rhetoric of his masters. Today, Gorbachev insists that he is trying to do essentially the same thing. As he has talked of the New Economic Policy as a potential model for economic reform, so he could point to Litvinov's example as a precedent for his own diplomatic reorientation.

After the end of World War II, Litvinov refused to sit back and simply ignore the disasters that were happening in Soviet foreign policy, which he attributed squarely to Stalin. So he spoke out bluntly and courageously, if off the record, to a few outsiders. If nothing else, he wanted to be sure that, after the war, his name would not be associated with the Soviet policy of those years. His success on this score was one of the few of his long career.

The final act of his rejection of Stalinism emphasizes a personal characteristic that ran through Litvinov's life: courage. As a young man, he risked his life repeatedly to further the cause of socialism. When it seemed to him, however, that the cause was lost in the years before World War I, he had the courage to accept the inevitable and get on with his life. Then the dream revived in 1917. He turned to diplomatic work for the young Soviet state, an occupation that involved frequent personal danger, as shown by Vorovskii's murder. In the 1930s, Litvinov waged a personal battle against the advocates of Rapallo. Defeat in any intraparty dispute often meant death, and one is struck by the serenity and tenacity with which Litvinov fought this perilous fight. Even his 1941 journey from the USSR to Washington, D.C., via the Pacific Ocean, put his life in jeopardy. In his condemnations of Stalin during and after the war with Germany, Litvinov's courage verged on wild recklessness. Yet he remained unflappable, seemingly more sad than outraged. Perhaps, like Bukharin before him, at the end he looked at his life's work and saw a "black vacuity." Nonetheless he surely found some consolation in the realization that the will to do what he thought right rarely left him.

Another issue regarding Litvinov and Stalinism is the puzzle of Litvinov's survival, something that will probably always remain a mystery. By every bizarre criterion conjured up by the People's Commissariat for Internal Affairs, Litvinov was a "traitor," if only because of his links to "hostile foreign elements." Yet Stalin spared Litvinov. For one thing, Litvinov was essentially a nonentity in domestic party affairs, a reputation he wisely did nothing to change, but a multitude of other nonentities, along with outright sycophants, were destroyed. Tatiana Litvinov suggested that the crucial factor was that her father had not been in Russia in 1917 and therefore did not witness the insignificant role that Stalin had played in the revolution. Mikhail Litvinov objected, observing that thousands of people perished who were scarcely familiar with even secondary accounts of 1917, much less having been an eyewitness. Both Tatiana and Mikhail agreed, however, that their father would probably have been consumed in the notorious "doctors' plot" that was threatening to become a second great purge at the time of Stalin's death in 1953.

One point must be emphasized. Had Stalin done away with Litvinov, he would have deprived himself of a man who could be useful should the Soviet Union need to rebuild relations with the west. If this was Stalin's thinking, events justified his sparing of Litvinov, but this interpretation suggests a certain degree of rationality on Stalin's part that some people might dispute. It does, however, offer at least a plausible explanation for an otherwise incongruous event.

Viewing Litvinov's career in a broad perspective, it is clear that he had definite ideas about the content of Soviet foreign policy and international relations. He wanted foremost to align the Soviet Union with western Europe and thereby check Germany, a nation that he believed was almost inherently dangerous to the USSR. He did not desire or seek bad relations with the Germans and was perfectly willing to coexist with them, but he always feared a resurgence of German militarism. Of course, in the 1920s, Germany had been effectively disarmed and the west refused to deal with the Soviet Union except on terms that almost the entire Soviet leadership rejected. There existed no choice then but to grasp the hand of Europe's other pariah, but Litvinov never liked the relationship with Germany and shed no tears when it collapsed in the early 1930s.

The 1930s held promise for a realization of a prowestern change in Soviet policy, and the failure to achieve collective security with the western powers during that decade was Litvinov's greatest disappointment. He was laboring, however, under conditions that virtually assured a lack of success. It seemed for a short time that with Hitler's unsolicited help, Litvinov and Louis Barthou might be able to bridge the enormous chasm between the capitalist west and the Stalinist east, but Barthou's assassination in 1934 was a grave blow to an effective Franco-Soviet pact. The majority of the other western statesmen thought they could bargain with Hitler, particularly with regard to his desire to revise the Versailles system, and the Soviet Union and Litvinov had no place in such a policy. If Barthou's assassination was a grave blow to Litvinov's policy, the execution of most of the leaders of the Red Army in 1937–1938 was fatal. Litvinov recognized this fact clearly; what is interesting, and unknown, is whether or not Stalin realized how much damage he had done to the Soviet Union's international position. Litvinov's search for a rapprochement with the west was thwarted by events and people both within and without the USSR.

Finally, the historian must address the matter of Litvinov's legacy in the broadest sense. For years, that legacy was slight, almost nonexistent. During the Cold War, his name was hardly mentioned except as an example of the Soviet Union's futile effort to achieve coexistence with the West. In 1976, the centenary of Litvinov's birth, there were no special articles or notices in the Soviet press.

After Mikhail Gorbachev came to power, however, the situation changed. In 1989, Sheinis's complete biography appeared, unchanged from what he wrote in the 1960s, and a commemorative plaque has been placed outside one of Litvinov's Moscow apartments. Shortly after Iraq's invasion of Kuwait in 1990, Thomas Pickering, the U.S. ambassador to the United Nations, even observed that "peace is indivisible," Litvinov's famous phrase from the 1930s. And more and more, one now hears of the need for "collective security" in Europe as NATO and the Warsaw Pact pass into history. It might not be a bad idea for the reunited Germany to understand with perfect clarity that aggression against one European state is tantamount to aggression against all. Maybe even the Poles would be responsive this time.

But Litvinov's true legacy is much broader. His is the example of a foreign minister who understood lucidly the international position and needs of the country he represented. Litvinov's clear-minded realism provided him with a remarkably accurate picture of the diplomatic milieu in which he moved. He came forth with specific proposals to meet potential threats and to exploit possible opportunities. His failure to see these proposals realized in no way diminishes his acumen as a statesman.

NOTES

CHAPTER 1

1. Arthur Upham Pope, *Maxim Litvinoff* (New York: L. B. Fischer, 1943), 32–33.

2. Ivy Litvinov Papers, Hoover Institution Archives, Stanford University, Box 4, "Statesman at Home," n.d. Ivy Litvinov was the commissar's wife, and this diverse collection consists of notes, drafts of diary entries, short stories and other memorabilia. Although the bulk of the material naturally relates to Ivy, there is a wealth of data on Maxim.

3. Pope, *Maxim Litvinoff*, 32–33.

4. Interview with Tatiana Litvinov, Brighton, England, 30–31 March 1981.

5. Ivy Litvinov Papers, Box 8, "The Frustrated Statesman," n.d. Young Meer, of course, had other adolescent concerns. According to Ivy, he wondered why girls would not "just raise their skirts." He felt it was "nothing to them, everything to me" (Ivy Litvinov Papers, Box 9, Diary 1973, Notes, n.d.)

6. Ivy Litvinov Papers, "Statesman at Home."

7. Ibid., Fragment, Box 7, n.d.

8. Ibid.

9. Pope, *Maxim Litvinoff*, 36–38.

10. Ibid. Also see Ivy Litvinov Papers, "Statesman at Home."

11. Pope, *Maxim Litvinoff*, 37–38.

12. Z. S. Sheinis, *Maksim M. Litvinov: Revoliutsioner, diplomat, chelovek* (Moscow: Politicheskaia literatura, 1989), 222.

13. N. Kornev, *Litvinov* (Moscow: Molodaia gvardiia, 1936), 16–17. Kornev's work was the first biography of Litvinov published in book form in the Soviet Union. Clearly meant as propaganda, it is of limited value at best. Perhaps the most significant thing about Kornev's book is the date of publication, 1936, which suggests that Stalin had not yet rejected Litvinov's foreign policy ideas, which favored collective security and the West.

14. Pope, *Maxim Litvinoff*, 38. The specifics of Litvinov's joining the party—for example, who recruited him—are not known.

15. The author of the party literature is not indicated in any of the sources (ibid., 39, Z. S. Sheinis, "Papasha," *Prometei* 7 [1969]:82). Sheinis wrote a biography of Litvinov in the late 1960s but until 1989 was only able to publish fourteen articles in various Soviet journals. The quality of his work is uneven, but it is worth noting that he had access to party and state archives. Litvinov's son and daughter believe firmly that former Soviet foreign minister Andrei Gromyko was responsible for blocking publication of Shein-is's complete study. They believe that Gromyko, who entered the Foreign Commissariat in 1939 as a result of the purge surrounding Litvinov's dismissal, carried a personal enmity toward their father and desired that he be forgotten (interviews with Tatiana Litvinov and with Mikhail Litvinov, Moscow, 3 November 1982). This suspicion is well founded. Gromyko took a personal interest in publications on Soviet foreign policy—for example, he helped edit the standard Soviet texts, *Istoriia diplomatii*, 5 vols. (Moscow: Politizdat, 1975), and *Istoriia vneshnei politiki SSSR 1917-1976*, 2 vols. (Moscow: Nauka, 1976)—and other foreign policy officials of the early Soviet period did receive biographical treatment—see, for example, V. V. Sokolov, *Na boevykh postakh diplomaticheskogo fronta: zhizn' i deiatel'nost' L. M. Karakhana* (Moscow: Politizdat, 1983), and Nikolai Zhukovskii, *Diplomaty novogo mira* (Moscow: Politizdat, 1982). After Mikhail Gorbachev came to power, Sheinis's articles began to reappear in Soviet journals, and Sheinis came to hope that his entire manuscript would be published in the near future (interview with Z. S. Sheinis, Moscow, 22 October 1986). Finally, in an article in *Moscow News*, Sheinis announced that his long-suppressed manuscript would be published soon (Z. S. Sheinis, "A Long Road," *Moscow News* 21 [1987]:16). It was finally published in 1989, but one point must be made: The *Moscow News* article suggests that Sheinis made no changes in the manuscript after 1967, and a great deal of new documentation on Litvinov's diplomatic career has become available since that time.

16. Litvinov said that a young man was responsible for turning the Social Democrats over to the police but that he held no animosity toward him. "The boy," said Litvinov, "was at an age when people easily change their minds" (interview with Tatiana Litvinov).

17. Pope, *Maxim Litvinoff*, 38-39; Sheinis, "Papasha," 82-83; and Leopold H. Haimson, *The Russian Marxists and the Origins of Bolshevism* (Boston: Beacon, 1966), 117-120.

18. Maxim M. Litvinov, "O leninskoi *Iskre*," *Istoricheskii arkhiv* 2 (1961):140, and interview with Tatiana Litvinov. Leopold Haimson has related that an early Russian Social Democrat, Solomon Schwarz, told him that it was quite the norm for the "most dedicated, the most active young Social

Democrats" to become followers of Lenin, who represented the more radical and decisive faction of the party (Leopold Haimson's Preface in Solomon Schwarz, *The Russian Revolution of 1905* [Chicago: University of Chicago Press, 1967], ix).

19. Sheinis, "Papasha," 84, and Pope, *Maxim Litvinoff*, 45.
20. Litvinov, "O leninskoi," 143–144, and Sheinis, "Papasha," 85–86.
21. Sheinis, "Papasha," 85.
22. Litvinov, "O leninskoi," 143.
23. Ibid., 144.
24. Ibid.
25. Ibid., 145–146.
26. Sheinis, "Papasha," 86.
27. Ibid., 87.
28. Litvinov, "O leninskoi," 146.
29. Ibid., 147.
30. Ibid., 148.
31. Ibid., 149. Litvinov argued unsuccessfully with Iurii Martov and other Menshevik leaders that Lenin should retain control of *Iskra* (see Adam Ulam, *The Bolsheviks* [New York: Collier, 1968], 195–196).
32. Sheinis, "Papasha," 93.
33. "Perepiska N. Lenina i N. K. Krupskoi s M. M. Litvinovym," *Proletarskaia revoliutsiia* 2 (1925):75.
34. Ibid., 76.
35. Ibid., 77–78.
36. Ibid., 78.
37. Donald W. Treadgold, *Twentieth Century Russia*, 7th ed. (Boulder: Westview Press, 1990), 55–57.
38. See Walter Sablinsky, *The Road to Bloody Sunday* (Princeton: Princeton University Press, 1976).
39. Nicholas Riasanovsky, *A History of Russia*, 2nd ed. (New York: Oxford University Press, 1969), 452.
40. Litvinov's memories of his days at *Novaia zhizn'* are recorded in M. Ol'minskii, ed., *Novaia zhizn': Pervaia legal'naia Bolsheviskaia gazeta* (Leningrad: Priboi, 1925) 1:vii–xi.
41. S. S. Khromov and A. L. Narochnitskii, chief eds., *Istoriia rabochego klassa SSSR* (Moscow: Nauka, 1979–), Vol. 2, *Rabochii klass v pervoi rossiiskoi revoliutsii, 1905–1907 gg* (Moscow: Nauka, 1981), 105. An interesting, if almost unrecognizable, photograph of Litvinov in 1905 appears on p. 113 of this volume.
42. Ibid., 240.
43. Pope, *Maxim Litvinov*, 74–75.
44. Z. S. Sheinis, "Vodvoritel' oruzhiia," *Nauka i zhizn'* 7 (1966):19.

45. Ibid., 20. Sheinis writes that his account is based on "what Litvinov later remembered," but he gives no sources.

46. Ibid., 21.

47. Ibid.

48. Ibid., 22. Sheinis writes only that Litvinov "vanished into the air."

49. Ibid., 23-24.

50. B. Bibineishvili, *Kamo* (Moscow: Starii Bol'shevik, 1934), 112. This biography of the eccentric and physically imposing revolutionary Kamo, who helped Litvinov with the smuggling mission, contains a brief note by Litvinov about the incident.

51. Sheinis, "Vodvoritel' oruzhiia," 25, and Pope, *Maxim Litvinoff*, 95-96.

52. Pope, *Maxim Litvinoff*, 96. Litvinov supplemented his income as a tour guide and language tutor (Ivy Litvinov, "Vstrechi i razluki," *Novyi mir* 7 [1966]:243). He also obtained "English agricultural machinery on commission to Russian firms" (Ivy Litvinov Papers, "Statesman at Home").

53. Ivy Litvinov Papers, "Litvinoff's Wife," n.d.

54. Ibid., Box 7, Fragment. n.d.

55. Ibid., "Litvinoff's Wife."

56. Ibid.

57. Ibid.

58. Ibid.

59. Ibid., Box 5, "Lucky Old Woman," n.d.

60. Ibid., Box 2, Fragment, n.d.

61. Ibid., "Litvinoff's Wife."

62. Ibid.

63. Ibid., Box 9, Fragment, n.d.

64. Ibid., Box 7, Fragment, n.d.

65. In Z. S. Sheinis, ed., "Neopublikovannye pis'ma M. M. Litvinova V. I. Leninu, 1913-1915 gg," *Novaia i noveishaia istoriia* 4 (1966):120. It is ironic that Litvinov thought Lenin's criticism of Luxemburg too harsh because she considered Litvinov "a complete idiot" (Elzbieta Ettinger, ed., *Comrade and Lover: Rosa Luxemburg's Letters to Leo Jogiches* [Cambridge, Mass., 1979], 182, cited in R. C. Elwood, "Lenin and the Brussels 'Unity' Conference of July 1914," *Russian Review* 39 [1980]:35, note 10).

66. Letter of Litvinov to Lenin and Krupskaia, 15 December 1913, in Sheinis, ed., "Neopublikovannye pis'ma," 125.

67. Litvinov to Lenin, 5 May 1914, in ibid., 125-126.

68. Interview with Tatiana Litvinov. According to Ivy Litvinov's biographer, Maxim "came to like England . . . and even to exaggerate the strength of its social system" (John Carswell, *The Exile: A Life of Ivy Litvinov* (Boston: Faber and Faber, 1983), 68.

69. Pope, *Maxim Litvinoff*, 96. I do not mean to suggest that Litvinov had fully repudiated Lenin or Bolshevism; were that the case, his behavior would have been very different after 1917. The point is simply that by 1915, Litvinov's hopes for a Bolshevik revolution in Russia were practically nil. Exactly when Litvinov was naturalized is not clear, but apparently it was after 1914.

CHAPTER 2

1. Ivan Maisky, *Journey into the Past* (London: Hutchinson, 1962), 57.

2. Ivy Litvinov, "Vstrechi i razluki," *Novyi mir* 7 (1966):247.

3. Maisky, *Journey*, 51–57.

4. The description of this incident and quotations are from Litvinov, "Vstrechi," 246–247.

5. Ivy Litvinov Papers, Box 4, "Litvinoff's Wife," n.d.; italics in the original.

6. Litvinov, "Vstrechi," 248. This story of a great interest in Litvinov on the part of London journalists may be true, but there is no evidence of such interest in the *Times*. Ivy probably exaggerated this account somewhat.

7. Z. S. Sheinis, *Maksim M. Litvinov: Revoliutsioner, diplomat, chelovek* (Moscow: Politicheskaia literatura, 1989), 113–114.

8. *Times*, 8, 10, 12, 14, 20 November 1917.

9. Richard H. Ullman, *Anglo-Soviet Relations, 1917–1921*, 2 vols. (Princeton: Princeton University Press, 1961), 1:60.

10. Maisky, *Journey*, 63.

11. Decree on Peace, 8 November 1918, Ministerstvo Inostrannykh Del, SSSR, *Dokumenty vneshnei politiki, SSSR* (Moscow: Politizdat, 1959–), 1:11–14 (hereafter cited as *D.V.P.*). This series is the most complete Soviet publication to date of foreign policy materials. As of 1992, twenty-one volumes had been issued, covering the years 1917–1938.

12. Circular telegram to all Russian embassies, 5 December 1918, ibid., 1:41.

13. S. V. Blinov, *Vneshniaia politika Sovetskoi Rossii: Pervyi god proletarskoi diktatury* (Moscow: Mysl', 1973), 66–68.

14. Ibid., 68.

15. Maisky, *Journey*, 62.

16. Ibid., 63. During the war, Litvinov worked for this commission purchasing agricultural machinery (Sheinis, *Maksim M. Litvinov*, 105).

17. N. Kornev, *Litvinov* (Moscow: Molodaia gvardiia, 1936), 28–38.

18. Maxim M. Litvinov, *The Bolshevik Revolution: Its Rise and Meaning* (Chicago: Socialist Party of the United States, 1920), 49–50.

19. Maisky, *Journey*, 64.

20. Ullman, *Intervention*, 60.

21. Richard K. Debo, "Litvinov and Kamenev—Ambassadors Extraordinary: The Problem of Soviet Representation Abroad," *Slavic Review* 34 (1975):466.

22. Ullman, *Intervention*, 34–35.

23. Debo, "Litvinov and Kamenev," 466.

24. Robert H. Bruce Lockhart, *British Agent* (London: G. P. Putnam's Sons, 1933), 200–202, and Lockhart, *The Diaries of Sir Robert Bruce Lockhart, 1915–1938* (New York: St. Martin's, 1973), 32.

25. Lockhart, *British Agent*, 201, and *Diaries*, 32.

26. Lockhart, *British Agent*, 201.

27. Maisky, *Journey*, 62–63.

28. *Times*, 23 January 1918, 8.

29. Ullman, *Intervention*, 80.

30. Debo, "Litvinov and Kamenev," 469, and Lockhart, *British Agent*, 275–277, 303, 312, and 313.

31. Ullman, *Intervention*, 80.

32. Leeper memo of a conversation with Litvinov, 29 June 1933 (Great Britain, Public Record Office, Foreign Office Papers, Series 371, vol. 17241, N4812, 5, 38; hereafter cited as F.O. 371, 17241, etc.).

33. Debo, "Litvinov and Kamenev," 469.

34. Maisky, *Journey*, 67.

35. Ullman, *Intervention*, 286–287.

36. Note from Chicherin to Oudenjik, 24 August 1918, *D.V.P.*, 1:433.

37. David Francis's note to Department of State, 25 August 1918, in U.S. Department of State, *Papers Relating to the Foreign Relations of the United States* [hereafter cited as F.R.U.S.], *1918, Russia*, 3 vols. (Washington, D.C.: Government Printing Office, 1931), 1:664–665, and Ullman, *Intervention*, 288.

38. Ullman, *Intervention*, 288–290.

39. Ibid., 290, and Maisky, *Journey*, 67. Soviet sources insist that Litvinov was arrested in retaliation for Lockhart's internment (see F. D. Volkov, "Zagovor poslov i provokatsionnaia rol Briusa Lokkarta," *Novaia i noveishaia istoriia* 5 [1976]:112–124), but in fact, it was Cromie's murder that precipitated Litvinov's arrest (Ullman, *Intervention*, 209, 291, note 25).

40. Ullman, *Intervention*, 294.

41. Ibid., 294–295.

42. Ibid., 295.

43. Ibid. and Leeper memo of conversation with Litvinov, 29 June 1933 (F.O. 371, 17241, N4812, 5, 38).

44. Ullman, *Intervention*, 295.

45. Maisky, *Journey*, 67–68.

46. Ullman, *Intervention*, 293–296.

CHAPTER 3

1. Valerii Shishkin, *V. I. Lenin i vneshneekonomicheskaia politika Sovetskogo gosudarstva, 1917–1923 gg* (Leningrad: Nauka, 1977), 154, and Z. S. Sheinis, *Maksim M. Litvinov: Revoliutsioner, diplomat, chelovek* (Moscow: Politicheskaia literatura, 1989), 138.

2. V. I. Lenin, *Polnoe sobranie sochinenii*, 5th ed., 55 vols. (Moscow: Politizdat, 1958–1964), 37:111–125.

3. John Thompson, *Russia, Bolshevism, and the Versailles Peace* (Princeton: Princeton University Press, 1966), 88.

4. Jane Degras, ed., *Soviet Documents on Foreign Policy*, 3 vols. (Oxford: Oxford University Press, 1951–53), 1:112–120.

5. Memo by William Buckler, undated [January 1919], William Buckler Papers, Yale University Archives, Box 6.

6. F.R.U.S., *1919, Russia*, 1.

7. Degras, ed., *Soviet Documents*, 1:130–131.

8. Ibid., 1:131–132. Litvinov told Buckler that his letter was intended to "make plain to the U.S. that the Soviet Government are [sic] genuinely anxious for real and permanent peace" (Buckler Papers, Box 6, Memo by Buckler, n.d.).

9. Louis Fischer, *Men and Politics* (New York: Duell, Sloan and Pearce, 1941), 127.

10. Buckler Papers, Box 6, Letter from Litvinov to Ludwig Meyer, 10 January 1919. The reference to small creditors was undoubtedly intended for French eyes as that nation had a multitude of Russian bond holders.

11. Interview with Tatiana Litvinov, Brighton, England, 30–31 March 1981. Also see Fischer, *Men and Politics*, 127–128.

12. Thompson, *Russia*, 90–91.

13. Ibid., 91.

14. F.R.U.S., *1919, Russia*, 15. Also see Buckler's undated memo in Box 6 of his papers.

15. F.R.U.S., *1919, Russia*, 16, and Buckler Papers, Box 6.

16. For example, Chicherin asserted that the League "serves the intrigues of imperialists" and that he had "always been an absolute, undiluted, unmixed, unwavering, unswerving enemy of Soviet membership in the League" (Chicherin letter to Louis Fischer, 10 March 1930, Louis Fischer Papers, Yale University Archives, Box 1).

17. F.R.U.S., *1919, Russia*, 15, 17, and Buckler Papers, Box 6.

18. Richard H. Ullman, *Anglo-Soviet Relations,1917–1921*, 2 vols. (Princeton: Princeton University Press, 1961), 2:109.

19. Telegram from Chicherin to Vorovskii, 14 January 1919, *D.V.P.*, 2:29. Chicherin reminded Litvinov that simultaneously with the beginning

of the foreign intervention, negotiations on economic concessions had opened with Britain in Moscow.

20. Radio address of Chicherin, 4 February 1919, *D.V.P.*, 57–59; Degras, ed., *Soviet Documents*, 1:137–139; and Ullman, *Anglo-Soviet Relations*, 2:112–113.

21. Thompson, *Russia*, 122–123.

22. Beatrice Farnsworth, *William C. Bullitt and the Soviet Union* (Bloomington and London: Indiana University Press, 1967), 35–39, and Ullman, *Anglo-Soviet Relations*, 2:147.

23. Degras, ed., *Soviet Documents*, 1:133–134, and Shishkin, *V. I. Lenin*, 155–156.

24. Farnsworth, *William C. Bullitt*, 39.

25. William C. Bullitt, *The Bullitt Mission to Russia: Testimony Before the Committee on Foreign Relations, United States Senate, 1919* (New York: Huebsch, 1919), 39.

26. Shishkin, *V. I. Lenin*, 160.

27. Ullman, *Anglo-Soviet Relations*, 2:148–149.

28. Shishkin, *V. I. Lenin*, 160.

29. Ibid., 161, and Ullman, *Anglo-Soviet Relations*, 2:149.

30. Thompson, *Russia*, 164.

31. Bullitt, *Bullitt Mission*, 45.

32. Farnsworth, *William C. Bullitt*, 47–51, and Sheinis, *Maksim M. Litvinov*, 146.

33. Teddy Uldrichs, *Diplomacy and Ideology: The Origins of Soviet Foreign Relations, 1917–1930* (London and Beverly Hills: Sage Publications, 1979), 62–63.

34. Ullman, *Anglo-Soviet Relations*, 2:340, and Richard K. Debo, "Prelude to Negotiations: The Problem of British Prisoners in Soviet Russia, November 1918–July 1919," *Slavonic and East European Review* 58 (January 1980):61.

35. Debo, "Prelude," 68–74.

36. Ivan Maisky, "Anglo-Sovetskoi torgovoe soglashenie 1921 v goda," *Voprosy istorii* (May 1975): 65. This article contains lengthy sections written by Litvinov concerning his role in the Copenhagen talks.

37. Z. S. Sheinis, "Diplomaticheskoe poruchenie," *Moskva* (October 1966): 149, and Shishkin, *V. I. Lenin*, 196.

38. Louis Fischer, *The Soviets in World Affairs*, 2 vols. (London: Jonathan Cape, 1930), 1:251.

39. Shishkin, *V. I. Lenin*, 196.

40. Sheinis, "Diplomaticheskoe," 148–149.

41. Ibid., 150.

42. Ibid., 151. Perhaps O'Grady should have pointed out that unlike the Bolsheviks, the English had executed only Charles I, not him *and* his entire family. Still, this conversation is an instance of Litvinov's benefiting from his knowledge of history.

43. Maisky, "Anglo-Sovetskoi," 65.

44. Ullman, *Anglo-Soviet Relations*, 2:342.

45. Ibid.

46. Maisky, "Anglo-Sovetskoi," 66–67. It is interesting that there is very little correspondence in *D.V.P.* between Litvinov and Moscow during these talks, suggesting that Litvinov was largely on his own.

47. Fischer, *Soviets in World Affairs*, 1:250–251. On 8 January, Litvinov had notified Moscow that the blockade would soon end (telegram from Litvinov to Chicherin, 8 January 1920, *D.V.P.*, 2:320).

48. Ibid., and Maisky, "Anglo-Sovetskoi," 68–69.

49. Maisky, "Anglo-Sovetskoi," 67–68.

50. Sheinis, "Diplomaticheskoe," 155. Litvinov gave no specific names.

51. Maisky, "Anglo-Sovetskoi," 68. Litvinov also obtained boots and fish from Norweign companies (see Unsigned report, 12 November 1920, F.O. 371, 5420, N2504, 33, 38).

52. Ivy Litvinov Papers, Box 9, "In Worlds Not Realised," n.d. Also see undated fragments in Boxes 6 and 7.

53. Sheinis, "Diplomaticheskoe," 155. For obvious reasons, Maxim had had to leave his wife and two infants behind when he left England. Ivy called the two years apart, the "most meaningless of my life," a situation aggravated by the early death of a third child. Maxim never saw his second son and asked Ivy what he had been like. He told her that he felt he had "lost a part of himself" (Ivy Litvinov Papers, Box 4, "Litvinoff's Wife," n.d.).

CHAPTER 4

1. Z. S. Sheinis, "V Genue i Gaage," *Novaia i noveishaia istoriia* (May–July 1968):53, and Louis Fischer, *Men and Politics* (New York: Duell, Sloan and Pearce, 1941), 137. This arrangement lasted until 1926 when the Western and Eastern Sections were abolished and the various regional sections were elevated to full department status (Teddy Uldrichs, *Diplomacy and Ideology: The Origins of Soviet Foreign Relations, 1917–1930* (London and Beverly Hills: Sage Publications, 1979), 81.

2. E. Gnedin, "Revoliutsioner-diplomat leninskoi shkoly," *Novyi mir* (February 1970):257.

3. Z. S. Sheinis, "Vodvoritel' oruzhiia," *Nauka i zhizn'* (1966):55.

4. Sheinis, "V Genue i Gaage," 52–53. Sheinis's source was the Central Party Archive in Moscow.

5. Telegram from Chicherin to Litvinov, 11 August 1921, *D.V.P.*, 4:262. For a stark and horrifying account of this famine, see Walter Duranty, *Duranty Reports Russia* (New York: Viking Press, 1934), 65-95.

6. Ivy Litvinov Papers, Hoover Institution Archives, Stanford University, Box 5, Fragment, n.d.

7. Benjamin Weissman, *Herbert Hoover and Famine Relief to Soviet Russia: 1921-1923* (Stanford, Calif.: Hoover Institution Press, 1974), 54.

8. Ibid., 58-62.

9. *New York Tribune*, 17 August 1921, cited in Weissman, *Hoover*, 62-63.

10. Barclay (Stockholm) to Foreign Office, 28 October 1921, F.O. 371, 6856, N12183, 5, 38.

11. Barclay (Stockholm) to Foreign Office, 11 November 1921, F.O. 371, 6893, N12701, 915, 38. Also see Stephen White, *The Origins of Detente: The Genoa Conference and Soviet-Western Relations, 1921-1922* (Cambridge: Cambridge University Press, 1985), Chapter 2. In a somewhat bizarre aside, Litvinov proposed that the United States might assume all Russia's debts "to other countries and thus reduce by equivalent amounts the debts of those countries to the U.S. In this manner it would be possible to settle a number of questions of vast importance for the whole world," and Russia would have only one creditor with which to "settle procedures and dates of payments." (Barclay [Stockholm] to Foreign Office, 15 November 1921, F.O. 371, 6893, N 12894, 915, 38).

12. E. H. Carr, *The Bolshevik Revolution, 1917-1923*, 3 vols. (London: Penguin Books, 1966), 3:357.

13. Ibid., 3:358-359, and Louis Fischer, *Russia's Road from Peace to War, 1917-1941* (New York: Harper and Row, 1969), 69.

14. Valerii Shishkin, *V. I. Lenin i vneshneekonomicheskaia politika Sovetskogo gosudarstva, 1917-1923 gg* (Leningrad: Nauka, 1977), 227.

15. Georgii Chicherin, *Stat'i i rechi po voprosam mezhdunarodnoi politiki* (Moscow: Politizdat, 1961), 230-231.

16. Shishkin, *V. I. Lenin*, 231-233.

17. Sheinis, "V Genue i Gaage," 58.

18. Carr, *Bolshevik Revolution*, 3:357.

19. Sheinis, "V Genue i Gaage," 58. The French invasion of the Ruhr would soon make it clear that France was still willing to act without British support so that Litvinov's suggestion to turn to London to restrain Paris would probably have failed—had the need arisen.

20. Ibid., 59.

21. Ibid. From Sheinis's account, it appears possible that these reasons were offered also by Litvinov to the Politburo, but that cannot be stated definitely. Also see A. Meerovich, "V Narkomindele, 1922-1939: Interv'iu s

E. A. Gnedinym," *Pamiat* 5 (1982):388. Gnedin, whom I interviewed in Moscow, was a friend and coworker of Litvinov, and he confirmed that Litvinov favored a pro-English foreign policy (interview with Evgenii Gnedin, Moscow, 3 November 1982). In a February 1921 conversation with a Professor Simpson, Litvinov complained that he was unable to understand why England and the new Russia could not be friends, and he found London's fear of Soviet propaganda especially puzzling: "What could a poor Russian that hardly knew English do that Sylvia Pankhurst could not do better?"—adding that the British fears were "quite unworthy" (letter from Simpson to the Foreign Office, 1 March 1921, F.O. 371, 6854, N3573, 5, 38). Speaking with Reginald Leeper in 1933, Litvinov said his "main desire had always been to establish satisfactory working relations" with Britain, but Leeper said that Litvinov, despite these feelings, was still "an out-and-out Communist of the Lenin school and will be quite unyielding on anything that he regards as a question of principle" (memorandum by Leeper, 29 June 1933, F.O. 371, 17241, N4812, 5, 38). It would indeed have been remarkable if Litvinov had jettisoned his Communist past by 1933.

22. Sheinis, "V Genue i Gaage," 58–59.

23. Ibid., 59. Sheinis does quote Litvinov as asserting that Russia should demand 35 million gold marks from Germany if the Allies refused to abandon the reparations program. This money, he felt, should be held solely as an asset against Allied claims against Russia. In other words, Litvinov was willing to enrage the Germans in order to facilitate a settlement with the capitalist countries.

24. Gustav Hilger and Alfred G. Mayer, *The Incompatible Allies* (New York: Macmillan and Company, 1953), 111. Hilger's remark that Litvinov measured all diplomatic policies purely on the basis of their expediency seems somewhat exaggerated.

25. Herbert von Dirksen, *Moscow, Tokyo, London: Twenty Years of German Foreign Policy* (New York: Hutchinson and Company, 1951), 130.

26. Martin Walsdorff, *Westorientierung und Ostpolitik: Stresemanns Russpolitik in der Locarno Ara* (Berlin: Schuenemann Universitätsverlag, 1971), 55.

27. Adam Ulam, *Expansion and Coexistence* (New York: Praeger, 1974), 144. Nevertheless, Ulam's work remains essential for any study of Soviet foreign policy.

28. Evgeny Chossudovsky, "Genoa Revisited: Russia and Coexistence," *Foreign Affairs* 50 (April 1972):554–564.

29. A. Gorokov, "Leninskaia diplomatiia: Printsipy i traditsii," *Mezhdunarodnaia zhizn'* (April 1968):63.

30. George Kennan, *Russia and the West Under Lenin and Stalin* (Boston: Little, Brown and Company, 1960), 211.

31. Telegram from Litvinov to *Narkomindel*, 5 April 1922, *D.V.P.*, 5:184–185.

32. Fischer, *Russia's Road*, 97.

33. Carol Fink, *The Genoa Conference* (Chapel Hill: University of North Carolina Press, 1984), 154. See also memo of Genoa delegation, 20 April 1922, *D.V.P.*, 5:235–238.

34. N. N. Liubimov and A. N. Erlikh, *Genuezskaia konferentsiia* (Moscow: Instituta mezhdunarodnykh otnoshenii, 1963), 51–52.

35. Ibid., 53.

36. Ibid., 54–55.

37. Carr, *Bolshevik Revolution*, 3:373–374.

38. Fischer, *Russia's Road*, 102–103, and Kennan, *Russia and the West*, 219–221.

39. Kennan, *Russia and the West*, 221.

40. Telegram from Litvinov to *Narkomindel*, 17 April 1922, *D.V.P.*, 5:226.

41. Statement by Litvinov, 17 April 1932, *D.V.P.*, 15:248.

42. M. Tanin [Litvinov], *10 let vneshnei politiki SSSR, 1917–1927* (Moscow and Leningrad: Government Publishing House, 1927), 109.

43. Richard K. Debo, "George Chicherin: Soviet Russia's Second Foreign Commissar" (Ph.D. dissertation, University of Nebraska, 1964), 259. For a more comprehensive study of Chicherin, see Timothy E. O'Connor, *Diplomacy and Revolution: G. V. Chicherin and Soviet Foreign Affairs, 1918–1930* (Ames: Iowa State University Press, 1988).

44. Gregory (Hague) to Foreign Office, 26 June 1922, F.O. 371, 8194, N6201, 646, 38.

45. Marling (Hague) to Foreign Office, 27 June 1922, F.O. 371, 8194, N6254, 646, 38.

46. British delegation (Hague) to Foreign Office, 30 June 1922, F.O. 371, 8194, N6365, 646, 38.

47. White, *Origins of Detente*, 140–141. Also see V. I. Lenin, *Selected Works: One Volume Edition* (New York: International Publishers, 1971), 498–499.

48. Lloyd-Greame (Hague) to Foreign Office, 1 July 1922, F.O. 371, 8194, N6382, 646, 38.

49. Maxse (Hague) to Foreign Office, 10 July 1922, F.O. 371, 8195, N6696, 646, 38.

50. Excerpts of Litvinov letter to *Narkomindel*, 18 July 1922, *D.V.P.*, 5:506.

51. Tanin, *10 let*, 110–111, and *New York Times*, 20 July 1922, 1, 7.

52. British delegation to Foreign Office, 19 July 1922, F.O. 371, 8196, N6977, 646, 38.

53. U.S. Embassy (London) to Balfour, 19 July 1922, F.O. 371, 8196, N6985, 646, 38, and British delegation (Hague) to Foreign Office, 20 July 1922, F.O. 371, 8196, N7029, 646, 38.

54. Note from Karakhan to Hodgson, 16 August 1922, D.V.P.; 5:553–554, and Hodgson (Moscow) to Foreign Office, 18 August 1922, F.O. 371, 8197, N8060, 646, 38.

CHAPTER 5

1. *New York Times*, 20 July 1922, 7.

2. Note of the Soviet government to the governments of Latvia, Poland, Finland, and Estonia, 12 June 1922, D.V.P., 5:448–450. Litvinov also invited Romania to the conference, but that country replied that it would accept only if Moscow recognized Romania's annexation of Bessarabia after World War I; Litvinov refused (see note of *Narkomindel* to government of Finland, 19 August 1922, D.V.P., 5:559).

3. V. I. Lenin, *Polnoe sobranie sochinenii*, 5th ed., 55 vols. (Moscow: Pulitizdat, 1958–1964), 28:223–224.

4. Robert Warth, *Soviet Russia in World Politics* (New York: Twayne, 1963), 100–101.

5. Bela Kun, ed., *Kommunisticheskii Internatsional v dokumentakh* (Moscow: Partiinoe izdatel 'stvo, 1933), 100.

6. E. H. Carr, *The Bolshevik Revolution,1917–1923*, 3 vols. (London: Penguin Books, 1966), 3:198.

7. Viktor M. Khaitsman, *SSSR i problema razoruzheniia mezhdu pervoi i vtoroi mirovymi voinami* (Moscow: Nauka, 1959), 7.

8. Mr. Hodgson (Moscow) to the Marquess Curzon of Kedleston, 24 October 1921, in Great Britain, Foreign Office, *Documents on British Foreign Policy 1919–1939*, 1st series, 20:792 (hereafter cited as D.B.F.P.), and note from the Soviet government to the governments of Britain, France, and Italy, 1 June 1921, D.V.P., 4:153.

9. T. H. Rigby, *Lenin's Government: Sovnarkom 1917–1922* (Cambridge: Cambridge University Press, 1979), 55.

10. Walter Clemens, Jr., "Origins of the Soviet Campaign for Disarmament: The Soviet Position on Peace, Security, and Revolution at the Genoa, Moscow, and Lausanne Conferences 1922–1923" (Ph.D. dissertation, Columbia University, 1961), 99.

11. Jane Degras, ed., *Soviet Documents on Foreign Policy*, 3 vols. (Oxford: Oxford University Press, 1951–1953), 1:249–250.

12. Ibid., 1:250–251.

13. Bohdan B. Budurowycz, *Polish-Soviet Relations, 1932–1939* (New York: Columbia University Press, 1963), 4.

14. Note from the Soviet government to the governments of Latvia, Poland, Finland, and Estonia, 12 June 1922, *D.V.P.*, 5:448.

15. Ibid., 5:448–449.

16. Ibid., 5:449; for discussions of the early Soviet-Romanian dispute over Bessarabia, see Alesksei A. Sheviakov, *Sovetsko-rumynstie otnosheniie; prolblema evropeiskoe bezopasnosti 1932–1939 gg* (Moscow: Nauka, 1977), 3–8, and Louis Fischer, *The Soviets in World Affairs*, 2 vols. (London: Jonathan Cape, 1930), 2:509–510.

17. Appendix to document number 183, *D.V.P.*, 5:450.

18. Ibid., 5:451. The Finns obviously had Lithuania in mind, and why the Russians did not formally invite Lithuania in June remains a mystery. Walter Clemens speculates that Moscow waited until 23 November to invite the Lithuanians (on the very eve of the conference) because the Russians wanted to first be certain that the Poles would definitely come. Because the Poles and Lithuanians were at loggerheads over Vilna, an early invitation to both might have resulted in a rejection by both (Clemens, "Origins," 178).

19. Appendix to document number 183, *D.V.P.*, 5:450–451.

20. Ibid., 5:450.

21. Note from the Soviet chargé to the Polish foreign minister, 19 August 1922, *D.V.P.*, 5:555–556.

22. Ibid., 5:556.

23. *Pravda*, 30 November 1922, 1.

24. Ibid.

25. Jonathan Haslam, *Soviet Foreign Policy, 1930–1933* (New York: St. Martin's Press, 1983), 7.

26. Francis P. Walters, *A History of the League of Nations* (Oxford: Oxford University Press, 1952), 50. Walters's work is an excellent survey of international events between the wars, but the book suffers unavoidably from a lack of documentation that has subsequently become available.

27. Ibid., 365.

28. Louis Fischer, *Men and Politics* (New York: Duell, Sloan and Pearce, 1941), 127–128.

29. Carr, *Bolshevik Revolution*, 3:436.

30. A. A. Gromyko and B. N. Ponomarev, eds. *Istoriia vneshnei politiki SSSR 1917–1976*, 2 vols. (Moscow: Nauka, 1976), 1:179. The account of the Rerel [Tallinn] meeting is based on Latvian archival materials.

31. *New York Times*, 15 December 1922, 14.

32. Litvinov's declaration on calling the Moscow Disarmament Conference, 24 August 1922, *D.V.P.*, 5:563.

33. Litvinov's declaration at the Moscow Disarmament Conference, 2 December 1922, ibid., 6:24–25. This document includes the responses of the various delegates.

34. Ibid., 6:25–26. The proposal regarding the disbanding of irregular forces was clearly aimed at Poland. In September 1922, Soviet Russia had protested twenty-three alleged recent violations of Soviet territory through the Polish border (note from *Narkomindel* to the Polish embassy in Moscow, ibid., 5:580–583).

35. Litvinov's declaration, 2 December 1922, ibid., 6:27.

36. *New York Times*, 4 December 1922, 3.

37. Clemens, "Origins," 218–219.

38. Estonian response to Soviet declaration of 2 December 1922, *D.V.P.*, 6:28. It subsequently became clear that by "political disarmament," the non-Russian delegates had in mind treaties of nonaggression and arbitration.

39. Ibid., 6:28–30.

40. Ibid., 6:30.

41. *New York Times*, 4 December 1922, 3, and Peters (Moscow) to the Marquess Curzon of Keldeston, 5 December 1922, *D.B.F.P.*, 1st series, 23:626–627.

42. Litvinov's declaration at the Moscow Disarmament Conference, 4 December 1922, *D.V.P.*, 6:39.

43. Ibid., 6:40.

44. Speech by Litvinov at the Moscow Disarmament Conference, 5 December 1922, *D.V.P.*, 6:44.

45. Ibid., 6:47.

46. Robert W. Lambert, *Soviet Disarmament Policy, 1922–1931* (Washington, D.C.: U.S. Arms Control and Disarmament Agency, 1964), 4.

47. Soviet proposal for agreement on arbitration and nonaggression, 7 December 1922, *D.V.P.*, 6:52.

48. Clemens, "Origins," 193.

49. *New York Times*, 12 December 1922, 2.

50. Clemens, "Origins," 203.

51. Litvinov's telegram to Chicherin, 11 December 1922, *D.V.P.*, 6:58.

52. Degras, ed., *Soviet Documents*, 1:351–353.

53. Declaration of Tenth All-Russian Congress of Soviets to the peoples of the world, 27 December 1922, *D.V.P.*, 6:114–115.

54. *New York Times*, 15 December 1922, 14.

CHAPTER 6

1. Edward L. Crowley, ed., *The Soviet Diplomatic Corps, 1917–1967* (Metuchen, N.J.: The Scarecrow Press, 1970), 117.

2. Max Eastman, *Love and Revolution* (New York: Random House, 1964), 431.

3. Maxim Litvinov, *Kak rabotaet komissariat mira* (Moscow: Udkniga, 1925), 4. I do not intend to suggest that Soviet policy during the interwar period was so simply ordered. Indeed, a recent Soviet work concedes that "armed struggle" was a basic tactic of the Moscow-dominated Comintern on the path to a "world, or at least, European Soviet government" (Viktor P. Makarenko, *Biurokratiia i stalinizm* [Rostov-on-the Don: Rostov State University Press, 1989], 276). The point is that Litvinov did not share such conceptions.

4. Litvinov, *Kak rabotaet*, 7–11.

5. Werner Angress, *Stillborn Revolution: The Communist Bid for Power in Germany, 1921–1923* (Princeton: Princeton University Press, 1963), 475, and Warren Lerner, *Karl Radek* (Stanford: Stanford University Press, 1970), 120–125.

6. Gerald Freund, *Unholy Alliance: Russian-German Relations from the Treaty of Brest-Litovsk to the Treaty of Berlin* (New York: Harcourt, Brace and Company, 1957), 174.

7. Ibid., 175.

8. Ibid., 237.

9. Leonard Harvey Dyck, *Weimar Germany and Soviet Russia, 1926–1933* (New York: Columbia University Press, 1966), 11.

10. Gabriel Gorodetsky, *The Precarious Truce* (Cambridge: Cambridge University Press, 1977), 73–85.

11. Dyck, *Weimar Germany*, 26, and Freund, *Unholy Alliance*, 169. After 1923, Stresemann served as Germany's Foreign Minister.

12. Dyck, *Weimar Germany*, 15, and Gorodetsky, *Precarious Truce*, 35–58. The "Zinoviev letter," dated 7 April 1924 and addressed to the Central Committee of the Communist Party of Great Britain, was signed by Zinoviev. It instructed the party to organize a mass demonstration for 1 May and ordered the British communists to "call the wide working masses into the street" in the event the ongoing Soviet-British trade talks failed. The letter's authenticity is extremely doubtful (Gorodetsky, *Precarious Truce*, 40–46).

13. Brockdorff-Rantzau to Stresemann, 9 March 1925, cited in Dyck, *Weimar Germany*, 15; see also George Kennan, *Soviet Foreign Policy, 1917–1941* (Princeton: D. Van Nostrand, 1960), 64. The best account of Soviet policy in China, the linchpin of the eastern strategy, is Dan N. Jacobs, *Borodin: Stalin's Man in China* (Cambridge: Harvard University Press, 1981).

14. Louis Fischer, *Men and Politics* (New York: Duell, Sloan and Pearce, 1941), 128. In a private conversation as early as February 1921, Litvinov asserted that in return for British economic aid and peace, London could have "security, as far as Russia was concerned, in Persia, India and Asia in general and that's a good deal" (letter from Simpson to Foreign Office, 1 March 1921, F.O. 371, 6854, N3573, 5, 38).

15. Valerii A. Shishkin, *"Polosa priznanii" i vneshneekonomicheskaia politika S.S.S.R. 1924–1928 gg* (Moscow: Nauka, 1983), 106–108.

16. Hodgson to MacDonald, 8 February 1924, *D.B.F.P.*, 1st series, 25:344.

17. Ibid.

18. Ibid., 25:345.

19. Gorodetsky, *Precarious Truce*, 16.

20. First plenary meeting of the London Anglo-Russian Conference, 14 April 1924, *D.B.F.P.*, 1st series, 25:464–466.

21. Ibid., 25:470.

22. Ibid., 25:470–471.

23. Record of conversation between the prime minister and Rakovskii and Litvinov, *D.B.F.P.*, 1st series, 25:543.

24. Ibid., 25:544.

25. *Pravda*, 28 June 1924.

26. Gorodetsky, *Precarious Truce*, 22–29, and Louis Fischer, *The Soviets in World Affairs*, 2 vols. (London: Jonathan Cape, 1930), 2:479–490.

27. Rakovskii to Litvinov, 19 January 1925, *D.V.P.*, 8:33–38.

28. Gorodetsky, *Precarious Truce*, 58, and Fischer, *Soviets in World Affairs*, 2:498.

29. Litvinov to Rozengoltz, 13 January 1926, *D.V.P.*, 9:24.

30. Jane Degras, ed., *Soviet Documents on Foreign Policy*, 3 vols. (Oxford: Oxford University Press, 1951–1953), 2:109.

31. Ibid., 2:110.

32. Adam Ulam, *Expansion and Coexistence* (New York: Praeger, 1974), 164.

33. Gorodetsky, *Precarious Truce*, 216.

34. An English employee of Arcos had told the police he had seen a British Army signals training pamphlet when it was being copied in Arcos (ibid., 221–222).

35. Note from the government of the USSR to the government of Great Britain, 17 May 1927, *D.V.P.*, 10:215.

36. Gorodetsky, *Precarious Truce*, 229–230.

37. Statement by Litvinov to representatives of the Soviet press, 26 May 1927, *D.V.P.*, 10:240–241.

38. Other than noting the hostility of Britain toward the Soviet Union, Litvinov played virtually no role in the war scare (see John P. Sontag, "The Soviet War Scare of 1926–1927," *Russian Review* 34 [January 1975]:66–77).

39. Richard K. Debo, "George Chicherin: Soviet Russia's Second Foreign Commissar" (Ph.D. dissertation, University of Nebraska, 1964), 313–315, and Gustav Hilger and Alfred G. Mayer, *The Incompatible Allies* (New York: Macmillan and Company, 1953), 229–230.

40. E. H. Carr, *German-Soviet Relations Between the Two World Wars* (Baltimore: Johns Hopkins Press, 1951), 79.

41. Memorandum of meeting between Litvinov and Radowitz, 17 October 1924, *D.V.P.*, 7:489–490.

42. Ibid., 7:490.

43. Ibid., 8:781, note 67. Article 16 provided for collective action against a state deemed an aggressor by the League (Francis P. Walters, *A History of the League of Nations* [Oxford: Oxford University Press, 1952], 51–52).

44. Hilger and Mayer, *Incompatible Allies*, 134.

45. Freund, *Unholy Alliance*, 213–214. It is ironic that Litvinov, upon gaining the leadership of the *Narkomindel*, would follow Stresemann's example of conciliation with the League, although Litvinov had to move much slower and against even greater opposition than Stresemann had faced.

46. Telegram from Litvinov to Soviet *polpred* in Germany, 26 August 1925, *D.V.P.*, 8:508.

47. Proposal of the Soviet government to the German government on the conclusion of a political agreement, 13 July 1925, ibid., 8:430–431.

48. Hilger and Mayer, *Incompatible Allies*, 145.

49. Ibid., 146.

50. Telegram from Krestinskii to Litvinov, 26 February 1926, *D.V.P.*, 9:137–138.

51. Hilger and Mayer, *Incompatible Allies*, 150.

52. Degras, ed., *Soviet Documents*, 2:107.

53. Jacques Nere, *The Foreign Policy of France from 1914 to 1945*, trans. Translance (London and Boston: Routledge and Kegan Paul, 1975), 63.

54. Max Beloff, *Foreign Policy of Soviet Russia, 1929–1941*, 2 vols. (New York: Oxford University Press, 1949), 1:123–125.

55. Note from Herriot to Kalinin, 28 October 1924, *D.V.P.*, 8:514–515.

56. Telegram from Chicherin to Herriot, 15 November 1924, ibid., 7:540, and Fischer, *Soviets in World Affairs*, 2:573.

57. Note from Herriot to Kalinin, 28 October 1924, *D.V.P.*, 7:515.

58. Lord Creive (Paris) to Chamberlain, 22 December 1924, *D.B.F.P.*, 1st series, 25:460.

59. Gorodetsky, *Precarious Truce*, 73–74, and Fischer, *Soviets in World Affairs*, 2:578.

60. A. A. Gromyko and B. N. Ponomarev, eds., *Istoriia vneshnei politiki SSSR 1917–1976*, 2 vols. (Moscow: Nauka, 1976), 2:207.

61. Memo of meeting between Litvinov and Herbette, 26 January 1925, *D.V.P.*, 8:99.

62. Ibid., 8:100.

63. Ibid.

64. Ibid., 8:101.

65. Memo of meeting between Litvinov and Herbette, 24 August 1926, ibid., 9:400–401. For the text of the treaty, see Arnold J. Toynbee, *Survey of International Affairs, 1926* (Oxford: Oxford University Press, 1928), 485–487.

66. Memo of meeting between Litvinov and Herbette, 22 September 1926, *D.V.P.*, 9:431–433.

67. For the position of the U.S. government, see press release issued by the State Department, 21 March 1923, F.R.U.S., *1923*, 2:757.

68. Letter from Litvinov to the unofficial representative of *Narkomindel* in the United States, B. E. Skvirskii, 13 January 1923, *D.V.P.*, 6:155–156, and letter from Litvinov to Skvirskii, 27 March 1923, ibid., 6:239.

69. Memo of meeting between Litvinov and the president of the New York Chamber of Commerce, 6 June 1923, ibid., 6:340–341. The reader should note that on 21 March 1923, the U.S. Secretary of State, Charles Evans Hughes, speaking specifically about the Soviet government had said: "Now the United States is not a harsh creditor. The U.S. is not seeking to press debtors who cannot pay beyond their means. But indulgence and proper arrangements are one things, repudiation quite another." (F.R.U.S., *1923*, 2:757).

70. Meeting between Litvinov and Bush, 6 June 1923, *D.V.P.*, 6:341.

71. Ibid.

72. Ibid., 6:342. There is no evidence in the published materials that Harding ever received such a report, although this by no means proves that Bush did not file one. My investigation of State Department archival materials relative to the 1930s and U.S. recognition of the Soviet Union revealed that the U.S. government was bombarded by ideas, suggestions, and even threats with regard to its policy regarding that nation.

73. For a brief biography of Goodrich, see James K. Libbey, *Alexander Gumberg and Soviet-American Relations, 1917–1933* (Lexington: University of Kentucky Press, 1977), 80–81.

74. James Goodrich to commissariat for foreign affairs, 11 January 1926, *D.V.P.*, 9:720, note 30.

75. Telegram from Litvinov to Rakovskii, 29 February 1926, ibid., 9:120.

76. Ibid., 9:120–121.

77. State Department Press Release, 4 November 1926, F.R.U.S., *1926*, 2:911.

78. Libbey, *Alexander Gumberg*, 170–174.

79. Chicherin's first Western biographer, who clearly respects the foreign commissar's considerable achievements, nonetheless recognizes that by 1926, Chicherin's policies had failed (Debo, "George Chicherin," 353–354; also see Timothy E. O'Connor, *Diplomacy and Revolution: G. V. Chicherin and Soviet Foreign Affairs, 1918–1930* [Ames: Iowa State University Press, 1988], 112).

80. Debo, "George Chicherin," 341.

81. Interview with Tatiana Litvinov, Brighton, England, 30–31 March 1981.

82. Fischer, *Men and Politics*, 147; Debo, "George Chicherin," 365. Chicherin's almost pathological hatred of the League of Nations must have received a mighty stimulus from Germany's entrance into that organization, an action Chicherin felt wrecked his cherished Rapallo connection.

83. See Litvinov to Dovgalevskii, 5 January 1926, *D.V.P.*, 9:10, for a succinct summary of this policy.

CHAPTER 7

1. George Kennan, *Soviet Foreign Policy, 1917–1941* (Princeton: D. Van Nostrand, 1960), 77; Jiri Hochman, *The Soviet Union and the Failure of Collective Security, 1934–1938* (Ithaca: Cornell University Press, 1984), 22; and Louis Fischer, *The Soviets in World Affairs*, 2 vols. (London: Jonathan Cape, 1930), 2:784.

2. Xenia J. Eudin and Robert M. Slusser, *Soviet Foreign Policy, 1928–1934, Documents and Materials* (University Park: Pennsylvania State University Press, 1966), 4.

3. Stalin at the plenum of the Central Committee of the party, 23 October 1927, in Xenia J. Eudin and Harold H. Fisher, *Soviet Russia and the West, 1920–1927, a Documentary Survey* (Stanford: Stanford University Press, 1957), 406. It must be noted that the German-Soviet Trade Agreement of 1925 provided Moscow with a credit of 100,000,000 reichsmarks, but the entire sum had to be repaid by 28 February 1926 at 8.5 percent interest. This type of arrangement was obviously of very limited benefit, and the Soviets constantly badgered the Germans for substantial long-term credits, which were not forthcoming. Stalin, when speaking of not getting any loans, obviously had in mind such long-term credits (Gustav Hilger and Alfred G. Mayer, *The Incompatible Allies* [New York: Macmillan and Company, 1953], 184–186).

4. Stalin's report to the Fifteenth Party Congress, 3 December 1927, in ibid., 408. Stalin's reference to "two tendencies" in the capitalist world was to be repeated by Litvinov in December 1933, although the positions of Britain and Germany would be reversed.

5. Ibid.

6. E. H. Carr, *Socialism in One Country, 1924–1926*, 3 vols. (New York: Macmillan Company, 1958–1964), 3:458. Litvinov was also acutely aware of the grave Soviet internal crisis and the consequent need for peace (see Michael Reiman, *The Birth of Stalinism: The USSR on the Eve of the "Second Revolution,"* trans. George Saunders [Bloomington: Indiana University Press,

1987] 138–142). I wish to thank Stephen Burant for bringing this information to my attention.

7. Carr, *Socialism in One Country*, 3:455. A useful survey of the early Soviet-League enmity is Donald Buzinkai, "Soviet-League Relations, 1920–1923: Political Disputes," *East European Quarterly* 13:1 (January 1980):25–45.

8. Kathryn W. Davis, *The Soviets at Geneva: The USSR and the League of Nations, 1919–1933* (Geneva: Librairie Kundig, 1934; reprint, Westport, Conn.: Hyperion Press, 1977), 297.

9. Telegram from Chicherin to General Secretary of the League of Nations Drummond, 15 December 1923, *D.V.P.*, 6:544.

10. Ibid.; Arnold J. Toynbee, *Survey of International Affairs, 1924* (Oxford: Oxford University Press, 1926), 78; and Davis, *The Soviets at Geneva*, 119.

11. Alfred Erich Senn, *Assassination in Switzerland: The Murder of Vatslov Vorovsky* (Madison: University of Wisconsin Press, 1981).

12. Alfred Erich Senn, "The Soviet Union's Road to Geneva, 1924–1927," *Jahrbucher für Geschichte Osteuropas* 27 (1979):69.

13. Ibid., 74–81.

14. Letter from Litvinov to Krestinskii, 19 March 1927, *D.V.P.*, 10:120, and Senn, "The Soviet Union's Road to Geneva," 79.

15. Senn, "The Soviet Union's Road to Geneva," 82. The fact that such bickering over language occurred reflects the lack of any compelling factors for a settlement. Relatively speaking, the second half of the 1920s was the most tranquil period of the interwar years.

16. Francis P. Walters, *A History of the League of Nations* (Oxford: Oxford University Press, 1952), 357.

17. Viktor M. Khaitsman, *SSSR i problema razoruzheniia mezhdu pervoi i vtoroi mirovymi voinami* (Moscow: Nauka, 1959), 177.

18. As late as 5 November, Stalin had reiterated that the Soviet Union "does not take part" in the League of Nations (Jane Degras, ed., *Soviet Documents on Foreign Policy*, 3 vols. (Oxford: Oxford University Press, 1951–1953), 2:274–275.

19. Ibid., 2:278. This remark is significant because it strongly implied that disarmament could be achieved only after the "system of wars" was abolished, a theory that placed Litvinov in a position virtually indistinguishable from the French policy of security first, then disarmament. Nonetheless, at the Preparatory Commission, Litvinov repeatedly ridiculed and rejected such an approach.

20. Ibid., 2:279.

21. Ibid., 2:280.

22. Ibid.

23. Most certainly the Germans were not surprised. In a Berlin meeting with Carl von Schubert (secretary of state 1924–1930), on 25 November, Litvinov told him the Soviet proposal would be for "complete disarmament" and, failing that, "partial disarmament" (Peter Grupp, general ed., *Akten zur deutschen auswartigen Politik 1918–1945*, Series B, 1925–1933 [Gottingen: Vandenhoeck and Ruprecht, 1974], 7:340; also see Leonard Harvey Dyck, *Weimer Germany and Soviet Russia, 1926–1933* [New York: Columbia University Press, 1966], 110).

24. John Carswell, *The Exile: A Life of Ivy Litvinov* (Boston: Faber and Faber, 1983), 113.

25. Arthur Upham Pope, *Maxim Litvinoff* (New York: L. B. Fischer, 1943), 223.

26. Aleksandr E. Ioffe, *Vneshniaia politika Sovetskogo Souiza, 1928–1932 gg* (Moscow: Nauka, 1968), 4.

27. League of Nations Secretariat, *Documents of the Preparatory Commission for the Disarmament Conference*, 11 vols. (Geneva: League of Nations, 1926–1931), 5:9 (hereafter cited as *Documents of the Preparatory Commission*). Litvinov's assertion that the profound postwar struggle of all countries "against imperialist wars . . . made it possible for the Soviet government" to participate in the Preparatory Commission's sessions totally ignores the serious obstacle of the Vorovskii affair. For a discussion of the actions (or inaction) of the Preparatory Commission before the arrival of the Soviet delegation, see Walters, *History of the League of Nations*, 361–370.

28. Documents of the Preparatory Commission, 5:10.

29. Ibid..

30. Fischer, *The Soviets in World Affairs*, 2:748.

31. *Documents of the Preparatory Commission*, 5:10–11.

32. Ibid., 5:11.

33. Ibid.

34. Ibid., 5:12.

35. Ibid.

36. Ibid.

37. Ibid., 5:18. At the same time, the commission voted to set up a Committee on Arbitration and Security. Asked by the president of the commission if the Soviet Union would participate in the new body, Litvinov refused, saying the committee would only divert attention from the "fundamental question of disarmament." The Soviet Union did, however, attach an observer to the committee (ibid., 5:19–20).

38. Ibid., 5:324–337.

39. Ibid., 5:239.

40. Litvinov refers here to the proposal that eventually became known as the Kellogg-Briand Pact, which is discussed in Chapter 8.

41. *Documents of the Preparatory Commission*, 5:241.

42. *F.R.U.S.*, *1928*, 1:243.

43. Ibid., 1:249, and *Documents of the Preparatory Commission*, 6:242–243.

44. *F.R.U.S.*, *1928*, 1:249.

45. Ibid.

46. *New York Times*, 21 March 1928.

47. Ibid.

48. *Documents of the Preparatory Commission*, 6:246.

49. Ibid., 6:250.

50. Telegram of Litvinov to *Narkomindel*, 23 March 1928, *D.V.P.*, 11:183.

51. *New York Times*, 21 March 1928, 6.

52. *Documents of the Preparatory Commission*, 6:285.

53. Ibid., 6:289.

54. For the text of the Soviet proposal, see ibid., 6:347–355.

55. Ibid., 6:347–348.

56. Ibid., 6:350–351.

57. Ibid., 6:351–352.

58. Ibid., 6:353.

59. Ibid., 6:354.

60. Ibid., 6:292–293, and Walters, *History of the League of Nations*, 368–369.

61. *Documents of the Preparatory Commission*, 6:295.

62. Ibid., 6:297–298.

63. Ibid., 6:299.

64. *New York Times*, 24 March 1928.

65. Ibid.

66. Telegram from Litvinov to *Narkomindel*, 25 March 1928, *D.V.P.*, 11:242. "The arrest of the engineers" referred to the imprisonment in Russia of five German employees of the German General Electric Corporation on charges of sabotage. Only one German was convicted, and he received a suspended sentence (Hilger and Mayer, *Incompatible Allies*, 217–220). It seems reasonable to assume that Litvinov's point in mentioning the affair at all was to underscore the need to end it before it further damaged German-Soviet relations.

67. Degras, ed., *Soviet Documents*, 2:304–309.

68. Ibid., 2:301–312.

69. Carswell, *The Exile*, 116–117.

70. Ibid., 118–119.

CHAPTER 8

1. Leonard Harvey Dyck, *Weimar Germany and Soviet Russia, 1926–1933* (New York: Columbia University Press, 1966), 111.

2. Jacques Nere, *The Foreign Policy of France from 1914 to 1945*, trans. Translance (London and Boston: Routledge and Kegan Paul, 1975), 86.

3. Robert D. Schulzinger, *American Diplomacy in the Twentieth Century* (New York: Oxford University Press, 1984), 137.

4. Jane Degras, ed., *Soviet Documents on Foreign Policy*, 3 vols. (Oxford: Oxford University Press, 1951–1953), 2:311–312.

5. State Department Press Statement, 27 August 1928, F.R.U.S., 1928, 1:131.

6. Memo of meeting between Litvinov and Herbette, 29 August 1928, *D.V.P.*, 11:489–490.

7. Aleksandr E. Ioffe, *Vneshniaia politika Sovetskogo Souiza, 1928–1932 gg* (Moscow: Nauka, 1968), 43.

8. Louis Fischer, *The Soviets in World Affairs*, 2 vols. (London: Jonathan Cape, 1930), 2:775.

9. Ioffe, *Vneshniaia politika*, 43.

10. Robert H. Ferrell, *Peace in Their Time: The Origins of the Kellogg-Briand Pact* (New Haven: Yale University Press, 1952), 261.

11. *D.V.P.*, 11:755, note 221.

12. Telegram from Litvinov to Rabinovich, 24 December 1928, ibid., 11:633.

13. Fischer, *Soviets in World Affairs*, 2:782.

14. Telegram from Litvinov to Rabinovich, 24 December 1928.

15. Bohdan B. Budurowycz, *Polish-Soviet Relations, 1932–1939* (New York: Columbia University Press, 1963), 6–7. For the text of the Soviet-Turkish Treaty of Friendship and Neutrality, see *D.V.P.*, 8:739–741.

16. Telegram from Litvinov to the chargé in France, 5 March 1926, *D.V.P.*, 9:152.

17. Memo of meeting between Litvinov and Patek, 29 December 1928, ibid., 11:639. The already poor relations had been further worsened by an attempt on the life of the Soviet trade representative in Warsaw in May 1928. Only eleven months had separated this event and the murder of *polpred* P. L. Voikov in Warsaw (ibid., 11:299).

18. Ibid., 11:639.

19. Ibid.

20. *Izvestiia*, 1 January 1929.

21. Litvinov himself emphasized to the French the peaceful and limited aims of the protocol (memo of meeting between Litvinov and Herbette, 29

December 1928, *D.V.P.*, 11:647–648). It can scarcely be doubted that the French, in turn, reassured the Poles.

22. Peter Grupp, general ed., *Akten zur deutschen auswärtigen Politik 1918–1945*, Series B, 1925–1933 (Gottingen: Vandenhoeck and Ruprecht, 1974), 11:53.

23. Brockdorff-Rantzau had died in December 1928.

24. Herbert von Dirksen, *Moscow, Tokyo, London: Twenty Years of German Foreign Policy* (New York: Hutchinson and Company, 1951), 94.

25. Memo of meeting between Litvinov and von Dirksen, 19 January 1929, *D.V.P.*, 12:37–38, and Dyck, *Weimar Germany*, 113.

26. Dyck, *Weimar Germany*, 113.

27. Polish foreign minister to *Narkomindel*, 10 January 1929, *D.V.P.*, 12:26.

28. Litvinov note to the Polish chargé, 11 January 1929, ibid., 12:24. The original signatories of the Litvinov Protocol were the Soviet Union, Poland, Romania, Latvia, and Estonia. Danzig, Lithuania, Persia, and Turkey subsequently adhered (Budurowycz, *Polish-Soviet Relations*, 7).

29. *New York Times*, 10 February 1929.

30. Budurowycz, *Polish-Soviet Relations*, 7–9.

31. Josef Korbel, *Poland Between East and West: Soviet and German Diplomacy Toward Poland, 1919–1933* (Princeton: Princeton University Press, 1963), 252.

32. *Documents of the Preparatory Commission*, 8:37.

33. Francis P. Walters, *A History of the League of Nations* (Oxford: Oxford University Press, 1952), 376.

34. Johann Bernsdorff, *Memoirs of Count Bernsdorff*, trans. Eric Sutton (New York: Random House, 1936), 362.

35. For a summary of this conflict, which began with a raid on the Soviet consulate in Harbin in May and the seizure of the Chinese Eastern Railroad, see Akira Iriye, *After Imperialism: The Search for a New Order in the Far East, 1921–1931* (Cambridge: Harvard University Press, 1965), 264–268. For Karakhan's crisis management, see the following documents in *D.V.P.*, 11: document numbers 334–337, 342, 362–363, 380–386, 388–392, 426–428, 463–464, 493, 530, 548–549, and 564–566.

36. *F.R.U.S.*, *1929*, 2:350–351.

37. Ibid., 2:405–406.

38. William N. Medlicott, *British Foreign Policy Since Versailles, 1919–1963* (London: Methuen and Company, 1968), 83–87, and A. A. Gromyko and B. N. Ponomarev, eds., *Istoriia vneshnei politiki SSSR 1917–1976*, 2 vols. (Moscow: Nauka, 1976), 1:256–257.

39. Note from Karakhan to the Norwegian chargé, 23 July 1929, *D.V.P.*, 11:407–408.

40. John Carswell, *The Exile: A Life of Ivy Litvinov* (Boston: Faber and Faber, 1983), 116–117.

41. Degras, ed., *Soviet Documents*, 1:396.

42. Ibid., 1:398–399.

43. Ibid.

44. Ovey to Henderson, 23 December 1929, F.O. 371, 14040, N6119, 55, 38.

45. Ovey to Foreign Office, 16 December 1929, F.O. 371, 14036, N6121, 18, 38. In a 1929 conversation with Ambassador Urbye of Norway, Litvinov sadly conceded that "the Comintern is of no use to us" (Lindley to Foreign Office, 10 June 1929, F.O. 371, 14039, N2840, 55, 38).

46. Ovey to Henderson, 25 February 1930, F.O. 371, 14860, N1404, 75, 38. In 1937, Litvinov still urged the capitalist countries to do as they wished with native Communists. He told Paris that Moscow "would view with complete equanimity the trial of [the French Communists] Thorez, Duclos and others of the same breed" (telegram from Lloyd Thomas [Paris] to Foreign Office, 27 April 1937, F.O. 371, 20702, C3753, 532, 62). Litvinov later emphasized that "all that interested Russia was the military alliance with France" (memo by Dutton [Paris], 17 June 1937, F.O. 371, 20686, C4517, 18, 17).

47. Ovey to Oliphant, 4 April 1930, F.O. 371, 14835, N2463, 12, 38.

48. Ibid.

49. Sir Leith Ross to Aliston Gwatkin (Office of the Exchequer), 26 May 1931, F.O. 371, 15596, N3657, 51, 38, and Medlicott, *British Foreign Policy*, 86–87.

50. See the "Chronology of Events" in Arnold J. Toynbee, *Survey of International Affairs, 1930* (Oxford: Oxford University Press, 1933), 553–574, and Toynbee, *Survey of International Affairs, 1931* (Oxford: Oxford University Press, 1931), 509–528.

51. Medlicott, *British Foreign Policy*, 99.

52. Schulzinger, *American Diplomacy in the Twentieth Century*, 151–153.

53. Interview with Tatiana Litvinov, Brighton, England, 30–31 March 1981, and Carswell, *The Exile*, 109.

54. Interview with Tatiana Litvinov. On Stalin's fear of war, see his famous speech of February 1931 in which he listed many of Russia's past military defeats, from the "Turkish beys" to the "Japanese barons." It was because of this military weakness, made even worse by the economic and political tensions between the Soviet Union and the rest of the world since 1917, that the country must spare no effort to industrialize and catch up. Stalin predicted that the Soviet Union had ten years to accomplish this task or it would face another defeat. Ten years and four months later, Nazi

Germany attacked (I. V. Stalin, *Works*, 13 vols. [Moscow: Foreign Languages Publishing House, 1954-1955], 13:40-41).

55. Interview with Tatiana Litvinov, who also speculates that Stalin may have actually respected her father's "openness and ability."

56. Ibid.

57. Ivy Litvinov Papers, Hoover Institution Archives, Stanford University, Box 6, Fragment, n.d.

58. Ilya Ehrenburg, *Post-War Years, 1945-1954*, trans. Tatiana Shebunina (Cleveland and New York: World Publishing Company, 1967), 278.

59. Ibid. In separate interviews with me, Litvinov's son, daughter, and an acquaintance Evgenii Gnedin dismissed this story as incredible. They all agreed that one did not do such things to Stalin (interviews with Tatiana Litvinov; Mikhail Litvinov, Moscow, 3 November 1982; and Evgenii Gnedin, Moscow, 3 November 1982). In other discussions with Soviet citizens and scholars from August 1982 to June 1983, I was unable to find anyone who could believe this incident ever took place.

60. Max Beloff, *Foreign Policy of Soviet Russia, 1929-1941*, 2 vols. (New York: Oxford University Press, 1949).

61. Max Beloff, "Soviet Foreign Policy, 1929-1941: Some Notes," *Soviet Studies* 11 (October 1950):127.

62. Adam Ulam, *Expansion and Coexistence* (New York: Praeger, 1974), 144, 204.

63. Jonathan Haslam, *Soviet Foreign Policy, 1930-1933* (New York: St. Martin's Press, 1983), 118.

64. Louis Fischer, *Russia's Road from Peace to War, 1917-1941* (New York: Harper and Row, 1969), 290.

65. Gustav Hilger and Alfred G. Mayer, *The Incompatible Allies* (New York: Macmillan and Company, 1953), 113.

66. Interview with Tatiana Litvinov.

67. Interview with Vladimir Trukhanovskii, Moscow, 19 October 1982.

68. Interview with Evgenii Gnedin; also see A. Meerovich, "V Narkomindele, 1922-1939: Interv'iu s E. A. Gnedinym," *Pamiat* 5 (1982):365-366. I discussed these points briefly with Gnedin, who said that he had given more information to Meerovich, which could be found in the *Pamiat* interview. Recently, Soviet historian V. M. Kulish essentially confirmed Gnedin's account of the consolidation of Stalin's control of foreign policy in the second half of the 1930s (V. M. Kulish, "U poroga viony," *Komsomolskaia pravda*, 24 August 1988, 3).

69. Maxim M. Litvinov, *Vneshniaia politika SSSR: Rechi i zaiavleniia 1927-1935* (Moscow: State Social-Economic Publishing House, 1935), 51-53. This collection consists of speeches and statements, all of which are available elsewhere, but it is useful for any study of Litvinov's public statements.

70. Ibid.

71. The campaign against Soviet dumping originated in Paris because such a practice was seriously hurting the agricultural economies of France's European allies to the east (Nere, *The Foreign Policy of France*, 101).

72. Gromyko and Ponomarev, eds., *Istoriia vneshnei politiki*, 2:263.

73. Degras, ed., *Soviet Documents*, 2:466.

74. Beloff, *Foreign Policy of Soviet Russia*, 1:40. The self-inflicted domestic tragedies of this time did not help.

75. This commission was the idea of Aristide Briand and was intended to discuss such matters as a European customs union, European stamps, and European coinage. Like other ideas and projects, it was wrecked by the blast of economic nationalism during the Great Depression (Walters, *History of the League of Nations*, 430–434). For Litvinov's almost comically complex reply to the Soviet Union's invitation to attend the commission, see Degras, ed., *Soviet Documents*, 2:492–494.

76. Maxim M. Litvinov, *The Soviet Dumping Fable* (New York: Workers' Library, 1931), 5–7. The Soviets considered the 1929 Young Plan for German reparation payments no solution at all, especially considering the rapid deterioration of the German economy and therefore of Germany's ability to pay (Degras, ed., *Soviet Documents*, 2:465).

77. Litvinov, *The Soviet Dumping Fable*, 14–16.

78. Ibid., 16–17.

79. Ibid., 25.

80. Degras, ed., *Soviet Documents*, 2:500–501.

81. Gromyko and Ponomarev, eds., *Istoriia vneshnei politiki*, 2:266, and Haslam, *Soviet Foreign Policy*, 52.

CHAPTER 9

1. Payart to Herriot, 19 October 1932, Ministere des Affaires Etrangeres, *Documents diplomatiques francais, 1932–1939*, 1st series, 8 vols. (Paris: Imprimerie Nationale, 1964–1981), 1:492 (henceforth cited as *D.D.F.*).

2. Leonard Harvey Dyck, *Weimar Germany and Soviet Russia, 1926–1933* (New York: Columbia University Press, 1966), 235, 244. As of the fall of 1930, at least two-fifths of the Reichstag deputies were openly committed to the destruction of the republic. The Nazis alone received almost one-third of the total votes in the September 1930 election (Raymond J. Sontag, *A Broken World, 1919–1939* [New York: Harper and Row, 1971], 160–161).

3. Telegram from Litvinov to Khinchuk, 25 March 1931, *D.V.P.*, 14:222, and A. Akhtamzian, *Rapall'skaia politika, 1922–1932* (Moscow: Mezhdunarodyne otnosheniia, 1974), 287.

4. Dyck, *Weimar Germany*, 237–252.

5. It must always be borne in mind, however, that Litvinov and *Narkomindel* were only one aspect of Soviet foreign policy. The other, the Comintern, which lies outside the limits of this book, aroused nothing but antagonism and suspicion in foreign capitals. Litvinov clearly realized this fact but could do nothing about it.

6. Memo of meeting between Litvinov and Herbette, 26 February 1930, *D.V.P.*, 13:111.

7. Memo of meeting between Litvinov and Herbette, 10 March 1931, ibid., 14:172-174. In this conversation, Litvinov's efforts to conciliate France went to extremes. For example, he asserted that although France had played a more active role in the foreign intervention after the revolution, he nonetheless considered Britain the real culprit.

8. Jacques Nere, *The Foreign Policy of France from 1914 to 1945*, trans. Translance (London and Boston: Routledge and Kegan Paul, 1975), 90-91.

9. Telegram from Dovgalevskii to *Narkomindel*, 20 April 1931, *D.V.P.*, 14:252.

10. Ibid.

11. Letter from Dovgalevskii to Krestinskii, 21 April 1931, ibid., 14:254-256. In fact, the Soviet Union had proposed such a pact five times (Iurii V. Borisov, *Sovetsko-Frantsuzskie otnosheniia, 1924-1945 gg* [Moscow: Mezhdunarodnye otnosheniia, 1964] 163).

12. Telegram from Litvinov to Dovgalevskii, 22 April 1931, *D.V.P.*, 14:266.

13. Ibid.

14. Jane Degras, ed., *Soviet Documents on Foreign Policy*, 3 vols. (Oxford: Oxford University Press, 1951-1953), 2:80. The occasion for this policy statement was the conclusion of the Soviet-Turkish Nonaggression Treaty.

15. Telegram from Ovey to Henderson, 26 July 1931, *D.B.F.P.*, 2d series, 7:215, and telegram from Ovey to Arthur Henderson, 28 July 1931, ibid., 7:216. It is interesting that Litvinov deplored the chance of a "fascist" takeover in Germany even though the Soviet Union got along well with fascist Italy. But he was familiar with Hitler's ideas of *lebensraum* and a racial "hierarchy."

16. Telegram from Dovgalevskii to *Narkomindel*, 10 August 1931, *D.V.P.*, 14:452-455. The talks for a commercial treaty broke down over the old problem of repudiated debts and other claims (memo of meeting between Litvinov and the French chargé, 22 August 1931, *D.V.P.*, 14:482).

17. Memo of meeting between Litvinov and the French chargé, 22 August 1931.

18. Chargé Strang (Moscow) to Secretary of State for Foreign Affairs, 25 August 1931, *D.B.F.P.*, 2d series, 7:218-219. The United Press broke the story, but apparently the leaks resulted from the need to inform many governments of the change in Franco-Soviet relations.

19. Dovgalevskii to *Narkomindel*, 23 September 1931, *D.V.P.*, 14:535–536.

20. Memo of Litvinov discussion with Massigli (a French diplomat at the League of Nations), September 1931, ibid., 14:817, note 195.

21. Josef Beck, *Dernier Rapport; Politique polonaise 1926–1936* (Neuchatel: Editions de la Baconniere, 1951), 10, cited by William Evans Scott, *Alliance Against Hitler* (Durham: Duke University Press, 1962), 31; also I. V. Mikhutina, "Sovetsko-pol'skii pakt o nenapadenii i vneshniaia politika Pol'shi v 1931–1932 gg." in *Sovetsko-pol'skie otnosheniia, 1918–1945*, ed. I. I. Kostiushko et al. (Moscow: Nauka, 1974), 137–138.

22. Memo of meeting between Litvinov and A. Zelezinskii, 14 October 1931, in I. A. Khrenov, chief ed., *Dokumenty i materialy po istorii sovetsko-pol'skhikh otnoshenii*, 6 vols. (Moscow: Nauka, 1964–1970), 2:501.

23. I. V. Mikhutina, "Sovetsko-pol'skii pakt," 149–165. It was not Litvinov's style to become enmeshed in all the details of Soviet negotiations. As he said to his longtime friend and colleague, Ivan Maisky, "The Commissariat gives you general instructions on serious problems; your job is to know how to translate these directives into practice—that is why you have a brain in your head" (Ivan Maisky, *Liude, sobytii, fakty* [Moscow: Mezhdunarodyne otnoshenii, 1973], 138). After talks began with France and Poland, similar pacts between the Soviet Union and the following states were signed: Finland, 21 January 1931; Estonia, 4 May 1932; Poland, 25 July 1932; France, 29 November 1932 (Nere, *Foreign Policy of France*, 159, and J. A. Large, "The Origins of the Soviet Collective Security Policy, 1930–1932," *Soviet Studies* 30 [April 1978]:224).

24. Memo of meeting between Litvinov and Hirota, 22 September 1931, *D.V.P.*, 14:531–532.

25. Memo of meeting between Litvinov and Strang, 24 September 1931, ibid., 14:537–538.

26. Degras, ed., *Soviet Documents*, 2:510–513.

27. Memo of meeting between Litvinov and Yoshizawa, 31 December 1931, *D.V.P.*, 14:746–747.

28. Ovey to Simon, 14 January 1932, *D.B.F.P.*, 2d series, 7:227–228.

29. A. A. Gromyko and B. N. Ponomarev, eds., *Istoriia vneshnei politiki SSSR 1917–1976*, 2 vols. (Moscow: Nauka, 1976), 1:279–280. The sale, however, was not completed until 1935.

30. Ovey to Simon, 14 January 1932, *D.B.F.P.*, 2d series, 7:227.

31. Francis P. Walters, *A History of the League of Nations* (Oxford: Oxford University Press, 1952), 501.

32. Ibid.

33. Maxim M. Litvinov et al., *The Soviets Fight for Disarmament* (New York: International Publishers, n.d.), 11, 13.

34. Nere, *Foreign Policy of France*, 119.

35. Litvinov et al., *Soviets Fight for Disarmament*, 15, 18. In fairness to Litvinov, it must be noted that his later advocacy for a definition of aggression came after an openly militarist and anti-Soviet regime had come to power in Germany. Nonetheless, it is hard to find much in Litvinov's February remarks that could be construed as promoting a feasible disarmament for Europe.

36. Alexander DeConde, *A History of American Foreign Policy*, 3d ed., 2 vols. (New York: Charles Scribner's Sons, 1978), 2:112.

37. Degras, ed., *Soviet Documents*, 2:529–530.

38. Litvinov et al., *Soviets Fight for Disarmament*, 20–21.

39. Telegram from Litvinov to *Narkomindel*, 12 February 1932, *D.V.P.*, 15:111.

40. Walters, *History of the League of Nations*, 506–507. Walters writes that this arrangement among Germany, Britain, the United States, and Italy was worked out in secret. There is no evidence in the official documents that Litvinov knew of it, but total ignorance on his part is difficult to believe because Litvinov frequently met with U.S., German, and Italian delegates (see *D.V.P.*, 15:178–348).

41. Scott, *Alliance Against Hitler*, 49–51.

42. Telegram from Khinchuk to *Narkomindel*, 27 June 1932, *D.V.P.*, 15:390.

43. Memo of meeting with Eden, 28 March 1935, ibid., 17:232.

44. Walters, *History of the League of Nations*, 508.

45. Ibid., 509.

46. Letter from Litvinov to Krestinskii, 23 June 1932, *D.V.P.*, 15:381–382.

47. Walters, *History of the League of Nations*, 510. Litvinov believed that French policy had mainly resulted in France's isolation at Geneva (letter from Litvinov to Krestinskii, *D.V.P.*, 15:382).

48. Walters, *History of the League of Nations*, 512.

49. Ibid., 515. Litvinov was not consulted (telegram from Litvinov to *Narkomindel*, 11 December 1932, *D.V.P.*, 15:679).

50. Walters, *History of the League of Nations*, 515.

51. Dejean to Paul-Boncour, 19 December 1932, *D.D.F.*, 1st series, 2:283–284.

52. Jonathan Haslam, *Soviet Foreign Policy, 1930–1933* (New York: St. Martin's Press, 1983), 95.

53. See A.J.P. Taylor, *The Origins of the Second World War*, 2d ed. (New York: Fawcett, 1966).

54. Gerhard Weinberg, *The Foreign Policy of Hitler's Germany: Diplomatic Revolution in Europe 1933–36* (Chicago: University of Chicago Press, 1970), 4–6.

55. Ibid., 6.

56. Ibid., 12.

57. Ibid., 13–14.

58. Ibid., 4, 16.

59. Ibid., 15–16. Litvinov, of course, was well aware of the essence of Hitler's thought (see, for example, memo of meeting between Litvinov and Eden, 28 March 1935, *D.V.P.*, 18:233.

60. Weinberg, *Foreign Policy of Hitler's Germany*, 8.

CHAPTER 10

1. William Evans Scott, *Alliance Against Hitler* (Durham: Duke University Press, 1962), 107.

2. Litvinov's speech at the Disarmament Conference, 6 February, 1933, *D.V.P.*, 15:73–75. The French proposal to which Litvinov was responding consisted of a "maximum" and a "minimum" plan for Europe. The former provided for "replacing permanent national forces with organically international forces" under control of the League. The "minimum" plan proposed that part of each state's armed forces was to be at the disposal of the League (Jacques Nere, *The Foreign Policy of France from 1914 to 1945*, trans. Translance [London and Boston: Routledge and Kegan Paul, 1975], 121).

3. Litvinov's speech at the Disarmament Conference, 6 February 1933, *D.V.P.*, 15:77.

4. Ibid., 15:80–81.

5. Ibid., 15:81.

6. Telegram from Litvinov to *Narkomindel*, 6 February 1933, ibid., 16:84.

7. Telegram from Dejean to Paul-Boncour, 11 April 1933, *D.D.F.*, 1st series, 3:206–207. Litvinov added significantly that the independence of the Baltic states was of "extreme importance" to the USSR.

8. Scott, *Alliance Against Hitler*, 109.

9. Jane Degras, ed., *Soviet Documents on Foreign Policy*, 3 vols. (Oxford: Oxford University Press, 1951–1953), 3:30–31.

10. Telegram from Litvinov to *Narkomindel*, 6 July 1933, *D.V.P.*, 16:416–417. The Soviet Union had just signed similar protocols with Persia, Afghanistan, Turkey, Poland, Romania, Yugoslavia, Czechoslovakia, Lithuania, Latvia, and Estonia (see ibid., 16:388–392, 403–406, and 408–411). Litvinov negotiated these pacts while at the London World Economic Conference; their importance was largely symbolic.

11. Telegram from Litvinov to *Narkomindel*, 6 July 1933, ibid., 16:417.

12. Scott, *Alliance Against Hitler*, 117.

13. Telegram from Litvinov to Stalin, 6 July 1933, *D.V.P.*, 16:846, note 172.

14. Ibid., 16:118–120.

15. Letter from Litvinov to Rozenberg, 19 September 1933, ibid., 16:521.

16. Memo of meeting between Litvinov and Cot, 20 September 1933, ibid., 16:523.

17. Scott, *Alliance Against Hitler*, 121. Scott's source was Joseph Paul-Boncour's memoirs, *Entre Deux Guerres*. Also see Elizabeth R. Cameron, "Alexis Saint-Leger Leger," in *The Diplomats*, ed. Gordon A. Craig and Felix Gilbert (Princeton: Princeton University Press, 1953), 383. The British also believed that Litvinov had made such a proposal (see Sir G. Clark to Sir J. Simon, 14 June 1934, *D.B.F.P.*, 2d series, 6:754), but Litvinov asserted that the suggestion for an alliance came from Paris. Indeed, even in 1935, the commissar maintained in a conversation with Anthony Eden that the pact was Paul-Boncour's idea (see telegram from Litvinov to *Narkomindel*, 31 October 1933, *D.V.P.*, 16:595, and memo between meeting of Litvinov and Eden, 28 March 1935, *D.V.P.*, 18:234).

18. Telegram from Alphand to Paul-Boncour, 28 September 1933, *D.D.F.*, 1st series, 4:432–433.

19. Telegram from Dovgalevskii to *Narkomindel*, 20 October 1933, *D.V.P.*, 16:577.

20. Telegram from Litvinov to *Narkomindel*, 31 October 1933, ibid., 16:595.

21. Ibid., and Scott, *Alliance Against Hitler*, 135–136.

22. Telegram from Litvinov to *Narkomindel*, 6 February 1933, *D.V.P.*, 16:84.

23. Memo by Neurath, 1 March 1933, in Paul R. Sweet, chief ed., *Documents on German Foreign Policy, 1918–1945*, Series C, 16 vols. (Washington, D.C.: Government Printing Office, 1957–1983), 1:91–92 (hereafter cited as *D.G.F.P.*).

24. Ibid., 1:92. Neurath was absolutely correct. As late as 19 December 1932, Litvinov had made such assurances to him (see E. H. Carr, *Twilight of the Comintern, 1930–1935* [New York: Pantheon Books, 1982], 80–81; Carr's source was a memo from the unpublished German Foreign Ministry Archives).

25. Telegram from Dirksen to the Foreign Ministry, 11 March 1933, *D.G.F.P.*, Series C, 1:144. It is interesting to note that one of France's main goals in signing a pact with Moscow was to prevent a German-Soviet rapprochement. Little wonder that an "alliance" with such negative goals never accomplished much.

26. Memo of meeting between Litvinov and Neurath, 13 June 1934, *D.V.P.*, 17:386–387.

27. *Pravda*, 10 May 1933.

28. *Izvestiia*, 6 August 1933.

29. Ibid., 9 August 1933.

30. Ibid., 12 September 1933.

31. For an excellent survey of the Soviet "skeptics" with regard to the rapprochement with France and the subsequent collective security campaign, see Paul Raymond, "Conflict and Consensus in Soviet Foreign Policy, 1933–1939" (Ph.D. dissertation, Pennsylvania State University, 1979), Chapter 4.

32. Robert Paul Browder, *The Origins of Soviet-American Diplomacy* (Princeton: Princeton University Press, 1953), 95.

33. Arthur Upham Pope, *Maxim Litvinoff* (New York: L. B. Fischer, 1943), 293.

34. Orville Bullitt, ed., *For the President, Personal and Secret: Correspondence Between Franklin D. Roosevelt and William C. Bullitt* (Boston: Houghton Mifflin Company, 1972), 43–50.

35. Z. S. Sheinis, "Vashingtonskaia missiia," *Moskva* 9 (1967):185–186.

36. Ibid., 186.

37. Bullitt, ed., *For the President*, 49.

38. Sheinis, "Vashingtonskaia," 186.

39. Bullitt, ed., *For the President*, 48.

40. *F.R.U.S., The Soviet Union, 1933–1939*, 26–27.

41. Ibid., 28–29.

42. Ibid., 31–33.

43. Telegram from Litvinov to *Narkomindel*, 17 November 1933, *D.V.P.*, 16:658–659. U.S. sources make no mention of such a discussion.

44. Beatrice Farnsworth, *William C. Bullitt and the Soviet Union* (Bloomington and London: Indiana University Press, 1967), 166.

45. Joseph C. Grew, *Ten Years in Japan* (New York: Simon and Schuster, 1944), 107.

46. Letter from Litvinov to Troianovskii, 10 April 1934, *D.V.P.*, 17:243.

47. Bullitt, ed., *For the President*, 67.

48. *F.R.U.S., The Soviet Union, 1933–1939*, 61.

49. Ibid.

50. Bullitt, ed., *For the President*, 71.

51. *F.R.U.S., The Soviet Union, 1933–1939*, 67.

52. Ibid.

53. Louis Fischer, *Russia's Road from Peace to War, 1917–1941* (New York: Harper and Row, 1969), 218.

54. Telegram from Troianovskii to the Central Committee, 23 February 1934, *D.V.P.*, 17:163–164.

55. Bullitt, ed., *For the President*, 83.

56. Adam Ulam, *Expansion and Coexistence* (New York: Praeger, 1974), 217.

57. Interview with Tatiana Litvinov, Brighton, England, 30–31 March 1981.

58. Memo of meeting between Davies and Litvinov, 3 March 1938, Joseph Davies Papers, Box 7, Manuscript Division, U.S. National Archives.

59. Telegram from John Wiley (Riga) to the secretary of state, 10 December 1938, National Archives Microfilm Publication Number T1241. Wiley noted that E. L. Packer had "recently" received this information from Duranty.

CHAPTER 11

1. Litvinov telegram to Dovgalevskii, 11 December 1933, *D.V.P.*, 16:735–736. Soviet-Italian relations were quite cordial at the time, as in September 1933, the two governments had signed a Treaty of Friendship, Nonaggression, and Neutrality. The issue for Russia was not fascism, but Hitler's wild ambitions (ibid., 16:494–495).

2. Telegram from de Chambrun to Paul-Boncour, 5 December 1933, *D.D.F.*, 1st series, 5:160–161.

3. Telegram from Alphand to Paul-Boncour, 4 January 1934, ibid., 1st series, 5:400–401.

4. Memo of meeting between Litvinov and Nadolny, 13 December 1933, *D.V.P.*, 16:741.

5. Ibid., 16:742. It should be noted that Hitler quite agreed with Litvinov that a Soviet-German rapprochement was impossible in 1933. The fuehrer had told Nadolny in May 1933 that he was willing to deal with Britain, "but he wanted nothing to do with Russia" (Rudolf Nadolny, *Mein Beitrag* [Wiesbaden: Limes Verlag, 1955], 167).

6. *D.V.P.*, 16:876, note 321; interview with Vladimir Trukhanovskii, Moscow, 19 October 1982; and A. A. Gromyko and B. N. Ponomarev, eds., *Istoriia vneshnei politiki SSSR 1917–1976*, 2 vols. (Moscow: Nauka, 1976), 1:308. In addition, two Soviet specialists with archival access have written that in "mid-December 1933, the People's Commissariat for Foreign Affairs drew up proposals for a system of collective security in Europe" (M. Andreyeva and L. Vidyasova, eds, "The Struggle of the USSR for Collective Security in Europe, 1933–1935," *International Affairs* [June 1963]:109).

7. *D.V.P.*, 16:877, note 321. The Soviets also understandably wanted the establishment of normal relations between their country and all League members, or at least an expression of willingness to do so. The French considered this desire an "insurmountable obstacle," and the Russians backed

down (Jiri Hochman, *The Soviet Union and the Failure of Collective Security, 1934–1938* [Ithaca: Cornell University Press, 1984], 41–42).

8. *D.V.P.*, 16:877, note 321. Both sides also agreed to maintain absolute secrecy until an agreement could be ironed out.

9. Writing from Moscow at this time, Lord Chilston remarked that a mutual assistance pact between Moscow and Paris would "contradict the basic principles of Soviet policy" and was conceivable only if the Russians "are really afraid of German aggression" (telegram from Chilston to the Foreign Office, 30 December 1933, F.O. 371, 18297, N1, 1, 38).

10. Litvinov to the Central Committee, 29 December 1933, *D.V.P.*, 16:782–783.

11. Ibid., 16:784.

12. Ibid., 16:784–785. This is a clear reference to France's refusal to cooperate with the Soviets against the Japanese.

13. Jonathan Haslam, *The Soviet Union and the Struggle for Collective Security in Europe, 1933–1939* (New York: St. Martin's Press, 1984), 30.

14. Litvinov to the Central Committee, *D.V.P.*, 16:788. Litvinov was hardly correct with respect to the last point. The "objective" basis for poor Anglo-Soviet relations was the recently settled "Metro-Vickers Affair," in which several British engineers in Russia had been arrested for espionage and sabotage. The sabotage charge was most likely groundless, but the espionage charge, especially by Soviet definitions, was more substantial (Haslam, *The Soviet Union*, 16–19). That the British government was enraged and disgusted cannot be doubted (Great Britain, Public Record Office, Cabinet Conclusions, Series 23 [33] item 2, 5 April 1933 [hereafter cited as *Cabinet 23*]).

15. Litvinov to the Central Committee, *D.V.P.*, 16:792–793.

16. Ibid., 16:793.

17. Adam Ulam, *Expansion and Coexistence* (New York: Praeger, 1974), p. 217. The Soviet documents indicate that these talks were handled mostly by Deputy Commissar for Far Eastern Affairs Lev Karakhan (for example, see telegram from Karakhan to Iurenev, 25 January 1934, *D.V.P.*, 17:69–70).

18. Telegram from Chilston to Foreign Office, 30 December 1933, F.O. 371, 18297, N1, 1, 38.

19. Jane Degras, ed. *Soviet Documents on Foreign Policy*, 3 vols. (Oxford: Oxford University Press, 1951–1953), 3:70–71. At the same party congress, Litvinov was elevated to membership in the Central Committee, further evidence of the party's disapproval of Hitler's policy.

20. William Evans Scott, *Alliance Against Hitler* (Durham: Duke University Press, 1962), 154–175. Also at this time, Litvinov fell ill and eventually had to be hospitalized (memo of meeting between Litvinov and Bullitt, 18 and 21 March 1934, *D.V.P.*, 17:193).

21. Scott, *Alliance Against Hitler*, 156.

22. Ibid., 157.

23. Interview with Tatiana Litvinov, Brighton, England, 30–31 March 1981.

24. Memo of meeting between Litvinov and Beck, 13–15 February 1934, *D.V.P.*, 17:132–133.

25. Ibid., 7:135.

26. Haslam, *The Soviet Union*, 42, and Scott, *Alliance Against Hitler*, 159. Almost ten years later, Litvinov was still infuriated with Beck, telling a British politician that "Poland, more than any other country, was responsible for the war. Beck has always been pro-Nazi" (memorandum by Lord Marley, 9 June 1943, U.S. National Archives, Record Group 59, Miscellaneous Files: "EUR/EE"; it is a pleasure to acknowledge that Ronald D. Landa of the Office of the Secretary of Defense Historical Office brought this document to my attention). Writing in the Soviet press during the war, Litvinov blasted Poland for basing its policy in the 1930s on "stupid dreams" of reviving Poland as it had existed in the eighteenth century (N. Malinin [pseudonym for Litvinov], "Po novodu stat'i tov. N. Baltiiskogo," *Voina i rabochii klass*, 15 February 1944, 15).

27. Memo of meeting between Litvinov and Nadolny, 28 March 1934, *D.V.P.*, 17:214–215, and 17:787, note 99.

28. Nadolny, *Mein Beitrag*, 167.

29. *Pravda*, 27 April 1934, and *Izvestiia*, 27 April 1934.

30. Telegram from Litvinov to Rozenberg, 28 April 1934, *D.V.P.*, 17:306. Jiri Hochman argues that statements like these were examples of the Russians merely blowing smoke and points out that they were even ready to include Berlin in a Franco-Soviet alliance (Hochman, *The Soviet Union*, 45–47). Also the Russians were ready to include the Germans in virtually any arrangement in eastern Europe that would "bind" them and preclude Nazi aggression— precisely the point of the Baltic guarantee proposal of March 1934. Hochman does not seem to realize that such proposals were made with the full knowledge that Hitler would not accept them. Even Barthou was ready to include Germany in Eastern Locarno, but the idea that Germany would accept such a reasonable commitment struck him as almost amusing. As Scott has pointed out, such offers to the Nazis were "empty" (Scott, *Alliance Against Hitler*, 179). A leading French diplomatic historian of the same era has observed that Barthou was a skeptic when it came to collective security but that he "would seek alliances" (Jean-Baptiste Duroselle, *La Decadence, 1932–1939* [Paris: Imprimerie nationale, 1979], 98).

31. Scott, *Alliance Against Hitler*, 167.

32. Ibid., 162–168.

33. Telegram from Alphand to Barthou, 8 May 1934, *D.D.F.*, 1st series, 6:436.

34. Ibid., 6:168–169, and Rozenberg to *Narkomindel*, 20 April 1934, *D.V.P.*, 17:279–280.

35. Note by the Direction Politique, Geneva, 3 June 1934, *D.D.F.*, 1st series, 6:602. Unfortunately for Litvinov, the French refused to insert clear-cut military plans into the alliance.

36. Telegram from Litvinov to *Narkomindel*, 18 May 1934, *D.V.P.*, 17:340.

37. Scott, *Alliance Against Hitler*, 168–169. The German diplomat Neurath told the Finnish politican Anti-Verner Hackzell that his government would never accept "Litvinov's eastern Locarno schemes" (telegram from Sperling [Helsinki] to the Foreign Office, 13 June 1934, F.O. 371, 18298, N3554, 2, 38).

38. Litvinov's address to the Disarmament Conference, 29 May 1934, *D.V.P.*, 17:357.

39. Telegram from Litvinov to *Narkomindel*, 4 June 1934, ibid., 17:371.

40. Telegram from Litvinov to *Narkomindel*, 6 June 1934, ibid., 17:375.

41. Scott, *Alliance Against Hitler*, 171.

42. Telegram from Litvinov to *Narkomindel*, 6 June 1934, *D.V.P.*, 17:375.

43. Scott, *Alliance Against Hitler*, 171–172.

44. Telegram from Hoesch to the Foreign Ministry, 7 July 1934, *D.G.F.P.*, Series C, 3:146.

45. Great Britain, Public Record Office, Miscellaneous Correspondence of John Simon, Simon to King George V, 10 July 1934, F.O. 800/289, 5:161. The German ambassador to London, Hoesch, told the British government that he found the suggestion of Russian aid to Germany "astonishing" (memo of conversation among Eden, Simon, and Hoesch, 19 July 1934, F.O. 371, 17748, C4902, 247, 18).

46. Great Britain, Public Record Office, Miscellaneous Correspondence of John Simon, 5:162–163.

47. Scott, *Alliance Against Hitler*, 179.

48. Memo of Anglo-French meeting, 9 July 1934, *D.B.F.P.*, 2d series, 6:821–822.

49. Scott, *Alliance Against Hitler*, 181.

50. Ibid., 182.

51. Telegram from Twardowski to the Foreign Ministry, 5 August 1934, *D.G.F.P.*, Series C, 3:292–293.

52. Memo by Neurath, 27 August 1934, ibid., 3:360.

53. Ibid. Presumably without the knowledge of the Poles, Hitler rejected an eastern pact because acceptance "seemed to imply fresh recognition of Germany's eastern frontiers, including the Polish corridor" (telegraph from Phipps to the Foreign Office, 19 July 1934, F.O. 371, 17748, C4907, 247, 18).

54. Twardowski to the foreign minister, 30 July 1934, *D.G.F.P.*, Series C, 3:270.

55. Memo of meeting between Litvinov and the French chargé, 23 July 1934, *D.V.P.*, 17:495.

56. Ivy Litvinov Papers, Hoover Institution Archives, Stanford University, Box 7, Fragment, n.d. Eduard Beneš was the president of Czechoslovakia.

57. Maxim Litvinov, *The USSR and the League of Nations* (New York: Workers' Library Publisher, 1934), 21–22. This pamphlet consists of Litvinov's address of 18 September to the League of Nations.

58. Ibid., 29.

59. Ibid., 30.

60. Ibid., 31.

61. Ibid.

62. Haslam, *The Soviet Union*, 43. The murderer was a Macedonian whose target was the visiting king of Yugoslavia, Alexander I. Barthou was simply in the wrong place at the wrong time.

63. Telegram from Alphand to Doumergue, 12 October 1934, *D.D.F.*, 1st series, 7:718.

64. Telegram from Rozenberg to *Narkomindel*, 19 October 1934, *D.V.P.*, 17:647–648.

65. Telegram from Litvinov to Rozenberg, 19 October 1934, ibid., 17:824, note 275.

66. Telegram from Litvinov to *Narkomindel*, 21 November 1934, ibid., 17:683–685, and protocol between the Soviet Union and France, 5 December 1934, ibid., 17:725–726.

67. Scott, *Alliance Against Hitler*, 212.

68. Ibid.

69. Ibid., 214–217.

70. Telegraph from Alphand to Laval, 7 January 1935, *D.D.F.*, 1st series, 8:600.

71. Molotov speech to the Seventh Congress of Soviets, 28 January 1935, *D.V.P.*, 18:43.

72. Ibid., 18:47.

73. Ibid.

74. Haslam, *The Soviet Union*, 46–47, and Scott, *Alliance Against Hitler*, 219–222.

75. Telegram from Litvinov to Potemkin, 4 February 1935, *D.V.P.*, 18:63.

76. Neurath to German embassies in Italy, Great Britain, France, and Poland, 16 March 1935, *D.G.F.P.*, Series C, 3:1005–1006.

77. Memo of meeting between Litvinov and Alphand, 17 March 1935, *D.V.P.*, 18:184–185. Also see Robert J. Young, *In Command of France: French*

Foreign Policy and Military Planning, 1933–1940 (Cambridge: Harvard University Press, 1978), 92.

78. By early 1935, Laval had finally realized that Poland would not defy Germany by agreeing to Eastern Locarno (Scott, *Alliance Against Hitler*, 218–219). Some Frenchmen continued to hope that Beck would change his mind, but to no avail (see telegram from Ia. Kh. Davtian to Litvinov, 8 April 1935, *D.V.P.*, 18:268).

79. Telegram from Litvinov to Potemkin, 2 April 1935, *D.V.P.*, 18:259.

80. Telegram from Potemkin to *Narkomindel*, 9 April 1935, ibid., 18:280.

81. Telegram from Litvinov to Potemkin, 10 April 1935, ibid., 18:280.

82. Andreyeva and Vilyasova, eds. "The Struggle of the USSR for Collective Security," *International Affairs* (October 1963):115.

83. Telegram from Litvinov to *Narkomindel*, 18 April 1935, *D.V.P.*, 18:292–293. This question about the need for a decision on the "principle" of the pact seemingly contradicts other Soviet sources that assert the Politburo had affirmed such a principle in December 1933.

84. Franco-Soviet Mutual Assistance Treaty, 2 May 1935, ibid., 18:311.

85. Franco-Soviet Mutual Assistance Treaty, ibid., 18:309, and Scott, *Alliance Against Hitler*, 247. The part of the covenant referred to stated: "If the Council fails to reach a report which is unanimously agreed to by the members thereof, other than the Representatives of one or more of the parties to the dispute [that is likely to lead to a rupture], the Members of the League reserve to themselves the right to take such action as they shall consider necessary for the maintenance of right and justice" (Francis P. Walters, *A History of the League of Nations* Oxford: Oxford University Press, 1952), 51.

86. Scott, *Alliance Against Hitler*, 241.

87. Haslam, *The Soviet Union*, 51. The well-known difference between the Czech and French treaties was that "aid to Czechoslovakia or the USSR by the other signatory would be conditional upon France taking action first"—the Czechs insisted upon this proviso (ibid.).

CHAPTER 12

1. William Evans Scott, *Alliance Against Hitler* (Durham: Duke University Press, 1962), 196.

2. Ibid., 197.

3. *Cabinet 23*, Series 3 (36), 29 January 1936. In March 1937, the French continued to emphasize this essentially negative view of the 1935 pact (telegram from Clerk [Paris] to Foreign Office, 8 March 1937, F.O. 371, 21094, N1522, 45, 38).

4. Jane Degras, ed., *Soviet Documents on Foreign Policy*, 3 vols. (Oxford: Oxford University Press, 1951-1953), 3:125.

5. M. Andreyeva and L. Vidyasova, eds., "The Struggle of the USSR for Collective Security," *International Affairs* (August 1963):138.

6. Telegram from Nadolny to Foreign Ministry, 8 May 1935, *D.G.F.P.*, Series C, 4:121. In a dispatch to the Soviet ambassador in Berlin, Litvinov said only that he had asked the Germans how to "establish more correct relations" between Berlin and Moscow (telegram from Litvinov to Suritz, 9 May 1935, *D.V.P.*, 18:323).

7. See Jonathan Haslam, *The Soviet Union and the Struggle for Collective Security in Europe, 1933-1939* (New York: St. Martin's Press, 1984), 86, 96, 127-128, and 144.

8. Memo of meeting between Litvinov and Eden, 28 March 1935, *D.V.P.*, 18:234-235.

9. Adam Ulam, *Expansion and Coexistence* (New York: Praeger, 1974), 224, and Scott, *Alliance Against Hitler*, 264-265.

10. Memo of conversation between Hoare and Litvinov, 13 September 1935, F.O. 371, 19452, N4675, 17, 38.

11. Telegram from Litvinov to Potemkin, 4 October 1935, *D.V.P.*, 8:523.

12. Francis P. Walters, *A History of the League of Nations* (Oxford: Oxford University Press, 1952), 654.

13. Ibid., 656.

14. Telegram from Krestinskii to Litvinov, 15 October 1935, *D.V.P.*, 18:531.

15. Anthony Eden, *The Memoirs of Anthony Eden: Facing the Dictators* (Boston: Houghton Mifflin, 1962), 292.

16. Raymond J. Sontag, *A Broken World, 1919-1939* (New York: Harper and Row, 1971), 290. It is significant that Litvinov called this deal the "Laval-Hoare" pact (telegram from Litvinov to Potemkin, *D.V.P.*, 18:591).

17. Sontag, *A Broken World*, 290-291.

18. Thomas M. Verich, *The European Powers and the Italo-Ethiopian War, 1935-1936* (Salisbury, N.C.: Documentary Publications, 1980), 130-131.

19. Telegram from Litvinov to Potemkin, 15 December 1935, *D.V.P.*, 18:591.

20. Telegram from Litvinov to Potemkin, 16 December 1935, ibid., 18:592.

21. Telegram from Eden to Foreign Office, 22 January 1936, F.O. 371, 19879, C452, 92, 62.

22. Sontag, *A Broken World*, 294.

23. Telegram from Corbin to Flandin, 30 January 1936, *D.D.F.*, 2d series, 1:161.

24. Great Britain, University of Birmingham, Neville Chamberlain Papers, Political Diary, N.C. 2/23A, entry for 12 March 1936.

25. Ibid. Flandin also told Litvinov he was ready to use "even military pressure" (telegram from Litvinov to *Narkomindel*, 14 March 1936, *D.V.P.*, 19:142).

26. *Cabinet 23*, Series 21 (36), 18 March 1936.

27. Litvinov to Potemkin, 9 March 1936, *D.V.P.*, 19:129.

28. Telegram from Litvinov to Maisky, 9 March 1936, Ibid., 19:130.

29. Sontag, *A Broken World*, 293.

30. Hajo Holborn, *A History of Modern Germany, 1840–1945* (New York: Alfred A. Knopf, 1969), 768–769.

31. Telegram from Litvinov to Stalin, 21 March 1936, *D.V.P.*, 19:179.

32. Telegram from Krestinskii to Litvinov, 22 March 1936, ibid., 19:181–182.

33. Telegram from Litvinov to *Narkomindel*, 28 March 1936, ibid., 19:734, note 55.

34. Or, as a Romanian diplomat asked the French diplomat Yvon Delbos at the time, "How can [France] protect us if you can't protect yourselves?" (Aleksei Roschchin, "Soviet Prewar Diplomacy: Reminiscences of a Diplomat" *International Affairs* [December 1987]:117).

35. Degras, ed., *Soviet Documents*, 3:171.

36. Ibid., 3:177–178.

37. Ibid.

38. Great Britain, Public Record Office, Personal Papers of Anthony Eden, Earl of Avon, Telegram from Eden to the Foreign Office, 1 October 1936, F.O. 954, 24 SU/36/16 (hereafter cited as F.O. 954).

39. Ibid.

40. Sontag, *A Broken World*, 301.

41. Ibid., 304–316.

42. Telegram from Eden to the Foreign Office, 1 October 1936.

43. Ibid. In an earlier conversation, Eden had brought up a Soviet proposal regarding naval armaments. "To my surprise M. Litvinoff seemed to know very little of this subject" (F.O. 954, telegram from Eden to the Foreign Office, 27 June 1936).

44. Telegram from Litvinov to Aleksandrovskii, 25 October 1936, *D.V.P.*, 19:517.

45. Jiri Hochman, *The Soviet Union and the Failure of Collective Security 1934–1938* (Ithaca: Cornell University Press, 1984), 112–113.

46. Roshchin, "Soviet Prewar Diplomacy," 118.

47. Interview with Tatiana Litvinov, Brighton, England, 30–31 March 1981.

48. Ibid.

49. A. Meerovich, "V Narkomindele, 1922–1939: Interv'iu s E. A. Gnedinym," *Pamiat* 5 (1982):386.

50. United States Library of Congress, Manuscript Division, Joseph Davies Papers, Box 7, 4 March 1938.

51. Interview with Tatiana Litvinov.

52. Ibid.

53. George von Rauch, *A History of Soviet Russia*, trans. Peter and Annette Jacobsonn, 6th ed. (New York: Praeger Publishers, 1972), 249.

54. Eden, *Memoirs*, 181.

55. Ibid.

56. Jean-Baptiste Duroselle, *La Decadence, 1932–1939* (Paris: Imprimerie nationale, 1979), 322. It is worth noting that even before the slaughter of the Red Army officers, the French government had decided to "reduce to the smallest possible compass any further development" of the Franco-Soviet pact "for which the Russian government had been pressing" (memo by Robert Vansittart, 28 May 1937, F.O. 371, 20702, DC3910, 532, 62).

57. Degras, ed., *Soviet Documents*, 3:262.

58. Telegram from Coulondre to Delbos, 4 May 1937, *D.D.F.*, 2d series, 5:676.

59. Telegram from Coulondre to Delbos, Enclosure, 27 December 1937, ibid., 2d series, 7:785–788.

60. Copy of a letter from Maxim to Ivy Litvinov, 11 June 1938, Ivy Litvinov Papers, Hoover Institution Archives, Stanford University, Box 9.

61. Degras, ed., *Soviet Documents*, 3:282–294. The human cost of World War II was approximately 50 million lives.

62. Great Britain, Public Record Office, Viscount Halifax Private Papers, F.O. 800, 309, record of conversation with Beneš, 14 March 1938.

63. Telegram from Coulondre to Bonnet, 28 April 1938, *D.D.F.*, 2d series, 9:553. A full exposition of the Czechoslovakia crisis of 1938 is beyond the parameters of this book, but the reader can profitably consult the works of Telford Taylor, Anthony Adamthwaite, Gerhard Weinberg, and Jonathan Haslam to name but a few.

64. Telegram from Coulondre to Bonnet, 31 May 1938, *D.D.F.*, 2d series, 9:965.

65. Telegram from Payart to Bonnet, 30 August 1938, ibid., 2d series, 10:874–875. In his memoirs, Coulondre asserted that Litvinov told him that if war came to Czechoslovakia, the Russians would "hold to our obligations." The ambassador added that this "reaffirmation of Soviet policy manifested itself uniformly in the diverse incidents of this epoch" (Robert Coulondre, *De Staline à Hitler: Souvenirs de deux ambassades, 1936–1939* [Paris: Hatchette, 1950], 139).

66. Telegram from Schulenburg to Foreign Ministry, 26 September 1938, *D.G.F.P.*, Series D, 3:946–948.

67. Telegram from Payart to Bonnet, 2 September 1938, *D.D.F.*, 2d series, 10:934–935, and telegram from Litvinov to Aleksandrovskii, 2 September 1938, *D.V.P.*, 21:470–471. The Payart telegram contains two "gaps in the text," which is rather remarkable for such an important document. There are no gaps in Litvinov's telegram.

68. Anthony Adamthwaite, *France and the Coming of the Second World War* (London: Frank Cass, 1977), 203, and Note on Political Direction, 6 September 1938, *D.D.F.*, 2d series, 11:43–44.

69. Great Britain, Public Record Office, Neville Henderson Papers, 4 January–20 September 1938, F.O. 800, 269, entry for 4 September 1938.

70. Telegram from Chilston to Foreign Office, 18 October 1938, F.O. 371, 22289, N5164, 97, 38.

71. Gustav Hilger and Alfred G. Mayer, *The Incompatible Allies* (New York: Macmillan and Company, 1953), 289.

72. Telegram from Coulondre to Bonnet, 18 October 1938, *D.D.F.*, 2d series, 12:275–276.

73. A. A. Gromyko, et al., eds., *Soviet Peace Efforts on the Eve of World War II* (Moscow: Progress Publishers, 1976), 273–274.

74. Winston S. Churchill, *The Gathering Storm* (New York: Bantam Books, 1961), 324.

75. *Cabinet 23*, Series 26 (39), 3 May 1939, and Haslam, *The Soviet Union*, 213.

76. Interview with Tatiana Litvinov. According to Louis Fischer, Litvinov and Molotov argued for an hour before Stalin ordered the former's resignation (Louis Fischer, *The Life and Death of Stalin* [New York: Harper and Brothers, 1952], 55–56).

77. *Pravda*, 4 May 1939.

78. Aleksei Roshchin, "V Narkomindele nakanune voiny," *Mezhdunarodnaia zhizn'* 4 (1988):124–125.

79. Interview with Tatiana Litvinov.

CHAPTER 13

1. W. Averell Harriman and Elie Abel, *Special Envoy to Churchill and Stalin, 1941–1946* (New York: Random House, 1975), 91.

2. Ibid., 199.

3. Letter from Ivy Litvinov to Joseph Freeman, 20 January 1943, Joseph Freeman Papers, Hoover Institution, Stanford, California, Box 175, Folder 1.

4. Elena Danielson, "The Elusive Litvinov Memoirs," *Slavic Review* 48:3 (1989):477–483.

5. Interview with Mikhail Litvinov, Moscow, 24 June 1990.

6. Memo of conversation between Welles and Litvinov, 7 May 1943, U.S. National Archives, Microfilm Publication Number T1242.

7. Ibid.

8. See Teddy Uldrichs, "The Effect of the Purges on the Peoples Commissariat for Foreign Affairs," *Slavic Review* 36 (1977):187–204.

9. Harriman and Abel, *Special Envoy*, 199.

10. Letter from Maxim to Ivy Litvinov, n.d. (October 1943?), Freeman Papers, Box 175.

11. Ibid., Maxim to Ivy Litvinov, n.d.

12. U.S. National Archives, Washington, D.C., Department of State Papers, Record Group 59, 500. CC/9-1944, Harriman to Hull, 19 September 1944.

13. Author's telephone interview with Richard C. Hottelet, New York, 19 August 1985.

14. *New York World Telegram and the Sun*, 28 January 1953.

15. Ibid.

16. Ibid.

17. Ibid., 29 January 1953.

18. Ibid.

19. Ibid., 28 January 1953. Litvinov made similar remarks to other Westerners, but the Hottelet interview was the most comprehensive and the final statement of his views (see Harriman and Abel, *Special Envoy*, 518; Alexander Werth, *Russia at War, 1941–1945* [New York: E. P. Dutton and Company, 1964], 938; and Edgar Snow, *Journey to the Beginning* [London: Gollancz, 1959], 357). In an analysis of these statements, Vojtech Mastny asserts that Litvinov's remarks support "the conclusion that the Soviet leaders realized they had options" in formulating their postwar policy (Vojtech Mastny, "The Cassandra in the Foreign Office," *Foreign Affairs* 54 [1976]:375). The essence of Mastny's statement is probably true, but it cannot be fully substantiated on the basis of Litvinov's remarks. As he had told Welles, he could not even get a message to Stalin. Also, Litvinov explicitly told Hottelet that he had not offered the Soviet leaders his opinions and "they will certainly not call on me" (*New York World Telegraph and the Sun*, 28 January 1953).

20. Letter from Ivy to Tatiana Litvinov, May 1950, Ivy Litvinov Papers, Hoover Institution Archives, Stanford University, Box 3.

21. Ivy Litvinov Papers, Box 6, Fragment, n.d.

22. Z. S. Sheinis, ed., "Moemu dal'neishemu potomstvu," *Iunost'* 7 (July 1966):92.

23. Interview with Tatiana Litvinov, Brighton, England, 30–31 March 1981.

24. Interview with Flora Litvinov, Moscow, 24 June 1990.

CONCLUSION

1. Telegram from Wiley to Hull, 17 November 1934, U.S. National Archives, Microfilm Publication Number T1249.

SELECTED BIBLIOGRAPHY

WORKS BY MAXIM M. LITVINOV

Litvinov, Maxim M. *The Bolshevik Revolution: Its Rise and Meaning*. Chicago: Socialist Party of the United States, 1920.

M. Tanin [pseud.]. *10 let vneshnei politiki SSSR, 1917–1927*. Moscow and Leningrad: Government Publishing House, 1927.

Litvinov, Maxim M. *Kak rabotaet komissariat mira*. Moscow: Udkniga, 1925.

_____. "O leninskoi *Iskre*." *Istoricheskii arkhiv* 2 (1961):140–147.

N. Malinin [pseud.]. "Po novodu stat'i tov. N. Baltiiskogo." *Voina i rabochii klass*, 15 February 1944, 13–16.

Litvinov, Maxim M. *The Soviet Dumping Fable*. New York: Workers' Library, 1931.

_____. *The USSR and the League of Nations*. New York: Workers' Library, 1934.

_____. *Vneshniaia politika SSSR: Rechi i zaiavleniia 1927–1935*. Moscow: State Social-Economic Publishing House, 1935.

Litvinov, Maxim M., et al. *The Soviets Fight for Disarmament*. New York: International Publishers, n.d.

UNPUBLISHED DOCUMENTS AND PAPERS

Great Britain. Public Record Office. Cabinet Conclusions, Series 23 (33) item 2. 5 April 1933.

Great Britain. Public Record Office. Foreign Office Papers. Series 371.

Great Britain. Public Record Office. Miscellaneous Correspondence of John Simon.

Great Britain. Public Record Office. Neville Henderson Papers.

Great Britain. Public Record Office. Personal Papers of Anthony Eden, Earl of Avon.

Great Britain. University of Birmingham. Neville Chamberlain Papers, Political Diary.

Ivy Litvinov Papers, Hoover Institution Archives, Stanford University.
Joseph Freeman Papers, Hoover Institution, Stanford, California.
Louis Fischer Papers, Yale University Archives.
Washington, D.C. National Archives. Department of State Papers.
William Buckler Papers, Yale University Archives.

PUBLISHED DOCUMENTS AND PAPERS

Andreeva, M., and L. Viliasova, eds. "Bor'ba SSSR za kollektivnuiu bezopos-
nost' v Evrope v 1933-1935 godakh." *Mezhdunarodnaia zhizn'* 10 (June
1963):152-162.

Andreyeva, M., and L. Vidyasova, eds. "The Struggle of the USSR for
Collective Security in Europe, 1933-1935." 4 parts. *International Affairs*
(June, July, August, October 1963).

Bullitt, Orville, ed. *For the President, Personal and Secret: Correspondence
Between Franklin D. Roosevelt and William C. Bullitt.* Boston: Houghton
Mifflin Company, 1972.

Bullitt, William C. *The Bullitt Mission to Russia: Testimony Before the Committee on Foreign Relations, United States Senate, 1919.* New York:
Huebsch, 1919.

Chicherin, Georgii. *Stat'i i rechi po voprosam mezhdunarodnoi politiki.* Moscow: Politizdat, 1961.

Degras, Jane, ed. *Soviet Documents on Foreign Policy.* 3 vols. Oxford: Oxford
University Press, 1951-1953.

Eudin, Xenia J., and Harold H. Fischer. *Soviet Russia and the West, 1920-
1927, a Documentary Survey.* Stanford: Stanford University Press, 1957.

Eudin, Xenia J., and Robert M. Slusser. *Soviet Foreign Policy, 1928-1934,
Documents and Materials.* University Park: Pennsylvania State University Press, 1966.

Great Britain. Foreign Office (*D.B.F.P.*). *Documents on British Foreign Policy
1919-1939.* 1st series, vols. 20, 23, 25; 2d series, vols. 6, 7.

Gromyko, A. A., et al. eds. *Soviet Peace Efforts on the Eve of World War II,*
Moscow: Progress Publishers, 1976.

Grupp, Peter, general ed. *Akten zur deutschen auswartigen Politik 1918-1945.*
Series B, 1925-1933, vols. 7, 11. Gottingen: Vandenhoeck and Ruprecht,
1974.

Khrenov, I. A., chief ed. *Dokumenty i materialy po istorii sovetsko-pol'skikh
otnoshenii.* 6 vols. Moscow: Nauka, 1964-1970.

Kun, Bela, ed. *Kommunisticheskii Internatsional v dokumentakh.* Moscow:
Partiinoe izdatel 'stvo, 1933.

League of Nations Secretariat. *Documents of the Preparatory Commission for the Disarmament Conference.* 11 vols. Geneva: League of Nations, 1926–1931.

Lenin, V. I. *Polnoe sobranie sochinenii.* 5th ed. 55 vols. Moscow: Politizdat, 1958-1964.

————. *Selected Works: One Volume Edition.* New York: International Publishers, 1971.

Ministere des Affaires Etrangeres (*D.D.F.*). *Documents diplomatiques francais, 1932-1939.* 1st series. 8 vols. Paris: Imprimerie Nationale, 1964–1981.

Ministerstvo Inostrannykh Del, SSSR (*D.V.P.*) *Dokumenty vneshnei politiki, SSSR.* Moscow: Politizdat, 1959–

Ol'minskii, M., ed. *Novaia zhizn': Pervaia legal'naia Bolsheviskaia gazeta.* Leningrad: Priboi, 1925.

"Perepiska N. Lenina i N. K. Krupskoi s M. M. Litvinovym." *Proletarskaia revoliutsiia* 2 (1925):75–88.

Sheinis, Z. S., ed. "Moemu dal'neishemu potomstvu." *Iunost'* 7 (July 1966):84–92.

————. "Neopublikovannye pis'ma M.M. Litvinova V. I. Leninu, 1913–1915 gg." *Novaia i noveishaia istoriia* 4 (1966):118–126.

Stalin, I. V. *Works.* 13 vols. Moscow: Foreign Languages Publishing House, 1954-1955.

Sweet, Paul R., chief ed. (*D.G.F.P.*). *Documents on German Foreign Policy, 1918-1945.* Series C. 16 vols. Washington, D.C.: Government Printing Office, 1957-1983.

Toynbee, Arnold J. *Survey of International Affairs, 1924.* Oxford: Oxford University Press, 1926.

————. *Survey of International Affairs, 1926.* Oxford: Oxford University Press, 1928.

————. *Survey of International Affairs, 1930.* Oxford: Oxford University Press, 1933.

————. *Survey of International Affairs, 1931.* Oxford: Oxford University Press, 1931.

U.S. Department of State (*F.R.U.S.*). *Papers Relating to the Foreign Relations of the United States, 1918, Russia,* 3 vols. Washington, D.C.: GPO, 1931.

————. *F.R.U.S., 1919, Russia.* Washington, D.C.: GPO, 1937.

————. *F.R.U.S., 1923,* 2 vols. Washington, D.C.: GPO, 1938.

————. *F.R.U.S., 1926,* 2 vols. Washington, D.C.: GPO, 1941.

————. *F.R.U.S., 1928,* 3 vols. Washington, D.C.: GPO, 1942.

————. *F.R.U.S., 1929,* 3 vols. Washington, D.C.: GPO, 1943.

————. *F.R.U.S., The Soviet Union, 1933-1939.* Washington, D.C.: GPO, 1952.

U.S. National Archives. Records of the Department of State Relative to the Political Relations Between the U.S. and the Soviet Union, 1940–1944. Microfilm Publication No. T1242.

AUTOBIOGRAPHIES AND MEMOIRS

Beck, Josef. *Dernier Rapport; Politique polonaise 1926–1936*. Neuchatel: Editions de la Baconniere, 1951.

Bernsdorff, Johann. *Memoirs of Count Bernsdorff*. Translated by Eric Sutton. New York: Random House, 1936.

Churchill, Winston S. *The Gathering Storm*. New York: Bantam Books, 1961.

Coulondre, Robert. *De Staline à Hitler: Souvenirs de deux ambassades, 1936–1939*. Paris: Hachette, 1950.

Dirksen, Herbert von. *Moscow, Tokyo, London: Twenty Years of German Foreign Policy*. New York: Hutchinson and Company, 1951.

Duranty, Walter. *Duranty Reports Russia*. New York: Viking Press, 1934.

Eastman, Max. *Love and Revolution*. New York: Random House, 1964.

Eden, Anthony. *The Memoirs of Anthony Eden: Facing the Dictators*. Boston: Houghton Mifflin Company, 1962.

Ehrenburg, Ilya. *Post-War Years, 1945–1954*. Translated by Tatiana Shebunina. Cleveland and New York: World Publishing Company, 1967.

Fischer, Louis. *Men and Politics*. New York: Duell, Sloan and Pearce, 1941.

Grew, Joseph C. *Ten Years in Japan*. New York: Simon and Schuster, 1944.

Harriman, W. Averell, and Elie Abel. *Special Envoy to Churchill and Stalin, 1941–1946*. New York: Random House, 1975.

Hilger, Gustav, and Alfred G. Mayer. *The Incompatible Allies*. New York: Macmillan and Company, 1953.

Litvinov, Ivy. "Early Days." *Blackwoods Magazine* 313 (1973):235–250.

———. "Vstrechi i razluki." *Novyi mir* 7 (1966):235–250.

Liubimov, N. N., and A. N. Erlikh. *Genuezskaia konferentsiia*. Moscow: Instituta mezhdunarodnykh otnoshenii, 1963.

Lockhart, Robert H. Bruce. *British Agent*. London: G. P. Putman's Sons, 1933.

———. *The Diaries of Sir Robert Bruce Lockhart, 1915–1938*. New York: St. Martin's, 1973.

Maisky, Ivan. *Journey Into the Past*. London: Hutchinson, 1962.

———. *Liudi, sobytii, fakty*. Moscow: Mezhdunarodyne otnoshenii, 1973.

Nadolny, Rudolf. *Mein Beitrag*. Wiesbaden: Limes Verlag, 1955.

Roshchin, Aleksei. "Soviet Prewar Diplomacy: Reminiscences of a Diplomat." *International Affairs* (December 1987):115–121.

_____. "V Narkomindele nakanune voiny." *Mezhdunarodnaia zhizn'* 4 (1988):120–126.

Snow, Edgar. *Journey to the Beginning.* London: Gollancz, 1959.

SECONDARY WORKS

Adamthwaite, Anthony. *France and the Coming of the Second World War.* London: Frank Cass, 1977.

Akhtamzian, A. *Rapall'skaia politika, 1922–1932.* Moscow: Mezhdunarodyne otnosheniia, 1974.

Angress, Werner. *Stillborn Revolution: The Communist Bid for Power in Germany, 1921–1923.* Princeton: Princeton University Press, 1963.

Beloff, Max. *Foreign Policy of Soviet Russia, 1929–1941.* 2 vols. New York: Oxford University Press, 1949.

Bibineishvili, B. *Kamo.* Moscow: Starii Bol'shevik, 1934.

Blinov, S. V. *Vneshniaia politika Sovetskoi Rossii: Pervyi god proletarskoi diktatury.* Moscow: Mysl', 1973.

Borisov, Iurii V. *Sovetsko-Frantsuzskie otnosheniia, 1924–1945 gg.* Moscow: Mezhdunarodnye otnosheniia, 1964.

Browder, Robert Paul. *The Origins of Soviet-American Diplomacy.* Princeton: Princeton University Press, 1953.

Budurowycz, Bohdan B. *Polish-Soviet Relations, 1932–1939.* New York: Columbia University Press, 1963.

Carr, E. H. *The Bolshevik Revolution, 1917–1923.* 3 vols. London: Penguin Books, 1966.

_____. *German-Soviet Relations Between the Two World Wars.* Baltimore: Johns Hopkins Press, 1951.

_____. *Socialism in One Country, 1924–1926.* New York: Macmillan Company, 1958–1964.

_____. *Twilight of the Comintern, 1930–1935.* New York: Pantheon Books, 1982.

Carswell, John. *The Exile: A Life of Ivy Litvinov.* Boston: Faber and Faber, 1983.

Clemens, Walter, Jr. "Origins of the Soviet Campaign for Disarmament: The Soviet Position on Peace, Security, and Revolution at the Genoa, Moscow, and Lausanne Conferences 1922–1923." Ph.D. dissertation, Columbia University, 1961.

Crowley, Edward L., ed. *The Soviet Diplomatic Corps, 1917–1967.* Metuchen, N.J.: Scarecrow Press, 1970.

Dallin, David J. *The Rise of Russia in Asia.* New Haven: Yale University Press, 1949.

Davis, Kathryn W. *The Soviets at Geneva: The USSR and the League of Nations, 1919–1933*. Geneva: Librairie Kundig, 1934. Reprint. Westport, Conn.: Hyperion Press, 1977.

Debo, Richard K. "George Chicherin: Soviet Russia's Second Foreign Commissar." Ph.D. dissertation, University of Nebraska, 1964.

DeConde, Alexander. *A History of American Foreign Policy*. 3d ed. 2 vols. New York: Charles Scribner's Sons, 1978.

Duroselle, Jean-Baptiste. *La Decadence, 1932–1939*. Paris: Imprimerie nationale, 1979.

Dyck, Leonard Harvey. *Weimar Germany and Soviet Russia, 1926–1933*. New York: Columbia University Press, 1966.

Ettinger, Elzbieta, ed. *Comrade and Lover: Rosa Luxemburg's Letters to Leo Jogiches*. Cambridge, Mass., 1979.

Farnsworth, Beatrice. *William C. Bullitt and the Soviet Union*. Bloomington and London: Indiana University Press, 1967.

Ferrell, Robert H. *Peace in Their Time: The Origins of the Kellogg-Briand Pact*. New Haven: Yale University Press, 1952.

Fink, Carol. *The Genoa Conference*. Chapel Hill: University of North Carolina Press, 1984.

Fischer, Louis. *The Life and Death of Stalin*. New York: Harper and Brothers, 1952.

————. *Russia's Road from Peace to War, 1917–1941*. New York: Harper and Row, 1969.

————. *The Soviets in World Affairs*. 2 vols. London: Jonathan Cape, 1930.

Freund, Gerald. *Unholy Alliance: Russian-German Relations from the Treaty of Brest-Litovsk to the Treaty of Berlin*. New York: Harcourt, Brace and Company, 1957.

Gorodetsky, Gabriel. *The Precarious Truce*. Cambridge: Cambridge University Press, 1977.

Gromyko, A. A., and B. N. Ponomarev, eds. *Istoriia vneshnei politiki SSSR 1917–1976*. 2 vols. Moscow: Nauka, 1976.

Haimson, Leopold H. *The Russian Marxists and the Origins of Bolshevism*. Boston: Beacon, 1966.

Haslam, Jonathan. *Soviet Foreign Policy, 1930–1933*. New York: St. Martin's Press, 1983.

————. *The Soviet Union and the Struggle for Collective Security in Europe, 1933–1939*. New York: St. Martin's Press, 1984.

Hochman, Jiri. *The Soviet Union and the Failure of Collective Security 1934–1938*. Ithaca: Cornell University Press, 1984.

Holborn, Hajo. *A History of Modern Germany, 1840–1945*. New York: Alfred A. Knopf, 1969.

Ioffe, Aleksandr E. *Vneshniaia politika Sovetskogo Souiza, 1928–1932 gg.* Moscow: Nauka, 1968.

Iriye, Akira. *After Imperialism: The Search for a New Order in the Far East, 1921–1931.* Cambridge: Harvard University Press, 1965.

Jacobs, Dan N. *Borodin: Stalin's Man in China.* Cambridge: Harvard University Press, 1981.

Kennan, George. *Russia and the West Under Lenin and Stalin.* Boston: Little, Brown and Company, 1960.

————. *Soviet Foreign Policy, 1917–1941.* Princeton: D. Van Nostrand, 1960.

Khaitsman, Viktor M. *SSSR i problema razoruzheniia mezhdu pervoi i vtoroi mirovymi voinami.* Moscow: Nauka, 1959.

Khromov, S. S. and A. L. Narochnitskii, chief eds. *Istroiia rabochego klassa SSSR.* Moscow: Nauka, 1979– .

Korbel, Josef. *Poland Between East and West: Soviet and German Diplomacy Toward Poland, 1919–1933.* Princeton: Princeton University Press, 1963.

Kornev, N. *Litvinov.* Moscow: Molodaia gvardiia, 1936.

Lambert, Robert W. *Soviet Disarmament Policy, 1922–1931.* Washington, D.C.: U.S. Arms Control and Disarmament Agency, 1964.

Lerner, Warren. *Karl Radek.* Stanford: Stanford University Press, 1970.

Libbey, James K. *Alexander Gumberg and Soviet-American Relations, 1917–1933.* Lexington: University of Kentucky Press, 1977.

Makarenko, Victor P. *Biurokratiia i stalinizm.* Rostov-on-the Don: Rostov State University Press, 1989.

Medlicott, William N. *British Foreign Policy Since Versailles, 1919–1963.* London: Methuen and Company, 1968.

Mikhutina, I. V. "Sovetsko-pol'skii pakt o nenapadenii i vneshniaia politika Pol'shi v 1931–1932 gg." In *Sovetskho-pol'skie otnosheniia, 1918–1945.* Edited by I. I. Kostiushko, et al. Moscow: Nauka, 1974.

Nere, Jacques. *The Foreign Policy of France from 1914 to 1945.* Translated by Translance. London and Boston: Routledge and Kegan Paul, 1975.

O'Connor, Timothy E. *Diplomacy and Revolution: G. V. Chicherin and Soviet Foreign Affairs, 1918–1930.* Ames: Iowa State University Press, 1988.

Pope, Arthur Upham. *Maxim Litvinoff.* New York: L. B. Fischer, 1943.

Rauch, Georg von. *A History of Soviet Russia.* 6th ed. Translated by Peter and Annette Jacobsonn. New York: Praeger Publishers, 1972.

Raymond, Paul. "Conflict and Consensus in Soviet Foreign Policy, 1933–1939." Ph.D. dissertation, Pennsylvania State University, 1979.

Reiman, Michael. *The Birth of Stalinism: The USSR on the Eve of the "Second Revolution."* Translated by George Saunders. Bloomington: Indiana University Press, 1987.

Riasanovsky, Nicholas. *A History of Russia,* 2d ed. New York: Oxford University Press, 1969.

Rigby, T. H. *Lenin's Government: Sovnarkom 1917–1922.* Cambridge: Cambridge University Press, 1979.

Sablinsky, Walter. *The Road to Bloody Sunday.* Princeton: Princeton University Press, 1976.

Schulzinger, Robert D. *American Diplomacy in the Twentieth Century.* New York: Oxford University Press, 1984.

Scott, William Evans. *Alliance Against Hitler.* Durham: Duke University Press, 1962.

Senn, Alfred Erich. *Assassination in Switzerland: The Murder of Vatslov Vorovsky.* Madison: University of Wisconsin Press, 1981.

Sheinis, Z. S. *Maksim M. Litvinov: Revoliutsioner, diplomat, chelovek.* Moscow: Politicheskaia literatura, 1989.

Sheviakov, Alesksei A. *Sovetsko-rumynstie otnosheniie; prolblema evropeiskoe bezopasnosti 1932–1939 gg.* Moscow: Nauka, 1977.

Shishkin, Valerii. *"Polosa priznanii" i vneshneekonomicheskaia politika S.S.S.R. 1924–1928 gg.* Moscow: Nauka, 1983.

———. *V. I. Lenin i vneshneekonomicheskaia politika Sovetskogo gosudarstva, 1917–1923 gg.* Leningrad: Nauka, 1977.

Sokolov, V. V. *Na boevykh postakh diplomaticheskogo fronta: Zhizn' i deiatel'- nost' L. M. Karakhana.* Moscow: Politizdat, 1983.

Sontag, Raymond J. *A Broken World, 1919–1939.* New York: Harper and Row, 1971.

Taubman, William. *Stalin's American Policy: From Entente to Détente to Cold War.* New York: W. W. Norton, 1982.

Taylor, A.J.P. *The Origins of the Second World War.* 2d ed. New York: Fawcett, 1966.

Thompson, John. *Russia, Bolshevism, and the Versailles Peace.* Princeton: Princeton University Press, 1966.

Treadgold, Donald W. *Twentieth Century Russia.* 2d ed. Chicago: Rand McNally and Company, 1964; 7th ed. Boulder: Westview Press, 1990.

Ulam, Adam. *Expansion and Coexistence.* New York: Praeger, 1974.

Uldrichs, Teddy. *Diplomacy and Ideology: The Origins of Soviet Foreign Relations, 1917–1930.* London and Beverly Hills: Sage Publications, 1979.

Ullman, Richard H. *Anglo-Soviet Relations, 1917–1921.* 2 vols. Princeton: Princeton University Press, 1961.

Verich, Thomas M. *The European Powers and the Italo-Ethiopian War, 1935–1936.* Salisbury, N.C.: Documentary Publications, 1980.

Walsdorff, Martin. *Westorientierung und Ostpolitik: Stresemanns Russpolitik in der Locarno Ara.* Berlin: Schuenemann Universitätsverlag, 1971.

Walters, Francis P. *A History of the League of Nations.* Oxford: Oxford University Press, 1952.

Warth, Robert. *Soviet Russia in World Politics.* New York: Twayne, 1963.

Weinberg, Gerhard. *The Foreign Policy of Hitler's Germany: Diplomatic Revolution in Europe 1933–36.* Chicago: University of Chicago Press, 1970.

Weissman, Benjamin. *Herbert Hoover and Famine Relief to Soviet Russia: 1921–1923.* Stanford, Calif.: Hoover Institution Press, 1974.

Werth, Alexander. *Russia at War, 1941–1945.* New York: E. P. Dutton and Company, 1964.

White, Stephen. *The Origins of Detente: The Genoa Conference and Soviet-Western Relations, 1921–1922.* Cambridge: Cambridge University Press, 1985.

Young, Robert J. *In Command of France: French Foreign Policy and Military Planning, 1933–1940.* Cambridge: Harvard University Press, 1978.

Zhukovskii, Nikolai. *Diplomaty novogo mira.* Moscow: Politizdat, 1982.

ARTICLES

Beloff, Max. "Soviet Foreign Policy, 1929–1941: Some Notes." *Soviet Studies* 11 (October 1950):124–128.

Buzinkai, Donald. "Soviet-League Relations, 1920–1923: Political Disputes." *East European Quarterly.* 13:1 (January 1980):25–45.

Cameron, Elizabeth R. "Alexis Saint-Leger Leger." In *The Diplomats,* ed. Gordon A. Craig and Felix Gilbert. Princeton: Princeton University Press, 1953.

Chossudovsky, Evgeny. "Genoa Revisited: Russia and Coexistence." *Foreign Affairs* 50 (April 1972):554–577.

Debo, Richard K. "Litvinov and Kamenev—Ambassadors Extraordinary: The Problem of Soviet Representation Abroad." *Slavic Review* 34 (1975):463–482.

―――. "Prelude to Negotiations: The Problem of British Prisoners in Soviet Russia, November 1918–July 1919." *Slavonic and East European Review* 58 (January 1980):58–75.

Elwood, R. C. "Lenin and the Brussels 'Unity' Conference of July 1914." *Russian Review* 39 (1980):32–49.

Gnedin, E. "Revoliutsioner-diplomat leninskoi shkoly." *Novyi mir* (February 1970):256–261.

Gorokov, A. "Leninskaia diplomatiia: Printsipy i traditsii." *Mezhdunarodnaia zhizn'* (April 1968):60–65.

Kulish, V. M. "U poroga viony." *Komsomolskaia pravda,* 24 August 1988.

Large, J. A. "The Origins of the Soviet Collective Security Policy, 1930–1932." *Soviet Studies* 30 (April 1978):212–236.

Maisky, Ivan. "Anglo-Sovetskoi torgovoe soglashenie v 1921 goda." *Voprosy istorii* (May 1975):60–77.

Mastny, Vojtech. "The Cassandra in the Foreign Office." *Foreign Affairs* 54 (1976):366–376.

Meerovich, A. "V Narkomindele, 1922–1939: Interv'iu s E. A. Gnedinym." *Pamiat* 5 (1982):357–393.

Mikhutina, I. V. "Sovetsko-pol'skii pakt o nenapadenii i vneshniaia politika Pol'shi v 1931–1932 gg." In *Sovetsko-pol'skie otnosheniia, 1918–1945,* ed. I. I. Kostiushko, P. N. Ol'shanskii, and I. A. Khrenov. Moscow: Nauka, 1974.

Senn, Alfred Erich. "The Soviet Union's Road to Geneva, 1924–1927." *Jahrbucher für Geschichte Osteuropas* 27 (1979):67–86.

Sheinis, Z. S. "Diplomaticheskoe poruchenie." *Moskva* (October 1966):145–155.

———. "Papasha." *Prometei* 7 (1969):82–93.

———. "Vashingtonskaia missiia." *Moskva* 9 (1967):174–191.

———. "V Genue i Gaage." *Novaia i noveishaia istoriia* (May–July 1968):52–62.

Uldrichs, Teddy. "The Effect of the Purges on the Peoples Commissariat for Foreign Affairs." *Slavic Review* 36 (1977):187–204.

INTERVIEWS

Gnedin, Evgenii. Moscow. 3 November 1982.

Hottelet, Richard C. New York. 19 August 1985.

Litvinov, Flora. Moscow. 24 June 1990.

Litvinov, Mikhail. Moscow. 29 September 1982, 3 November 1982, and 24 June 1990.

Litvinov, Tatiana. Brighton, England. 30–31 March 1981.

Sheinis, Z. S. Moscow. 22 October 1986.

Trukhanovskii, Vladimir. Moscow. 19 October 1982.

ABOUT THE BOOK AND AUTHOR

This is the first complete biography of Maxim Litvinov, a Bolshevik revolutionary who began his professional life running guns into Tsarist Russia and eventually became the leading Soviet diplomat in the turbulent 1930s. His was a spectacular career, spanning some of the most dramatic decades of the twentieth century and including an unsuccessful effort to contain Hitler with the cooperation of the Western Allies. Litvinov's subsequent replacement as Soviet foreign minister by Molotov in 1939 signaled the dramatic shift in Soviet foreign policy that led directly to the outbreak of World War II.

After the war, Litvinov's final public act was to bluntly warn the West of the danger presented by Stalin's cold war policies—a threat Litvinov even dared to compare with that posed by Hitler a decade earlier. Litvinov's career ended in the relative obscurity from which it had sprung, his consistently pro-Western policies no longer consonant with the reemerging Soviet hostility toward the West. Passing away from remarkably natural causes in 1951, Litvinov left behind a political legacy that lay dormant for forty years until its recent revival by Mikhail Gorbachev.

Between the Revolution and the West is based on extensive research in the Soviet Union and the West, including previously unavailable archives and interviews with Litvinov's friends and family. Hugh Phillips' work casts light not only on Litvinov the man but also on Soviet foreign policy during crucial and dramatic times.

Hugh D. Phillips is associate professor of history at Western Kentucky University.

INDEX